FLORIDA FLAVORS II

Environmental Studies Council, Inc.

> The young are wonderful. They are the promise of the future. Protecting the young, teaching the young to survive are elemental expressions of love.
>
> ~"The Last Cracker Barrel," by Ernest Lyons

Mission Statement of the Environmental Studies Council, Inc.

To protect and enhance the educational programs at the Environmental Studies Center and to promote and extend environmental awareness through community education.

ISBN 0-916629-04-X
Library of Congress Catalog Card Number:
1st Edition 2006

ENVIRONMENTAL
STUDIES COUNCIL
JENSEN BEACH, FLORIDA

WIMMER
COOKBOOKS

A CONSOLIDATED GRAPHICS COMPANY

800.548.2537 wimmerco.com

COOKBOOK COMMITTEE

Dagmar Bothwell   Sharyon Daigneau   Patty Henderson

Gretchen Hurchalla   Mary Hutchinson   Kathy Walker

Production Assistance: Ampersand Graphics, Bonnie Brashear, Dorothy Dicks, Jean Gallagher, Gary Hawkins, Schuyler Hodgins, Fran Howard, Val Martin, Lisa Massing, Adrienne Moore, Katie Preston, Elsie Stewart, Janel Weigt and Cecilia Wright.

ARTWORK

Cover: Kevin Hutchinson

Pen and Ink Drawings - Section Pages:
James Hutchinson and Kevin Hutchinson

Other Pen and Ink Drawings:
Children of Martin County's School System

ACKNOWLEDGEMENTS

We thank James and Kevin Hutchinson,
a wonderful father and son team, for graciously giving so
much of their time to provide such beautiful artwork for our cookbook.
It is greatly appreciated and we thank you.

We sincerely thank Val Martin, publisher,
for allowing us the use of excerpts from "My Florida" and
"The Last Cracker Barrel", written by Ernest Lyons. In both of these
books Mr. Lyons describes Martin County's nature the way it was
when he was growing up. Mr. Lyons passed away in 1990.

We also wish to thank the Cookbook Committee
of the original Florida Flavors for having the insight to begin such
a worthwhile project to support the Environmental Studies Center.

We sincerely appreciate the generous contributions of recipes.
We regret that we were unable to use all of them either
due to similarity or lack of space.

CAUGHT BY AN ENVIRONMENTAL STUDIES CENTER SEINE NET
BY SANDRA THURLOW

The Thurlow family was caught by an Environmental Studies Center seine net in 1975. This came about when I called Ella "Mike" Clark, one of the Center's founders, and asked if we could borrow a seine to use when my world-traveling brother came to visit. I thought seining would be a great thing for my kids to do with their uncle. I was right. We had a ball, and memories of that particular visit are still with us.

After I returned the net, I wrote a Letter to the Editor of *The Stuart News* praising the Environment Studies Center and, as they say, "the rest is history." From that point on the Jensen Beach Environmental Studies Center has been a part of our lives.

Before I knew it, I found myself on the Environmental Studies Council Board of Trustees. Barbara Hendry and Joan Hutchinson were spearheading the publication of a cookbook to be named *Florida Flavors*. I pitched in and was asked to launch the cookbook with a special event. The Celebration of *Florida Flavors* held on October 6, 1984 in the courtyard of the newly constructed Harbour Bay Plaza was a huge success. Mike Clark, to whom the original cookbook was dedicated, Ernie Lyons whose wise and wonderful words were sprinkled throughout, and Jim Hutchinson, whose beautiful painting of the South Fork graced the cover, were on hand to autograph books. Hundreds of Martin County residents came out to sample recipes and buy cookbooks.

Funds received from sales of *Florida Flavors* along with Annual Kitchen Tours that were initiated to promote the cookbook have helped sustain the Center.

My kids, like all children in Martin County Schools, visited the Environmental Studies Center and participated in numerous field trips where the Center's special hands-on brand of learning gave them a deep and lasting appreciation of the environment and the need to protect it.

Now my children are passing on their love of nature to their own kids and my grandchildren are now visiting the Environmental Studies Center.

Florida Flavors II, produced by a new generation of nature lovers on the Environmental Studies Council, will help ensure the Jensen Beach Environmental Studies Center's future. Enjoy.

A HISTORY OF THE
ENVIRONMENTAL STUDIES CENTER
1972 – 2006

In the beginning there was a dream...

Teachers "Mike" Clark and Olive Ashby wanted to introduce their students to the local environment using a "hands-on" curriculum. They wanted to spark students' interest in the mangroves, rivers, fresh water habitats, and beaches in hopes that the students would help to preserve our "Good Nature" for future generations.

Ashby and Clark took the students on field trips to the beach, the lagoons and even their own Stuart Junior High School pond. The students learned first hand about the delicate environmental balance of the area where they lived. With a small state grant, the teachers ran a marine science summer program which was expanded to include students in other county schools. The success of this summer program attracted the interest of administrators and the Martin County School Board. They became aware of its importance to Martin County and the students.

Funding for programs are always vital and luckily several events came together to allow the teachers to make this program available to all public and private schoolchildren in the county. Federal money, under Title III of the Elementary and Secondary Education Act, was available for marine science education, and the district had an empty building, the old Jensen Beach Elementary School, on the shores of the Indian River.

In 1971, Superintendent V. James Navitsky, and two of his assistants, Gilbert Miller and Terrance Horrigan, attended an administrative meeting in Tallahassee. On the long drive back home, they discussed the empty building, the federal money and the teachers' passion for their subject. By the time they arrived back in Stuart, the three had a plan.

Horrigan and Miller wrote the original funding grant and submitted it for approval. Superintendent Navitsky, Clark and Ashby prepared a presentation for the grant review committee in Tallahassee. The presentation was strongly received, but turned down as being "too slick" and all funding dollars went to Dade County that year. However, the Martin County group was advised to resubmit the grant the next year. They changed very little in their application, but called the project the Marine Environmental Studies Center. The addition of this word must have been what the committee was looking for, because this time approval came and the Martin County School District was granted funding for three years. The word marine was dropped from the name shortly after the center opened.

Verbal approval of the grant was given in June of 1972 and the work began immediately. The staff spent the summer writing the goals and objectives to comply with federal requirements. Each objective had to be "measurable" by behavioral and objective observations of the students learning.

The grant allowed the district three years to fully develop the program. The staff began writing the curriculum for kindergarten through third grade. As each grade level of curriculum was finished, they would bring groups of children from that level to the Center to test the materials. The materials were rewritten and refined after each visit. When satisfied with the grade level materials, the staff would move on to the next level and continue the process of writing, testing and rewriting until they were satisfied with their product.

The grant contained funding for the rental of a boat. The Center teachers felt that it would be far wiser to use the money to purchase a boat. Through friends, they arranged for a custom-designed boat to be built by Thompson T-Craft in Titusville. The company and its owner, Rodney Thompson, donated a large portion of the cost in order to build the boat for the $9,000.00 which was allotted in the grant which left no money for motors. Thompson donated the motors also.

A contest was held for the students and the boat was named River Scout. The River Scout continues to be widely used in river expeditions for the students, largely because of the care and maintenance of Outboard Marine Corporation. OMC/Evinrude has replaced and maintained the motors over the years for the center and the value of these contributions from OMC/Evinrude Corporation has been immeasurable.

With the boat in place and the K-8 curriculum completed, the staff began scheduling regular classroom visits to the Center during the third year of operation. In the spring of the third year, the evaluation report was submitted and accepted and the district then became eligible for a dissemination grant under Title IV-C. This grant paid for half of the staff cost and the district paid for the other half.

As the dissemination grant came to an end, the Center faced the first of many financial crises. The grant was no longer renewable and the school district could not make up the costs that had been borne by the grant money. Toward the end of the summer, the School Board regretfully announced that the program would be closed. The Staff pleaded to retain the Center. The Superintendent relented and the Environmental Studies Center opened again that fall and has remained a vital part of the community.

In the early to mid-'80s, the Center began to offer Summer Camp programs for area students. The programs were fee-based and first started as half-day sessions. At the request of parents, the camps became full-day programs as Day Camp and Sailing Camp. In 1983, Camp SAMACAWAY, yet-to-be-named Camp W.E.T. (Water, Environment, Technology) was funded by a grant from the Department of Education.

During the next few years, the Center grew, not only in the number of students participating in the environmental education programs, but in changes to its facilities. Thanks to grants from several organizations and individuals, the Center was able to redesign the Wet Lab, establish a garden area and an outdoor turtle tank where a sea turtle is one of its main attractions. An alligator came to the center in 2005 to share the spotlight next to the turtle tank with its own enclosure.

Today more than 34 years since it's inception, the dream of two Martin County teachers, and many others who followed in their footsteps, has become a reality, with many officials, individuals, businesses and Martin County school children to thank for it's continued success.

ENVIRONMENTAL STUDIES COUNCIL, INC.

What started as an Advisory Committee, required by the original federal grant establishing the Environmental Studies Center, later evolved into a 501 (c) (3) non-profit organization to provide supplemental funding to the Center. The Environmental Studies Council, Inc. has become a fundraising and support group for the Center. The Council was created as a five-year federal grant program came to an end and future funding became conditional on grants and School Board support.

The Environmental Studies Council, addressing the need for financial support and long term funding for the Center, established the Environmental Studies Council Trust Fund, and set a goal for that fund at $1,000,000.00. This Fund continues to grow through the dedicated support of the public and provides the much needed contributions to avoid further cutbacks in staffing levels at the Center. This Trust Fund offers a guarantee that a program so lovingly created, so carefully protected, and so well supported by the community will continue to offer the finest in environmental education to the students of Martin County. The School Board, the Center Staff, the Council, the community can be proud that such a unique program is here to stay in Martin County.

To obtain some of its initial funding, the Council coordinated various fundraising activities in the community. However, its two primary fundraisers - an annual Kitchen Tour and the popular Florida Flavors cookbook - have brought the majority of funding to the trust fund.

The Council is currently spending $50,000 per year to pick up the tab for one teacher's salary and provides about $30,000 per year through different accounts for equipment, training and other requests from Center staff. In the Spring, 2000, the Council authorized funding for an annual scholarship to be presented to a graduating senior from an area high schools who will be pursuing environmental studies.

The Council also provides the Dr. Walter R. Stokes Summer Camp Scholarships to students who have a special interest learning more about the environment. In 2005, the first Ross Witham Summer Camp Scholarships for children of 2nd and 3rd grades were established in memory of Martin County's Turtle Man. The Council has also assisted with funding for Camp W.E.T. during times when full funding was not available

In more recent years, walking tours, seining adventures, and kayaking trips have contributed to the funding of the Council, and brought about new adventures for the community—parents and children alike.

TABLE OF CONTENTS

Party Fare

Breads and Brunch

Salads and Soup

Entrées

TABLE OF CONTENTS *(continued)*

Seafood Entrées

Vegetables and Side Dishes

Desserts

Pet Pages

Recipes with this logo are from the original Florida Flavors published over 20 years ago.

W e need quiet, wild places to cut ourselves down to size. They have the therapy that restores a proper sense of values: that all men and all creatures are common passengers on a wondrous space ship, living in that strange river of light always flowing from the sun. We need to lift our eyes to the mystery of a starry sky at night and to wonder.

~"The Last Cracker Barrel," by Ernest Lyons

Party
Fare

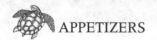

RONDELE WITH
CARAMELIZED ONION TARTLETS

1-3 tablespoons butter
1   large Vidalia onion, diced
2   teaspoons sugar
1   (2-ounce) package frozen
    prebaked phyllo tartlet shells

1   (5-ounce) package Rondele garlic
    spread, flavor of choice
2   tablespoons finely chopped fresh
    parsley

Preheat oven to 375 degrees.

Melt butter in a medium skillet over medium heat. Add onions and sauté until golden brown. Add sugar and stir until well blended and caramelized. Fill each tartlet with about 1 teaspoon garlic spread and top with about ½ teaspoon onions. Place on a baking sheet and bake 5 to 7 minutes. Garnish with parsley and serve immediately.

Serves: 15

Jill Levy

FRESH TOMATO TART

½ (15-ounce) package refrigerated
    pie crust
2   cups shredded mozzarella cheese
3   tablespoons chopped fresh basil,
    divided

3   medium-size ripe tomatoes,
    peeled and sliced ½-inch thick
1½ tablespoons olive oil
¼   teaspoon salt
¼   teaspoon black pepper

Preheat oven to 400 degrees.

Fit pie crust into a 10-inch tart pan according to package directions; trim any excess pastry along edges. Generously prick bottom and sides of crust with a fork. Bake 5 minutes.

Sprinkle cheese evenly over pie crust. Top with 2 tablespoons basil. Arrange tomato slices on top and brush with olive oil. Sprinkle with salt and pepper and place tart on a baking sheet. Bake on lower rack of oven for 35 to 40 minutes. Remove from oven and sprinkle with remaining 1 tablespoon basil. Let stand 5 minutes before serving.

Serves: 8 to 10

Susie Brock

CHILI SAUSAGE SQUARES

1   cup baking mix
⅓   cup milk
¼   cup mayonnaise, divided
1   pound pork sausage
½   cup chopped onion

1   egg, beaten
2   cups shredded sharp Cheddar cheese
2   (4-ounce) cans chopped green chiles, drained

Preheat oven to 350 degrees.

Combine baking mix, milk and 2 tablespoons mayonnaise and stir well. Spread mixture in a greased 9x13-inch pan; set aside. Cook sausage and onions in a skillet until sausage is browned; drain. Layer sausage mixture over crust in pan. Combine eggs, cheese, chiles and remaining 2 tablespoons mayonnaise. Spread mixture over sausage. Bake 30 minutes. Let stand 5 minutes before cutting into squares.

Serves: 40

Patty Henderson

COCKTAIL TOASTS

6   slices hearty white bread, crusts removed
½   cup fresh pesto

¼   cup sun-dried tomatoes packed in oil
¼   cup kalamata olives
1   tablespoon finely chopped parsley

Preheat oven to 400 degrees.

Spread one side of each slice of bread with pesto. Cut each slice into 4 squares and place on a baking sheet. Bake 10 minutes or until bottom of bread is lightly browned. Bread squares can be prepared up to a few hours before serving.

Soak tomatoes and olives in warm water for about 10 minutes; drain and dry with paper towel. Finely chop tomatoes and olives into chunks or slivers. Toss tomatoes and olives with parsley. Just before serving, spoon tomato mixture onto bread squares.

Marie Servinsky

CONCH FRITTERS

1 cup flour	2 teaspoons finely chopped parsley
1 teaspoon baking powder	⅓ cup finely chopped green bell
¼ teaspoon cayenne pepper	peppers (optional)
2 eggs	½ teaspoon salt
½ cup milk	¼ teaspoon black pepper
2 cups minced conch (a food	Dash of hot pepper sauce to taste
processor can be used)	Oil for frying

Mix together flour, baking powder and cayenne pepper. Beat eggs with milk and add to dry ingredients. Blend well and let stand 30 minutes. Stir in conch, parsley, bell peppers, salt, pepper and hot sauce.

Heat oil in a deep skillet to 375 degrees. Drop batter by teaspoonfuls into hot oil and fry until golden brown. Serve with cocktail sauce or mustard sauce.

Lillie Davis

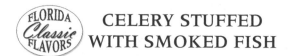

CELERY STUFFED WITH SMOKED FISH

1 (3-ounce) package cream cheese, softened	6 stalks celery
	Lettuce
1 cup Mrs. Peters' smoked fish	2 cups grapefruit segments, chilled
2 tablespoons mayonnaise	French dressing
Salt to taste	

Mash cream cheese. Blend in fish, mayonnaise and salt well. Pack mixture into the grooves of celery stalks. Cut stalks into ¾-inch pieces. Arrange on a bed of lettuce leaves with grapefruit segments. Drizzle dressing on top.

Florence Werle

> In Stuart, if you put on a coat you are going to church, a funeral or an installation. Add a hat and you are going to New York.
>
> ~ Ernest Lyons

ELEGANT ASPARAGUS ROLLS

50 thin fresh asparagus spears
    (do not use frozen or canned)
1 (8-ounce) package cream cheese,
    softened
4 ounces blue cheese

1 egg
25 slices thin white sandwich bread,
    crusts removed, Pepperidge
    Farms
5 tablespoons butter, melted

Preheat oven to 400 degrees.

Snap off ends of asparagus spears. Steam 2 to 3 minutes or until crisp-tender; dry in a single layer on paper towel. Combine cream cheese, blue cheese and egg in a food processor on medium speed until smooth; set aside. Use a rolling pin to flatten bread slices. Spread cheese mixture on each slice and lay 2 asparagus spears, in opposite directions, on top. Roll bread over spears and press edge to seal. Brush with melted butter. Bake 12 to 15 minutes or until browned.

Susie Brock

MARINATED GREEN BANANAS

4 pounds green bananas
1 cup milk
1 medium onion, chopped
1 medium-size green bell pepper,
    chopped
1 small can roasted red peppers,
    chopped

½ cup green olives, or more to taste
4-5 bay leaves
    Garlic powder to taste
    Salt and pepper to taste
1¼ cups olive oil
¾ cup vinegar

Rinse bananas well. Slightly slash the skin of each banana vertically to separate some of the skin from the meat of the banana. Fill a large pot part way with water. Add milk and some salt and bring to a boil. Add bananas and boil 20 minutes or until tender. Drain bananas and rinse with cold water; drain and set aside until completely cool.

In a large container, mix onions, bell peppers, roasted peppers, olives, bay leaves, garlic powder and salt and pepper. Mix olive oil and vinegar together in a separate jar. Add oil marinade to vegetable mixture and stir well. Peel bananas, cut into pieces and add to vegetable mixture. Cover and marinate 24 hours. Serve with a slotted spoon.

Judy Simmons

PECAN-BRIE QUESADILLAS

3 ounces Brie cheese, chopped	2 tablespoons chopped fresh
2 (9-inch) flour tortillas	parsley
2 tablespoons chopped pecans,	Parsley sprigs for garnish
toasted	¼ cup sour cream

Sprinkle cheese over half of each tortilla. Top with pecans and parsley. Fold tortillas in half, pressing gently. In a lightly greased 10-inch skillet, cook quesadillas over medium heat for 2 to 3 minutes or until lightly browned, turning once.

Cut quesadillas into wedges. Garnish with parsley sprigs and serve with sour cream on the side.

Patty Henderson

GORGONZOLA TOASTS

2 tablespoons pignoli nuts	8-10 fresh basil leaves, finely
4 tablespoons butter, softened	chopped
8-10 tablespoons Gorgonzola cheese	Very thin white bread

Preheat oven to 375 degrees.

Toast nuts in oven for 5 to 7 minutes; cool. Combine nuts with butter, cheese and basil in a bowl. Spread a thin layer of mixture over bread slices and place on a baking sheet. Bake until brown and crisp. Remove from oven and transfer toasts to a cutting board. Cut away crusts and cut each slice of toast into triangles. Serve warm.

Gretchen Hurchalla

WONTON PIES

2 pounds sausage	½ cup chopped green bell peppers
3 cups shredded cheese	1 cup Ranch dressing
½ cup chopped onions	1 package wonton wrappers

Preheat oven to 350 degrees.

Brown sausage and drain off grease. In a bowl, mix sausage, cheese, onions, bell peppers and dressing. Spray muffin tins with baking spray. Place wonton wrappers in muffin tins. Bake wrappers 5 minutes. Remove from oven and spoon filling into wrappers. Bake 5 to 8 minutes longer.

Lori Slaughter

FLORIDA Classic FLAVORS BACON-WRAPPED WATER CHESTNUTS

1 (8½-ounce) can water chestnuts, drained	¼ cup soy sauce
8 slices bacon, halved	½ teaspoon ground ginger
	½ teaspoon garlic salt

Wrap each water chestnut in a half-slice of bacon and secure with a toothpick. Combine soy sauce, ginger and salt and pour over wrapped water chestnuts. Refrigerate several hours; drain. Marinade can be stored in refrigerator and reused. Place water chestnuts in a microwave-safe dish and cover with paper towel. Cook in microwave on high for 3 minutes. Turn dish and cook 3 minutes longer. Serve hot.

Serves: 16

Pam Kahle

FRESH ASPARAGUS APPETIZERS

2 (8-ounce) cans refrigerator crescent rolls	1 pound fresh asparagus, cut into 1-inch pieces, tips reserved
3 tablespoons butter	¼ teaspoon black pepper
1 sweet onion, chopped	1 cup shredded mozzarella cheese
2 cloves garlic, minced	1 cup shredded Swiss cheese

Preheat oven to 375 degrees.

Unroll crescent rolls and press dough onto an ungreased baking sheet, pressing to seal perforations. Prick dough with a fork. Bake on lower rack of oven for 6 to 8 minutes or until lightly browned. Melt butter in a large skillet over medium-high heat. Add onion and sauté 5 minutes. Add garlic and sauté 2 minutes longer. Add asparagus pieces and sauté 4 to 6 minutes or until crisp-tender. Add pepper and asparagus tips and sauté 1 to 2 minutes or until tender. Spoon asparagus mixture over prepared crust. Sprinkle with cheeses. Bake on low rack of oven for 6 to 8 minutes or until cheese melts. Cut into squares.

Patty Henderson

SHRIMP AND PICKLED JALAPEÑOS

1½ pounds fresh shrimp, lightly cooked	¼ cup fresh lime juice
1 bunch cilantro, chopped	1 (12-ounce) can pickled green jalapeño peppers

Combine all ingredients in a serving dish and chill. Serve with toothpicks.

Elaine Clark

WALNUT-BLUE CHEESE SLICES

1 stick butter	1¼ cups flour
1 (4-ounce) package blue cheese, softened	⅓ cup finely chopped walnuts

Preheat oven to 350 degrees.

Process butter, cheese and flour in a food processor until smooth. Spoon mixture into a bowl and mix in walnuts. Cover with plastic wrap and chill 10 minutes. Shape dough into two 8-inch logs. Wrap in plastic wrap and refrigerate 1 hour. Unwrap and slice into ¼-inch thick slices. Bake on an ungreased baking sheet for 10 to 12 minutes. Store in an airtight container.

Patty Henderson

 ## BOURBON HOT DOGS

1 pound hot dogs	1 small onion, sliced
¾ cup bourbon	1½ cups ketchup
½ cup dark brown sugar	

Cut hot dogs into ½-inch slices and place in a electric skillet. Add bourbon, sugar, onions and ketchup to skillet. Simmer at least 1 hour. If sauce cooks down too much, add more bourbon. When ready to serve, transfer to a chafing dish and keep warm.

The amount of hot dogs can be increased without increasing the amount of sauce. Stores well in refrigerator.

Salli Campbell

PESTO DELIGHT

Round Melba toast	Fresh pesto
Whipped cream cheese	Freshly grated Parmesan cheese

Cover Melba toast with cream cheese. Spread about ½ teaspoon pesto per toast over top. Sprinkle with Parmesan cheese.

Michelle Wright

DOTTIE'S SECRET RECIPE MEATBALLS

Meatballs

¾ pound lean ground beef
¼ pound lean ground pork
¾ cup rolled oats
½ cup milk
¼ cup finely chopped water chestnuts
1 tablespoon Worcestershire sauce

½ teaspoon garlic salt
½ teaspoon onion salt
  Few drops of Tabasco sauce, or to taste
2 tablespoons butter

Sweet and Sour Sauce

1 cup sugar
¾ cup vinegar
1 teaspoon paprika

½ teaspoon salt
2 tablespoons cornstarch
1 tablespoon cold water

Combine all meatball ingredients except butter. Mix and shape into 48 balls. Brown meatballs well in butter; drain on paper towel. Simmer meatballs in Sweet and Sour Sauce in a skillet for 30 minutes. Serve hot as an appetizer with toothpicks.

To make sauce, mix sugar, vinegar, paprika and salt in a small saucepan. Dissolve cornstarch in water and add to saucepan. Cook and stir over medium heat until thickened.

Yield: 48 meatballs

Dottie Childs/Submitted by Dale Hipson

JUST IN THYME TARTLETS

15 cherry tomatoes, halved
1 teaspoon dried thyme
1 teaspoon olive oil
¼ teaspoon salt
⅛ teaspoon freshly ground black pepper

2 (2-ounce) packages prebaked phyllo tartlet shells
12 ounces Gruyère cheese, cut into 30 cubes (about ¾-inch cubes)

Preheat oven to 425 degrees.

Combine tomatoes, thyme, oil, salt and pepper and toss. Transfer mixture to a jelly roll pan. Roast tomatoes, cut-side up, for 12 minutes or until tomatoes soften. Cool in pan 5 minutes. Reduce oven temperature to 350 degrees. Arrange tartlet shells on a large baking sheet. Place a piece of cheese and a tomato half side-by-side in each shell. Bake 5 to 8 minutes or until cheese is melted and bubbly. Cool 3 minutes before serving.

Susie Brock

SPINACH ROLLUPS

1 (10-ounce) package frozen chopped spinach, thawed and drained	1 bunch scallions, chopped
	1 (1-ounce) package Ranch dressing mix
1 cup mayonnaise	3 ounces real bacon bits
1 (8-ounce) container sour cream	9 (10-ounce) flour tortillas

Combine spinach, mayonnaise, sour cream, scallions, dressing mix and bacon bits. Spread mixture evenly over tortillas. Roll up tortillas jelly roll fashion, pressing edges to seal. Wrap in plastic wrap and chill 4 hours. Cut into ½-inch thick slices.

Yield: 6 dozen

Patty Henderson

COFFIED BEEF SKEWERS

1 pound boneless beef sirloin steak	¾ teaspoon black pepper
¼ cup strong brewed coffee	½ teaspoon salt
¼ cup dry white wine	⅛ teaspoon cayenne pepper

Cut steak across the grain into long, thin strips and place in a resealable plastic bag. In a bowl, combine coffee, wine, black pepper, salt and cayenne pepper. Pour mixture over beef, seal and turn bag to coat beef. Chill 2 to 4 hours. Thread beef onto skewers and grill over hot coals until done.

Colleen Hynes

STUFFED MUSHROOMS

⅓ cup Parmesan cheese	20 mushrooms, stems removed
1 (3-ounce) package cream cheese, softened	Melted butter

Preheat oven to 350 degrees.

Mix cheeses together. Spoon a scant teaspoon of mixture into each mushroom cap. Dip mushrooms in melted butter and place on a baking sheet. Bake 15 minutes.

Serves: 4

Lynn Siegel

CURRIED CRAB APPETIZERS

7   ounces crabmeat, drained and
    flaked
1   cup shredded Swiss cheese
1½ cups mayonnaise
1   tablespoon finely chopped
    scallions

1   teaspoon lemon juice
¼   teaspoon curry powder
1   (8-ounce) package butter flake
    refrigerated rolls
1   (5-ounce) can sliced water
    chestnuts

Preheat oven to 400 degrees.

Combine crabmeat, cheese, mayonnaise, scallions, lemon juice and curry powder. Split rolls in half. Spoon crab mixture onto each half and top with water chestnuts. Bake 10 to 12 minutes or until bubbly and brown.

Marion Paul

BBQ CHICKEN PIZZA

¼   cup olive oil
1   pound boneless chicken breast
    Salt and pepper to taste
1½ cups hickory BBQ sauce, divided

14 ounces smoked Gouda cheese,
    shredded, divided
2   large prebaked pizza crusts
1½ cups thinly sliced red onions
4   scallions, chopped

Preheat oven to 450 degrees.

Heat olive oil over medium heat in a medium skillet. Season chicken with salt and pepper. Sauté chicken in oil for 5 minutes per side or until tender; cool. Slice into ⅓-inch slices and mix with ¾ cup BBQ sauce; set aside.

Sprinkle half of cheese over pizza crusts. Spoon remaining BBQ sauce evenly over both pizzas. Arrange chicken over sauce and top with red onions. Spread any remaining sauce from chicken over top. Sprinkle with remaining cheese and scallions. Bake pizzas, one at a time, for 14 minutes or until bottom is crisp and cheese is melted. Let stand 5 minutes before slicing.

Serves: 12 appetizers or 6 main dish

Zazu Williams

CHEESY BACON BITES

8   slices bacon, cooked and
       crumbled
1   cup shredded Swiss cheese
¼   cup mayonnaise
1   tablespoon grated onion

1   tablespoon chopped fresh chives
½   teaspoon celery salt
⅛   teaspoon cayenne pepper
6   slices hearty white bread, crusts
       removed

Preheat oven to 325 degrees.

Combine bacon, cheese, mayonnaise, onion, chives, celery salt and cayenne pepper. Spread mixture over bread slices and place on a lightly greased baking sheet. Bake 10 to 12 minutes. Cut into squares.

Yield: 2 dozen

Patty Henderson

CURRIED STUFFED EGGS

8   hard cooked eggs, peeled and
       halved crosswise
¼   cup mayonnaise
2   tablespoons sour cream
1   tablespoon chutney

½   teaspoon curry powder
¼   teaspoon cayenne pepper
     Salt to taste
     Paprika

Remove egg yolks and place in a bowl. Cover egg white shells and set aside. Add mayonnaise, sour cream, chutney, curry and cayenne pepper to yolks and mix until smooth. Season with salt. Fill egg white shells with yolk mixture. Sprinkle with paprika. Cover tightly and refrigerate until ready to serve.

Ev Roarke

SHRIMP PÂTÉ

1½ pounds shrimp, cooked and
       chopped
1   small onion, minced

1   stick butter, melted
⅓   cup mayonnaise
1   teaspoon lemon juice

Combine all ingredients and press into a mold. Chill thoroughly. Unmold and serve with cocktail sauce and crackers. Garnish with lemon wedges.

Dutchess Kiiorja

GRILLED GREEN QUESADILLAS WITH BRIE AND HERBS

4 (12-inch) spinach tortillas	2 tablespoons chopped fresh tarragon leaves
¾ pound Brie cheese with herbs, sliced	Sour cream
¼ cup chopped fresh chives	Tomato salsa or mango salsa

Lightly grill or brown tortillas on both sides. While still over heat, arrange a layer of Brie across half of each tortilla. Sprinkle with chives and tarragon. Fold tortilla over, covering cheese. Lightly press down on quesadilla, turn and cook 30 seconds longer. Cut into wedges. Serve with sour cream and salsa.

For a party, I sometimes put the quesadilla together, fold and lay on a baking sheet. Just before ready to serve, bake them on low until the cheese melts.

You can also experiment with different herb combinations.

Marie Servinsky

VEGGIE BARS

2 (8-ounce) packages refrigerated crescent rolls	½ cup milk
1 (1-ounce) package Ranch dressing mix	½ cup chopped scallions
2 (8-ounce) packages cream cheese, softened	1 large carrot, grated
	1 cup snipped broccoli florets
	1 cup shredded Cheddar cheese

Preheat oven to 350 degrees.

Unroll dough onto a jelly roll pan. Press together perforations to make 2 sheets of dough. Bake 10 minutes; cool.

Mix dressing mix and cream cheese. Slowly add milk until a frosting consistency is reached. Spread mixture over cooled crust. Sprinkle with scallions, carrot and broccoli. Top with cheese. Chill before cutting into squares.

Pat Ries

SPINACH APPETIZER SQUARES

2 eggs	1 (10-ounce) package frozen
½ cup milk	chopped spinach, thawed and
2 tablespoons butter, melted and	squeezed dry
cooled	3 scallions, minced
½ cup flour	8 ounces Monterey Jack or
1 teaspoon baking powder	Muenster cheese, shredded

Preheat oven to 350 degrees.

Beat together eggs, milk, butter, flour and baking powder in a medium bowl. Stir in spinach, scallions and cheese. Spread mixture in a greased 8-inch square pan and smooth top. Bake 35 minutes or until brown. Let stand 10 minutes. Cut into small squares and serve warm.

Serves: 12

Jill Levy

MOM'S GLAZED NUTS

1 teaspoon cinnamon	5 tablespoons water
⅛ teaspoon nutmeg	1 teaspoon vanilla
1 cup sugar	2 cups pecans or walnuts
¼ teaspoon salt	

Combine cinnamon, nutmeg, sugar, salt, water and vanilla in a 2-quart saucepan. Cook over medium heat to soft-ball stage. (To test, a teaspoon of mixture forms a soft ball when dropped into a cup of water.) Stir in nuts. Spread nuts onto a wax paper-lined baking sheet; cool. Store nuts in an airtight container for up to a month.

Makes a great hostess or teacher gift.

Dorothy Young

> I find peace in the upper rivers. Their charm is that you can still be alone on them look up to the clouds or stars and think. They unlock the mind and it's friend, the spirit.
>
> ~ Ernest Lyons

APRICOT-PECAN-BRIE TARTS

25 pecan halves
1 (8-ounce) package Brie cheese, chilled

1½ (16-ounce) packages frozen puff pastry sheets, thawed (or pie crust)
⅓ cup apricot preserves

Preheat oven to 350 degrees.

Bake pecans in a shallow pan for 10 to 15 minutes or until toasted; cool. Remove cheese rind and cut cheese into 24 cubes; set aside.

Roll pastry into a 15x10-inch rectangle on a lightly floured surface. Cut into 24 squares. Fit squares into mini muffin tins, extending corners slightly above rims. Bake pastry at 425 degrees for 10 to 12 minutes or until it begins to brown. Remove from oven and gently press into center of each pastry, forming tart shells. Spoon ½ teaspoon preserves into each shell. Place a cheese cube in each shell and top with a pecan half. Bake 5 minutes longer or until cheese melts. Serve immediately.

Serves: 24

Susie Brock

DOROTHY'S BREAD AND BUTTER PICKLES

12 medium pickling cucumbers, unpeeled, washed and sliced
3 red or yellow bell peppers, sliced
3 medium onions, sliced
3 cups cider vinegar

6 cups sugar
1 teaspoon celery seed
1 teaspoon turmeric seed
1 teaspoon mustard seed
1 teaspoon salt

Soak cucumbers, peppers and onions in ice water for 3 hours. Heat vinegar and sugar in a saucepan. Add drained vegetables and cook 5 minutes. Add celery seed, turmeric seed, mustard seed and salt. Mix well. Pack into sterilized jars and seal.

Bryna Potsdam

FETA DIP

6   cloves garlic, minced
6   basil leaves, chopped
¼   cup olive oil
½   teaspoon salt (optional)

4   ounces black olives, sliced
4   ounces grape tomatoes, chopped
1   (8-ounce) block feta cheese

Combine garlic, basil, olive oil, salt, olives and tomatoes. Drizzle mixture over feta. Let stand at room temperature 1 hour. Taste improves if made ahead and refrigerated overnight. If making ahead, add tomatoes just before serving. Serve with crackers, such as Triscuits.

Michelle Narson Kassay

CRABMEAT DIP

1   (8-ounce) package cream cheese, softened
1   tablespoon milk
1   (6½-ounce) can crabmeat, flaked (or use fresh crab)

2   tablespoons grated onion
½   teaspoon prepared horseradish
¼   teaspoon salt
    Dash of black pepper to taste
½   cup sliced almonds for garnish

Preheat oven to 375 degrees.

Combine cream cheese and milk. Add crabmeat, onion, horseradish, salt and pepper. Pour mixture into a shallow 2-quart baking dish. Top with almonds. Bake 15 minutes. Serve hot with your favorite crackers. Recipe may be doubled.

Kay Norris

FIRESIDE BRIE

1   (8-ounce) round Brie cheese
3   tablespoons sun-dried tomatoes in oil, chopped

1   tablespoon toasted pine nuts
1   tablespoon sliced fresh basil
    Sliced French bread or water crackers

Preheat oven to 350 degrees.

Place cheese in a lightly greased ovenproof serving dish. Bake, uncovered, for 8 to 10 minutes or until cheese is soft and partially melted. Lightly drain tomatoes. Sprinkle tomatoes, nuts and basil over cheese. Serve immediately with bread or crackers. Adjust topping amounts according to your liking. I like lots!

Lisa J. Massing

HOT CLAM DIP À LA LOIS GAILLARD

2   (8-ounce) cans minced or
      chopped clams with juice
1   tablespoon lemon juice
1   stick butter
1   medium onion, chopped
1   teaspoon dried oregano

1   clove garlic, chopped
1   tablespoon dried parsley, plus
      extra for garnish
1   teaspoon dried hot pepper flakes,
      or to taste
1   cup unseasoned dry bread crumbs
      Paprika

Preheat oven to 350 degrees.

Mix together undrained clams and lemon juice; set aside. In a saucepan, combine butter, onions, oregano, garlic, parsley and pepper flakes. Simmer 15 minutes. Add clam mixture to saucepan and simmer 15 minutes longer. Add bread crumbs and mix well. Transfer to a baking dish and sprinkle with paprika. Sprinkle parsley around the rim of dish for garnish. Bake 15 minutes. Serve with crackers or small rounds of pumpernickel bread.

Lois Gaillard

VIDALIA ONION DIP

2   cups finely chopped Vidalia
      onions

2   cups shredded Swiss cheese
2   cups mayonnaise

Preheat oven to 325 degrees.

Combine all ingredients and transfer to a shallow baking dish. Bake 20 minutes. Serve with crackers.

Jill Roberts

MISSISSIPPI CAVIAR

3   (16-ounce) cans black-eyed peas, rinsed and drained
¾   cup diced green bell peppers
½-¾ cup diced sweet onions
1   (4-ounce) jar pimientos, drained
½   cup diced canned jalapeño peppers, or ¾ cup fresh

3   large cloves garlic, minced
1   cruet Good Seasons Italian Dressing, prepared according to directions with red wine vinegar and vegetable oil

Combine all ingredients in a non-reactive bowl. Marinate overnight, if possible. Adjust all ingredients according to taste. Drain slightly and serve with corn chips. Store in refrigerator for up to 1 week, if it is not all eaten.

Patty Henderson

GUACAMOLE-AVOCADO DIP

6   avocados, peeled with pit removed
1   onion, chopped

1   large tomato, chopped
1   (6-ounce) can chopped green chiles

Mash avocado, then mix avocado with onions and tomatoes. Add chiles and blend thoroughly.

Gloria Gary

NACHO DIP

1   (8-ounce) package cream cheese, softened
1   (8-ounce) container sour cream
1   (10½-ounce) can jalapeño bean dip
1   (1¼-ounce) package chili seasoning dip

5   drops hot pepper sauce
2   teaspoons dried parsley
¼   cup taco sauce
1¼ cups shredded Cheddar cheese, divided
1¼ cups shredded Monterey Jack cheese, divided

Preheat oven to 325 degrees.

Combine cream cheese and sour cream and beat until smooth. Stir in bean dip, chili seasoning, hot sauce, parsley, taco sauce, ¾ cup Cheddar cheese and ¾ cup Monterey Jack cheese. Spoon mixture into a lightly greased 12x8x2-inch baking dish. Top with remaining cheeses. Bake 15 to 20 minutes. Serve with chips.

Sharyon Daigneau

CALCUTTA CHUTNEY CHICKEN SPREAD

1	envelope unflavored gelatin	1½	cups coarsely chopped skinless cooked chicken
½	cup milk		
1	chicken bouillon cube, crumbled	1	(12-ounce) jar chutney, divided
1	teaspoon curry powder	¼	cup chopped celery
¼	teaspoon salt	1	(2-ounce) jar diced pimiento, drained
1	cup creamed cottage cheese		
1	(3-ounce) package cream cheese, softened and cut into cubes	⅓	cup chopped scallions
		8-12	drops Tabasco
		½	cup whipping cream
½	cup sour cream		

Lightly oil a 9-inch tart pan with a removable bottom or a 9-inch quiche dish. To serve unmolded, choose and grease a 5- to 6-cup mold or two 3-cup molds and double the amount of gelatin.

Sprinkle gelatin over milk in a small saucepan and allow to stand 5 minutes or until gelatin is softened. Add bouillon and bring to a boil, stirring constantly, over medium heat until gelatin is dissolved. Stir in curry powder and salt. Remove from heat and cool slightly.

Combine cottage cheese, cream cheese and sour cream in a food processor fitted with a metal blade. Process until smooth. Add chicken, ½ cup chutney, celery, pimiento, scallions, Tabasco and gelatin mixture. Pulse processor on and off until mixture is just combined but still chunky. Adjust seasonings as needed.

In a large mixing bowl, whip cream until soft peaks form; do not beat stiff. Fold chicken mixture into cream. Pour mixture into prepared pans. Cover with plastic wrap and refrigerate until firm. The spread may be refrigerated, well covered, for up to 2 days, or it may be frozen. Thaw frozen spread overnight in refrigerator.

If using a tart pan, go around the inside edges with the tip of a sharp knife. Remove the sides of the pan and place bottom of pan with chicken spread on a platter. If using a mold, unmold onto a serving platter.

Stir remaining chutney in a small bowl. If chutney is very chunky, process in a food processor fitted with a metal blade until almost smooth. Spread chutney over the top of the spread. Refrigerate until ready to serve. Serve with crackers.

Serves: 12

Lloyd Wescoat

CRAB VEGETABLE DIP

1	(8-ounce) package reduced-fat cream cheese, softened		Dash of hot pepper sauce, or to taste
1	cup non-fat sour cream		Salt to taste
2	tablespoons chili sauce	1	(7-ounce) can crabmeat, drained and sliced
1	tablespoon grated onions		Vegetables for dipping
1	tablespoon lemon juice		
¼-½	teaspoon Worcestershire sauce		

Blend cream cheese with sour cream. Add chili sauce, onions, lemon juice, Worcestershire sauce and hot sauce. Season with salt. Mix in crabmeat. Serve with vegetables.

Bunny Moss

FRESH CORN DIP

2	tablespoons unsalted butter, divided	1	jalapeño pepper, seeded and minced
4	ears fresh yellow or white corn, kernels removed from cob	2	teaspoons minced garlic
½	teaspoon salt	1	cup mayonnaise
¼	teaspoon freshly ground black pepper	¼-½	teaspoon cayenne pepper, or to taste
1	large sweet onion, finely chopped (about 1 cup)	1	(8-ounce) package shredded Cheddar and Monterey Jack cheese mixture, divided
1	red bell pepper, finely chopped		Corn chips or tortilla chips
6-8	scallions, thinly sliced		

Preheat oven to 350 degrees.

Melt 1 tablespoon butter in a skillet over medium-high heat. Add corn kernels and salt and pepper. Cook about 5 minutes or until corn turns golden brown. Transfer to a large bowl; set aside.

Melt remaining 1 tablespoon butter in a skillet. Add onions and bell peppers and cook 2 to 3 minutes or until onions are clear. Add scallions, jalapeño and garlic and cook another 2 minutes. Add mixture to corn in bowl. Mix in mayonnaise, cayenne and three-fourths of cheese. Pour mixture into an 8- or 9-inch square or round baking dish. Sprinkle with remaining one-fourth of cheese. Bake 10 to 15 minutes or until golden brown on top. Serve with chips and enjoy.

Dip can be prepared, but not baked, 1 to 2 days ahead of time and refrigerated until ready to use. To serve, bake at 350 degrees for 13 to 18 minutes.

Susie Brock

SMOKED FISH DIP

1½ cups crumbled smoked fish
½ cup milk
1 (8-ounce) package reduced-fat
cream cheese, softened
¼ cup finely minced onions
1 stalk celery, finely chopped

1 tablespoon finely minced fresh
parsley
½ teaspoon Dijon mustard
½ teaspoon lemon juice
1 teaspoon Worcestershire sauce
Cayenne pepper to taste
Salt and pepper to taste

Place fish in a medium bowl. Add milk, cover and chill 30 to 60 minutes. Stir in cream cheese, onions, celery, parsley, mustard, lemon juice and Worcestershire sauce. Season with cayenne pepper, salt and pepper. Cover and chill 2 to 3 hours to allow flavors to blend.

Gretchen Hurchalla

EAST INDIAN STUFFED PINEAPPLE

1 pound cream cheese, softened
1 jar Major Gray's chutney
¾ cup salted pecans or almonds
½ cup finely chopped scallions

1 ripe pineapple
Sesame snack sticks or other
crackers of choice

Beat cream cheese with an electric mixer until fluffy; do not overbeat. Add chutney, pecans and scallions. Meanwhile, split pineapple in half lengthwise from top to bottom, leaving on top leaves. Cube and scoop out inside of pineapple; reserve for another use. Fill half of pineapple with chutney mixture. Serve with crackers.

Nancy Farrow

PACIFIC NORTHWEST SALMON SPREAD

1 (15-ounce) can red salmon, drained
1 (8-ounce) package cream cheese,
softened
¼ teaspoon liquid smoke
1 tablespoon lemon juice

¼ teaspoon salt
1 teaspoon prepared horseradish
2 teaspoons grated onions
3 tablespoons dried parsley
½ cup pecans

Combine all ingredients except pecans and form into a ball. Roll ball in pecans and refrigerate until ready to serve. Serve with crackers.

Darlene A. Rogers

SEAFOOD DIP

2   (8-ounce) packages reduced-fat
    cream cheese
1   package crab delight flakes
    (imitation crab)
2   tablespoons finely chopped
    onions

1   tablespoon prepared horseradish
1   teaspoon Worcestershire sauce
4-5 drops hot pepper sauce
⅓   cup finely chopped walnuts
    Paprika

Preheat oven to 375 degrees.

Stir cream cheese until slightly softened. Blend in crab flakes, onions, horseradish, Worcestershire sauce and hot sauce. Spread mixture in a 9-inch pie pan. Top with walnuts and sprinkle with paprika. Bake, uncovered, for 25 minutes or until lightly browned.

Jean Gallagher

HOT CRAB SPREAD

1   (7¾-ounce) can crabmeat,
    drained and shells removed
1   (8-ounce) package cream cheese,
    softened
3   tablespoons sherry or white wine

½   teaspoon horseradish
3   tablespoons minced onions
    Dash of hot pepper sauce
2   teaspoons Worcestershire sauce
    Paprika

Preheat oven to 350 degrees.

Combine all ingredients except paprika and transfer to a 1-quart casserole dish. Sprinkle with paprika. Bake 15 minutes or until bubbly and light brown. Serve with crackers or toast.

Cecilia Wright

VEGETABLE DIP

1   tablespoon anchovy paste
1   (8-ounce) package cream cheese
½   cup mayonnaise

¼   cup dried parsley
2   tablespoons dried minced onion
1   hard-boiled egg

Mix together anchovy paste, cream cheese, mayonnaise, parsley and onion. Separate white from yolk of egg. Grate egg white into dip mixture. Grate egg yolk over top of dip for garnish.

Ginger Baldwin

SMOKED MACKEREL ROQUEFORT LOG

7   ounces fresh smoked mackerel
2   (3-ounce) packages cream cheese, softened
2   ounces Roquefort cheese, crumbled
2   tablespoons finely chopped celery

1   teaspoon minced onions
⅛   teaspoon hot pepper sauce
⅛   teaspoon cayenne pepper
½   cup chopped pecans
2   tablespoons chopped fresh parsley

Combine mackerel, cream cheese, Roquefort cheese, celery, onions, hot sauce and cayenne. Mix thoroughly. Chill several hours. Combine pecans and parsley and shape into a log. Roll log in pecan mixture. Serve with crackers.

Kim Neall

SPINACH-ARTICHOKE DIP

3   cups finely chopped fresh spinach, stems removed, or one 10-ounce package frozen chopped spinach, thawed and drained
¾   cup freshly grated Parmesan cheese, plus extra for topping
1¼ cups shredded Monterey Jack cheese

1   (8-ouunce) package cream cheese, softened
½   cup mayonnaise
2   (14-ounce) cans artichoke hearts, drained and finely chopped
    Juice of ½ lemon
2   cloves garlic, chopped
3   tablespoons chopped shallots
    Cayenne pepper to taste
    Salt to taste

Preheat oven to 350 degrees.

Combine all ingredients and transfer to a baking dish. Sprinkle extra Parmesan cheese on top. Bake 30 minutes or until top starts to bubble. Serve on toasted baguette rounds, plain crackers or mini toasts.

Nancy Stanford

They say as the twig is bent, the tree will grow.

~ Ernest Lyons

SPINACH DIP WITH FETA CHEESE

5   tablespoons extra-virgin olive oil, divided
1   (6-ounce) package fresh baby spinach
1   cup crumbled feta cheese
¾   cup sour cream
1   teaspoon minced garlic
½   teaspoon lemon zest
Salt and pepper to taste

Heat 1 tablespoon oil in a skillet over medium heat. Add spinach and toss 3 minutes or until spinach is wilted but still bright green. Transfer spinach to a sieve and press out excess liquid. Chop spinach coarsely; set aside. Combine remaining 4 tablespoons oil, feta cheese, sour cream, garlic and lemon zest in a food processor. Blend until smooth and transfer to a bowl. Mix in spinach and season with salt and pepper. Cover and chill. Serve with breadsticks or vegetables.

Virginia Lueders

HOT CHEESY SPINACH DIP

2   tablespoons butter
¼   cup chopped onions
1   tablespoon all-purpose flour
1¾ cups half-and-half
2   (10-ounce) packages frozen chopped spinach, thawed and drained
1   (8-ounce) can sliced water chestnuts, drained
1   cup shredded Cheddar cheese
1   (1-ounce) package dry vegetable soup mix
¼   cup shredded Parmesan cheese

Preheat oven to 425 degrees.

Melt butter in a large saucepan over medium heat. Add onions and cook and stir 2 to 3 minutes or until tender. Stir in flour and cook and stir 1 minute longer. Add half-and-half and cook, stirring constantly, until mixture boils and thickens. Remove from heat. Stir in spinach, water chestnuts, cheese and soup mix. Spoon mixture into a 1-quart casserole dish. Sprinkle with Parmesan cheese. Bake 10 to 15 minutes or until dip is bubbly and cheese is melted. Serve warm.

Serves: 8

Kathy Walker

HAWAIIAN BREAD AND DIP

1	loaf King's Hawaiian bread	2	tablespoons dried parsley, or
1⅓	cups sour cream		¼ cup fresh
1⅓	cups mayonnaise	2	tablespoons Season-All
2	tablespoons dried minced onions	2	tablespoons dried dill weed
		1	(4½-ounce) can sliced black olives, drained

Slice top off loaf of bread. Hollow out loaf, cutting bread removed into chunks for dipping; set aside. Mix sour cream, mayonnaise, onions, parsley, Season-All, dill and olives in a bowl. Just before serving, transfer dip to bread shell. Serve with reserved bread chunks and additional crackers or bread. Tear apart bread shell to eat when almost empty.

Judy Schalk

 # REUBEN DIP

1	(3-ounce) package cream cheese, softened	4	ounces sliced corn beef, finely diced
¼	cup sour cream	¼	cup drained sauerkraut, chopped
½	cup shredded Swiss cheese	2-3	tablespoons milk

Combine all ingredients in a small saucepan. Heat over low heat, thinning with milk if dip is too thick. Serve with rye sticks.

Cheryl Kessel

CHRISTMAS CURRY-ALMOND CHEESE SPREAD

2	(8-ounce) packages cream cheese, softened	1	cup slivered almonds, toasted, plus extra for garnish
1	(9-ounce) jar mango chutney	1	tablespoon curry powder
		½	teaspoon dry mustard

Combine all ingredients in a food processor. Process, stopping occasionally to scrape down sides. Transfer mixture to a plate and mold into a round shape. Cover and chill. When ready to serve, sprinkle extra toasted almonds on top for garnish. Serve with crackers or Granny Smith apple wedges.

Mary Hutchinson

SCOOP'S HOT BEAN DIP

2 cups refried beans	1 (8-ounce) package cream cheese, cubed
1 (1¼-ounce) package taco seasoning	1 (8-ounce) container sour cream
5 ounces picante sauce, or to taste	8 ounces Cheddar cheese, shredded

Preheat oven to 350 degrees.

Mix beans, taco seasoning and picante sauce. Fold in cream cheese and sour cream and transfer to a baking dish. Top with Cheddar cheese. Bake 30 minutes or until bubbly. Serve with corn chips.

Fran Howard

BLUE CHEESE DIP

⅔ cup cottage cheese	⅛ teaspoon seasoning salt
½ cup plain yogurt	Dash of cayenne pepper
1 (4-ounce) package blue or Gorgonzola cheese	Paprika for garnish

Combine all ingredients except paprika in a small bowl. Sprinkle paprika on top. Serve with celery sticks.

Becky Arnold

HOT MACADAMIA SPREAD

1 (8-ounce) package cream cheese, softened	1 scallion, chopped
2 tablespoons milk	½ teaspoon garlic salt
½ cup sour cream	¼ teaspoon black pepper
2 teaspoons prepared horseradish	½ cup chopped macadamia nuts
¼ cup finely chopped green bell pepper	2 teaspoons butter

Preheat oven to 350 degrees.

Beat cream cheese and milk in a mixing bowl until smooth. Stir in sour cream, horseradish, bell pepper, scallion, garlic salt and pepper. Spoon mixture into an ungreased shallow 2-cup baking dish; set aside. In a skillet, sauté nuts in butter for 3 to 4 minutes or until lightly browned. Sprinkle nuts over cheese mixture. Bake, uncovered, for 20 minutes. Serve with crackers.

Becky Webber

PESTO TORTE

2 (8-ounce) packages cream cheese, softened
2 sticks butter, softened
½ tablespoon chopped garlic
1 (10-ounce) container refrigerated pesto

½ cup Parmesan cheese
1 small jar sun-dried tomatoes packed in oil, drained and chopped

Beat cream cheese, butter and garlic in a medium bowl until well blended. In a separate small bowl, mix pesto and Parmesan cheese. Line a 5x9-inch loaf pan with plastic wrap. Spoon one-third of cream cheese mixture into the bottom of prepared pan. Sprinkle with tomatoes. Spread another third of cream cheese over tomatoes. Spread pesto mixture on top. Use remaining third of cream cheese to make a layer over pesto mixture. Fold plastic wrap over top and seal well. Chill overnight or until firm. Unmold and remove plastic wrap. Serve with crackers or crusty bread.

Gretchen Hurchalla

CURRIED CRAB SALAD

1 cup fat-free sour cream
4 teaspoons chopped fresh cilantro
2 teaspoons curry powder

¼ teaspoon cayenne pepper
1½ pounds crabmeat, shells removed

Combine sour cream, cilantro, curry powder and cayenne in a bowl. Stir in crabmeat and mix well. Chill before serving. Serve with crackers.

Mary Hutchinson

FLUFFY PEANUT BUTTER DIP FOR FRUIT

½ cup creamy peanut butter
1 (8-ounce) container vanilla yogurt
⅛ teaspoon cinnamon

½ cup frozen whipped topping, thawed
Sliced apples, pears, bananas or strawberries

Combine all ingredients except fruit. Chill before serving. Serve with fruit for dipping.

Jodi Burger

CHICKEN PECAN CHEESE SPREAD

1 (8-ounce) package garlic and herb gourmet spreadable cheese
1 cup chopped cooked chicken
⅓ cup mayonnaise

2 tablespoons chopped mango chutney
1 tablespoon curry powder
2 tablespoons coarsely chopped fresh parsley
½ cup chopped pecans, toasted, for garnish

Combine all ingredients except pecans in a bowl. Transfer to a serving bowl and garnish with pecans. Refrigerate 2 hours or until chilled.

Ev Roarke

BACON, LETTUCE AND TOMATO DIP

1 (8-ounce) package cream cheese, softened
¾ cup mayonnaise
3 ounces real bacon bits

2 tomatoes, peeled, seeded and chopped
1 cup shredded lettuce

Blend together cream cheese and mayonnaise. Mix in bacon bits. Fold in tomatoes and lettuce.

Donna Teuscher

CONFETTI CHEESE BALL

8 ounces Cheddar cheese, shredded
1 (8-ounce) package cream cheese, softened
½ cup mayonnaise
1 tablespoon prepared mustard
  Dash of cayenne pepper
2 tablespoons Worcestershire sauce
2 tablespoons grated onions

1 tablespoon finely chopped red bell pepper
1 tablespoon finely chopped green bell pepper
1 tablespoon finely chopped black olives
  Chopped nuts or parsley (optional)

Combine cheeses, mayonnaise, mustard, cayenne, Worcestershire sauce and onions in a large mixing bowl. Blend with an electric mixer on low speed. Add all bell peppers and olives and mix until blended. Chill until firm. Divide mixture in half and shape into two balls, using wax paper to cover for shaping. Roll balls in chopped nuts or parsley to coat.

Jean Gallagher

39

PINEAPPLE HABANERO SALSA

½	pineapple, peeled (rind reserved), cored and coarsely chopped
2	tablespoons fresh pineapple juice squeezed from reserved rind
2	tablespoons fresh lime juice
1	tablespoon mild molasses
3	scallions, finely chopped
¼-½	teaspoon minced seeded habanero or Scotch bonnet pepper
1	teaspoon chopped fresh thyme
¾	teaspoon salt
¼	teaspoon allspice

Combine all ingredients in a bowl and toss to mix. Let stand, stirring occasionally, 30 minutes to allow flavors to blend.

Salsa can be made up to 1 day ahead, covered and chilled. Serve at room temperature.

Lauren Palmero

STRAWBERRY SALSA

2	tablespoons white balsamic vinegar
6	tablespoons olive oil
½	teaspoon salt
1	pint fresh strawberries, diced
6	scallions, chopped (including tops)
2	pints grape tomatoes, chopped
½	cup chopped fresh cilantro

Mix vinegar, olive oil and salt in a bowl. Stir in strawberries, scallions, tomatoes and cilantro. Refrigerate 1 hour. Serve with corn chips.

Elsie Stewart

KIWIFRUIT SALSA

2	cups chopped pineapple, fresh or canned
2	yellow or red bell peppers, chopped
3	kiwifruit, peeled and chopped
1	small red onion, finely chopped
¼	cup finely chopped fresh cilantro Juice of 1 lime

Combine all ingredients and toss well to mix. Serve with chicken or fish.

Serves: 6

Kathy Walker

AVOCADO-FETA SALSA

1 large avocado or 2 Haas avocados
   (preferred)
2 plum tomatoes
½ cup chopped red onions
1 clove garlic, minced

1 tablespoon chopped fresh
   oregano or parsley
1-2 tablespoons olive oil
1 tablespoon red wine vinegar
1 (4-ounce) block feta cheese, cut
   into small cubes

Peel avocado and discard pit. Chop avocado and tomato and combine in a bowl. Add onions, garlic, oregano, olive oil and vinegar and stir or toss gently to mix. Fold in cheese. Serve with tortilla chips or on burgers, fish or chicken. Serve immediately as this salsa doesn't keep well.

Susie Brock

FIRE AND ICE SALSA

3 cups chopped and seeded
   watermelon
½ cup chopped green bell peppers
2 tablespoons lime juice
2 tablespoons chopped fresh
   cilantro

1 tablespoon chopped scallions
1 tablespoon chopped jalapeño
   peppers
½ teaspoon garlic salt

Combine all ingredients in a bowl. Mix well and serve. Do not make more than a day ahead.

Gretchen Hurchalla

SIMPLE HOT SALSA

10 plum tomatoes
1 small to medium onion
3-4 cloves garlic, or more to taste
1 bunch cilantro

1 habanero pepper, seeded
Juice of ½ lime
Salt to taste

Chop tomatoes, onion, garlic, cilantro and habanero separately in a food chopper or processor. Combine tomatoes, onions, garlic, cilantro and lime juice. Add habanero a little at a time according to taste. Season with salt.

Add this salsa to mashed avocados to make guacamole.

Mary Hutchinson

PAPAYA SALSA

2 ripe papayas, peeled and cut into
½-inch cubes
1 cucumber, peeled and chopped
½ cup finely chopped red bell
pepper
1 jalapeño pepper, seeded and
finely chopped

½ cup finely chopped red onion
½ cup chopped fresh cilantro
1 large clove garlic, minced
1 tablespoon lime zest
½ cup fresh lime juice

Combine all ingredients in a bowl and toss lightly. Serve with chicken or grilled fish.

Yield: 2 cups

Karly Walker

TROPICAL FRUIT SALSA

½ cup diced pineapple
½ cup diced mango
½ cup diced papaya
¼ cup finely diced red bell pepper
½ teaspoon finely diced jalapeño
pepper

2 tablespoons finely diced red
onion
2 tablespoons lime juice
2 teaspoons chopped fresh cilantro
Salt to taste

Combine all ingredients in a bowl. Refrigerate 1 hour.

Jill Leserra

TOMATO BASIL SALSA

6 plum tomatoes, diced
6 cloves garlic, finely chopped
1 cup shredded Parmesan cheese

¼ cup chopped fresh basil leaves
1 teaspoon salt

Combine all ingredients and chill 2 hours. Serve with toasted bread.

Colleen Hynes

APPLE-BERRY SALSA WITH CINNAMON CHIPS

2   medium Granny Smith apples,
    peeled and chopped
1   cup sliced fresh strawberries
1   kiwifruit, peeled and chopped

Zest and juice of 1 small orange
2   tablespoons brown sugar
2   tablespoons apple jelly

Combine apples, strawberries and kiwifruit. Add orange zest and juice. Add brown sugar and jelly and mix gently. Serve with cooled Cinnamon Chips (recipe below).

Cinnamon Chips
10 (7-inch) flour tortillas
2   tablespoons sugar

1¼ teaspoons cinnamon

Preheat oven to 400 degrees.

Lightly spray tortillas with water. Combine sugar and cinnamon and sprinkle over tortillas. Using a pizza cutter, cut each tortilla into 8 wedges. Bake 6 to 8 minutes or until lightly brown and crisp. Cool completely before serving.

Dagmar Bothwell

CHERRY TOMATO AND SHRIMP SALSA

18 ounces grape tomatoes
¼   cup olive oil
1½ teaspoons paprika
¾   cup chopped white onions
2   cloves garlic, chopped
1½ teaspoons dried oregano
¼   cup fresh lime juice

1½ tablespoons chopped canned
    chipotle chiles
¾   pound cooked bay shrimp,
    coarsely chopped
¾   cup chopped scallions
½   cup chopped fresh cilantro
    Salt and pepper to taste

Combine grape tomatoes, olive oil, paprika, onions, garlic and oregano. Place mixture on a rimmed baking sheet and broil 8 to 10 minutes; cool. In a large bowl, stir together lime juice and chiles. Add shrimp, scallions and cilantro. Stir in cooled tomato mixture and toss to coat. Season with salt and pepper. Refrigerate until ready to serve.

Virginia Lueders

BLACK BEAN-CRANBERRY RELISH

2   cups canned black beans, rinsed
      and drained
1   cup dried cranberries, chopped
¼   cup chopped fresh cilantro
¼   cup olive oil

2   tablespoons lime juice
2   tablespoons honey
    Salt to taste
    Hot pepper sauce to taste

Combine all ingredients in a non-reactive bowl. Refrigerate at least 1 hour.

Patty Henderson

JERI'S BLACK-EYED PEA AND CORN SALSA

1   (15-ounce) niblets corn, drained
1   cup canned black-eyed peas,
      rinsed and drained
1   large tomato, diced
⅓   cup chopped onion
3   scallions, chopped

1   jalapeño pepper, finely chopped
1   green bell pepper, chopped
2   cloves garlic, chopped
⅓   cup chopped fresh cilantro, or
      ½ cup zesty Italian dressing

Combine all ingredients and chill. Serve with tortilla scoops.

Jeri Butler

SALSA GREEK STYLE

4   ounces crumbled feta cheese
½   cup chopped scallions
¼   cup chopped olives
2   teaspoons olive oil
6   pepperoncini chiles, chopped

½   cup chopped tomatoes
1   teaspoon minced garlic
2   grape leaves, chopped
2   serrano peppers, chopped

Combine all ingredients. Let stand at least 20 minutes before serving.

Holly Whitney

LIME RÉMOULADE

¼ cup chopped dill pickle
2 tablespoons finely diced onions
1 tablespoon chopped capers
1 cup mayonnaise
½ tablespoon chopped fresh parsley

½ teaspoon anchovy purée
2 teaspoons lime juice
1 teaspoon lime zest
Tabasco to taste
Worcestershire sauce to taste

Combine all ingredients in a bowl. Adjust seasonings to taste. Will keep in refrigerator for up to 3 to 4 weeks.

Jill Leserra

BBQ RUB

¼ cup paprika
2 tablespoons salt
2 tablespoons granulated sugar
2 tablespoons brown sugar

2 tablespoons ground cumin
2 tablespoons chili powder
2 tablespoons black pepper
1 tablespoon cayenne pepper

Combine all ingredients and store in an airtight container. Great on chicken, beef or pork.

Pete Lueders

ORIENTAL LIME MARINADE

⅓ cup lime juice, fresh preferred
1 tablespoon peanut oil

1½ teaspoons soy sauce
2 cloves garlic, chopped

Combine all ingredients in a glass jar or bowl.

Use to marinate 4 chicken breasts in a zip-top bag in the refrigerator for 1 hour before grilling. Double recipe for larger amounts of chicken.

Patty Henderson

RASPBERRY COCKTAIL SAUCE

¼ cup seedless raspberry jam   Prepared horseradish to taste

Mix jam with desired amount of horseradish until smooth. Serve with steamed or coconut shrimp.

Kathi Barry

ALL-PURPOSE MEAT MARINADE

½ cup soy sauce   1 teaspoon ground ginger
2½ tablespoons brown sugar   1 teaspoon minced garlic
2½ tablespoons lemon or lime juice

Combine all ingredients. Use to marinade meat for several hours or overnight before cooking.

John Wakeman

BEST EVER BBQ SAUCE

1 cup ketchup   ½ cup cider vinegar
1 cup sugar   1 tablespoon Worcestershire sauce
1 cup chopped onions

Combine all ingredients in a medium saucepan. Bring to a boil over medium-high heat, stirring frequently. Reduce heat to low and simmer 20 minutes or until sauce thickens. Cool and store in refrigerator.

Dora Dragseth

PARSLEY-GARLIC BUTTER

1 stick unsalted butter, softened   ½ teaspoon minced garlic
½ cup finely chopped fresh parsley   1 teaspoon salt
2 tablespoons minced shallots   ¼ teaspoon black pepper
2 tablespoons fresh lemon juice

Purée all ingredients together in a food processor until smooth. Brush on corn on the cob or you favorite veggies before or after grilling.

Hazel Fox

SAUCE FOR BARBECUED CHICKEN

1 medium onion, minced
1 clove garlic, minced
½ cup vegetable oil
2 teaspoons salt
1 teaspoon dry mustard
1 teaspoon paprika
1 tablespoon brown sugar

1 tablespoon chili powder
1 large dash cayenne pepper, or to taste
2 tablespoons plus ½ cup water, divided
2 cups tomato juice
½ cup lemon juice

Combine onions, garlic and oil in a saucepan. Simmer on low heat for 5 minutes or until onions are tender. In a bowl, mix together salt, mustard, paprika, brown sugar, chili powder, cayenne and 2 tablespoons water. Add mixture to saucepan. Stir in tomato juice, remaining ½ cup water and lemon juice. Boil, uncovered, for 10 to 15 minutes.

This is enough sauce for 6 chicken halves.

The Pelican Hotel, courtesy of Lillie King Davis

LEMON-THYME BUTTER

1 stick butter, softened
1 teaspoon dried thyme
1 tablespoon fresh lemon juice

1 teaspoon salt
¼ teaspoon black pepper

Purée all ingredients in a food processor until smooth. Brush on corn on the cob or you favorite veggies before or after grilling.

Hazel Fox

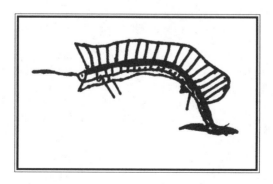

BLUEBERRY CHUTNEY

1	large Granny Smith apple, peeled and diced	¼	teaspoon dried crushed red pepper flakes
½	cup sugar	¼	teaspoon black pepper
½	cup orange juice	2	cups fresh or frozen blueberries
1	tablespoon orange zest	3	tablespoons balsamic vinegar
1	teaspoon ground ginger		

Combine apples, sugar, orange juice and zest, ginger, pepper flakes and black pepper in a medium saucepan. Bring to a boil. Reduce heat and simmer 15 minutes, stirring occasionally. Stir in blueberries and vinegar and bring to a boil. Reduce heat and simmer 40 minutes longer.

Dagmar Bothwell

GOLDEN PINEAPPLE CHUTNEY

½	cup sugar	¼	cup peeled and finely chopped fresh ginger
½	medium-size red onion, diced	2	tablespoons Caribbean hot sauce of your choice
1¼	cups diced mango		
1½	cups diced golden pineapple	½	teaspoon kosher salt
1	Granny Smith apple, peeled and diced	½	teaspoon freshly ground black pepper
1	Asian pear, peeled and diced		
¾	cup diced papaya	3	tablespoons allspice berries
1	tablespoon allspice	1	cup apple cider or white wine vinegar

Combine sugar, onions, mango, pineapple, apples, pears, papaya, allspice, ginger, hot sauce, salt and pepper in a large bowl. Let stand 30 minutes.

Meanwhile, toast allspice berries in a small saucepan until they just begin to smoke. Add vinegar and bring to a simmer. Cook until liquid is reduced to ¼ cup. Strain vinegar, discarding berries. Combine reduced vinegar with fruit mixture in a large heavy saucepan. Simmer over medium heat, stirring occasionally, for 20 to 30 minutes or until liquid is almost syrupy. Chutney will keep up to 3 months in the refrigerator.

Lauren Palmero

CRANBERRY RELISH

1 tangerine, seeded	¾-1 cup sugar
1 (16-ounce) package cranberries, fresh or frozen	

Grind whole seeded tangerine in a food processor until the rind is in small pieces. Add cranberries and sugar and process until berries are coarsely chopped. Refrigerate until needed.

Hillary Brandt

CHIMICHURRI

½ cup finely chopped fresh parsley	Pinch of salt
5 tablespoons extra virgin olive oil	¼ teaspoon seasoned pepper
3 tablespoons red wine vinegar	Pinch of hot pepper flakes
Juice of ½ lime or lemon	¼ teaspoon dried oregano
1 clove garlic, minced	

Stir together all ingredients and let stand 1 to 2 hours. Sauce can be stored at room temperature for up to 1 week, or up to 3 months in the refrigerator.

Lauren Palmero

 JEAN'S MUSTARD

3 (2-ounce) cans Colman's dry mustard	2 egg yolks
	¼ teaspoon salt
1 cup vinegar	1 cup sugar

Blend mustard and vinegar together. Cover and let stand overnight. Beat egg yolks with salt. Add sugar and mix with mustard and vinegar. Cook mixture in the top of a double boiler for 15 minutes or until mixture darkens and has a ribbon-like thickness.

Jean Hupfel

MANGO CHUTNEY

9	cups chopped mangoes	2	cups raisins
2	lemons, unpeeled, seeded and chopped	½	cup chopped fresh ginger
		1	teaspoon cayenne pepper
2	large cloves garlic, chopped	3	cups apple cider vinegar
3	cups brown sugar	2	medium onions, chopped
1	teaspoon mace	2	teaspoons salt
1	tablespoon cinnamon	½	cup sliced almonds
1	teaspoon allspice		

Combine all ingredients in a saucepan. Cook until tender, stirring often. Simmer slowly about 35 minutes longer. Spoon into sterilized jars and seal.

Peggy C. Clute

SPICY CILANTRO SAUCE

½	cup packed fresh cilantro leaves	¼	teaspoon hot pepper flakes
½	cup packed fresh flat-leaf parsley leaves	1	tablespoon plus ¼ cup water, divided
2	shallots, chopped	1	teaspoon vegetable oil
1	large clove garlic, chopped	2	tablespoons soy sauce
2	teaspoons grated fresh ginger		Salt and pepper to taste
½	teaspoon cumin seeds	2	tablespoons fresh lemon juice

Have a bowl of ice water ready. Blanch cilantro and parsley for 10 seconds in a small saucepan of boiling water. Drain in a sieve and refresh in ice water; drain again in sieve. Cook and stir shallots, garlic, ginger, cumin and pepper flakes in 1 tablespoon water and oil in a small nonstick skillet over medium-low heat until shallots are softened. In a blender, purée shallot mixture, blanched herbs, remaining ¼ cup water and soy sauce for 1 minute or until smooth. Season with salt and pepper. Sauce may be made a day ahead, covered and chilled. Bring sauce to room temperature before serving. Just before serving, stir in lemon juice.

Lauren Palmero

SORBET SMOOTHIE

1 (6-ounce) can unsweetened pineapple juice	1 cup lemon sorbet Mint leaves for garnish (optional)

Combine juice and sorbet in a blender. Cover and blend until smooth. Divide mixture between two 8-ounce glasses. Garnish with mint leaves and serve immediately.

Serves: 2

Michelle Wright

 # SURINAM CHERRY WINE

4 pounds cherries, pitted	4 pounds sugar
1 gallon water	1 (½-ounce) package yeast

Place cherries in a bowl and cover with 1 gallon water. Let stand 3 days, stirring daily. Strain mixture through a cheesecloth into a large pot with sugar in it. Heat to lukewarm, stirring well to dissolve sugar. Remove from heat and pour into a large jar or crock. Dissolve yeast in a small amount of warm cherry liquid, then add to jar with remaining liquid. Cover well with cheesecloth; do not cork or screw on a lid yet. After 4 weeks, siphon wine into bottles. Insert cotton wool into necks of bottles and do not cork until all fermentation has ceased.

Mike Clark

VANILLA LATTE

3 cups milk	2 cups freshly brewed coffee, any flavor
2 teaspoons vanilla	

Heat milk in a small saucepan until warm, stirring constantly with a wire whisk to create foam. Remove from heat and stir in vanilla. Stir in coffee and serve immediately.

Serves: 6

Karly Walker

 EGGNOG

¾ cup sugar, divided	4 cups whole milk, scalded
3 egg yolks	3 egg whites
¼ teaspoon plus a dash of salt, divided	½ teaspoon vanilla
	Nutmeg for garnish

Beat ½ cup sugar into egg yolks. Add ¼ teaspoon salt. Slowly stir in milk. Cook mixture over water, stirring constantly, until mixture coats a spoon; cool.

Add a dash of salt to egg whites and beat until stiff. Beat in remaining ¼ cup sugar. Add egg white mixture and vanilla to cooled custard. Mix thoroughly and chill at least 4 hours. Sprinkle individual servings with nutmeg.

Serves: 8 to 10

Beanie Ricou

BAHAMA MAMA

½ ounce dark rum	½ ounce coffee liqueur
½ ounce 151 rum	4 ounces pineapple juice
½ ounce coconut liqueur	¼ ounce lemon juice

Combine all ingredients. Pour over ice in 2 glasses.

Serves: 2

Cookbook Committee

BAHAMA MAMA II

¾ ounce rum	½ ounce grenadine
½ ounce Nassau Royale	¼ ounce lemon juice
½ ounce Cointreau	Dash of bitters
2 ounces orange juice	

Combine all ingredients and pour over ice.

Cookbook Committee

ELLIOT MUSEUM HOLIDAY PUNCH

⅓ punch cup Cointreau	2 bottles white champagne
2 punch cups brandy	(not pink)
3 punch cups rum	1 ice ring
1 (2-liter) bottle ginger ale	

Combine all ingredients except ice ring in a punch bowl. Float ice ring on top.

Janet Hutchinson, Elliot Museum

SWAMP WATER

2 ounces rum	1 ounce orange juice
¼ ounce blue curaçao	½ ounce lemon juice

Combine all ingredients and pour over ice.

Cookbook Committee

WATERMELON STRAWBERRY LEMONADE

4	cups seedless watermelon	1	(6-ounce) can frozen lemonade
1	heaping cup strawberries, hulled		concentrate
2	cups water, divided	8	ounces light rum (optional)

Purée watermelon and strawberries with 1 cup water in a blender. Stir in lemonade concentrate, rum and remaining 1 cup water.

Serves: 6

Kathy Walker

KENTUCKY BOURBON PUNCH

2	cups Kentucky bourbon	1	(12-ounce) can frozen orange
2	cups strong tea (4 bags per cup)		juice concentrate
¾	cup sugar	7	cups water
1	(12-ounce) can frozen lemonade		
	concentrate		

Combine all ingredients. Freeze and enjoy.

Denise Blanton

 # GOOMBAY SMASH

1	fifth (25 ounces) light rum	1	quart orange juice
1	fifth (25 ounces) coconut rum	1	(46-ounce) can pineapple juice

Mix together all ingredients. Serve over ice.

Ron Teal

SPICED CIDER

1	cup fresh orange juice	4	sticks cinnamon
¼	cup lemon juice	4	whole allspice
8½	cups apple cider	4	cloves
2⅛	cups dark rum		

Combine all ingredients in a saucepan. Bring to a boil. Remove from heat and allow to steep 4 hours or until cool. To serve, reheat or serve over ice.

Ginger Baldwin

MAI TAI

½ cup light rum
½ cup dark rum
½ cup fresh lemon juice
½ cup fresh orange juice

3 tablespoons orange curaçao or triple sec
3 tablespoons almond syrup

Combine all ingredients. Fill 4 small glasses with ice and pour rum mixture over top. Stir to chill.

Serves: 4

Virginia Lueders

OPEN HOUSE PUNCH

1 fifth Southern Comfort
¾ cup fresh lemon juice
1 (6-ounce) can frozen orange juice concentrate

1 (6-ounce) can frozen lemonade concentrate
3 quarts lemon-lime soda

Chill all ingredients. Combine all ingredients in a punch bowl, adding soda last. If desired, add a few drops of food coloring. Serve over ice with lemon and lime slices.

Serves: 32

Lorraine Berger

CRAN-RASPBERRY CHAMPAGNE PUNCH

1 (64-ounce) bottle cran-raspberry juice, chilled
2 bottles champagne or Asti Spumante, chilled

1 quart club soda or raspberry seltzer water, chilled
1 small bunch fresh mint sprigs for garnish

Mix all ingredients, except mint, in a large chilled punch bowl. Garnish each serving with a sprig of mint.

Serves: 38

Jill Levy

GIN AND COCONUT WATER

Shot of gin   Coconut water

Pour gin over ice. Add coconut water and stir.

Serves: 1

Cookbook Committee

CARIBBEAN BREEZE

1⅓ ounces dark rum   1¾ ounces cranberry juice
⅓   ounce crème de bananas   ⅓   ounce Rose's lime cordial
2⅓ ounces pineapple juice

Pour all ingredients into a shaker with ice. Shake and strain into a highball glass filled with crushed ice. Garnish with a slice of lime. Serve with a straw.

Cookbook Committee

MOJITO

1   teaspoon superfine sugar   1⅔ ounces white rum
⅔ ounce fresh lime juice   Sparkling water
1   bunch fresh mint

Put the sugar and lime juice in the bottom of a highball glass with a thick base. Add mint leaves to taste and muddle with the end of a spoon. Add rum and fill the glass with crushed ice. Fill glass with sparkling water and stir. Serve with a stirrer.

Cookbook Committee

PLANTER'S PUNCH

1   teaspoon sugar   3   ounces rum
    Juice of 1 lime   1   ounce club soda

Dissolve sugar in lime juice. Mix in rum and club soda. Pour over ice.

Cookbook Committee

LONG ISLAND ICED TEA

⅓ ounce light rum
⅓ ounce vodka
⅓ ounce gin
⅓ ounce tequila

⅓ ounce Cointreau
⅔ ounce fresh lime juice
Cola, chilled
Lime wedge for garnish

Pour all ingredients, except cola and lime wedge, into a highball glass filled with ice. Stir. Top off glass with cola. Garnish with lime wedge. Serve with a straw and a stirrer.

Cookbook Committee

EGGNOG

1 dozen eggs, separated
2 cups sugar, divided
1 quart whipping cream

1 quart milk
2 ounces rum
1 pint whiskey

Beat egg yolks in a bowl until light yellow. Add 1 cup sugar and mix well. In a separate bowl, beat egg whites until stiff. In a third bowl, beat cream until stiff. When stiff, add remaining 1 cup sugar to cream. In a large bowl, combine yolk mixture, whipped cream, milk, rum and whiskey. Fold in egg whites. Refrigerate to chill. Stir before serving.

Ginger Baldwin

Civilized men have drifted away from those simple, elemental basics with which mankind was conditioned through the countless centuries. The average man today has lost touch with which way the wind is blowing. It does not matter any more, so he pays no attention to the movement of the air.

~ Ernest Lyons

Alligators and black bass go together. I do not know why this is so, but if you see a 'gator or two in a pond there is usually good bass fishing.

~ Ernest Lyons

Fisherman will believe anything. They are innocent and pure of heart, trusting, guileless and should not be imposed upon.

~ Ernest Lyons

Breads
and
Brunch

JALAPEÑO CORN MUFFINS

1 cup flour	¾ cup whole milk
1 cup yellow cornmeal	¼ cup corn oil
¼ cup sugar	2 tablespoons seeded and minced
1 tablespoon baking powder	jalapeño peppers
1 teaspoon salt	2 cups frozen corn, thawed and
4 eggs	drained

Preheat oven to 375 degrees.

Combine flour, cornmeal, sugar, baking powder and salt in a mixing bowl. In a separate bowl, whisk together eggs, milk, oil and jalapeños. Add dry ingredients to egg mixture and stir until all is moistened. Fold in corn. Divide batter among 12 greased muffin cups. Bake 25 minutes. Serve warm.

Serves: 12

Colleen Hynes

JOHN'S BROWN BREAD

From George Wakeman, circa 1940

1 cup sugar	2 teaspoons baking soda
½ teaspoon salt	2 tablespoons molasses
2 cups flour	2 cups buttermilk
2 cups All Bran cereal	

Preheat oven to 325 degrees.

Combine sugar, salt, flour, cereal and baking soda in a bowl. Add molasses and buttermilk and stir just enough to combine. Pour batter into 5 greased (12- to 15-ounce) cans, filling less than two-thirds full. Bake 40 to 45 minutes. Allow to cool 15 minutes before removing bread from cans.

Delicious served with butter, cream cheese and assorted jellies.

Yield: 5 small round loaves

John Wakeman

HUSH PUPPIES

2 cups cornmeal	Salt to taste
1 cup flour	2 eggs, beaten
1 cup finely diced onions	1 cup buttermilk
¼ cup sugar, or to taste	Cooking oil
1 tablespoon baking powder	

Combine cornmeal, flour, onions, sugar, baking powder and salt in a medium bowl. Stir in eggs, then buttermilk; batter will be stiff. Pour cooking oil to 3 to 4 inches deep in a heavy skillet. Heat oil to 450 degrees. Drop batter by heaping tablespoons into hot oil. Fry until golden brown. Drain on paper towel and serve.

If buttermilk is not available, substitute regular milk mixed with 2 tablespoons vinegar.

Judy Schalk

BEER BREAD

3 cups self-rising flour	1 (12-ounce) can beer
½ cup sugar	2 tablespoons butter, melted

Preheat oven to 375 degrees.

Combine flour, sugar and beer in a large bowl and mix well; the batter will be sticky. Pour batter into a greased loaf pan. Bake 55 minutes. Three minutes before done baking, remove from oven, brush top with melted butter and return to oven.

This bread is easy and makes a delicious toast.

Barbara Norcia

GARLIC CHEESE BISCUITS

2 cups plus 2 tablespoons baking mix, divided	½ cup shredded Cheddar cheese
⅔ cup milk	2 tablespoons butter, melted
	⅛ teaspoon garlic powder

Preheat oven to 450 degrees.

Combine baking mix, milk and cheese in a bowl. Stir together until a soft dough forms. Drop by heaping tablespoons onto an ungreased baking sheet. Bake 8 to 10 minutes or until brown. Mix melted butter and garlic powder and brush over top of warm biscuits.

Fran Howard

IRISH SODA BREAD

2 eggs	1½ teaspoons baking soda
1½ cups buttermilk	1 teaspoon salt
2 tablespoons butter, melted	¾ cup sugar
2 tablespoons caraway seeds	1 cup raisins
4 cups flour	

Preheat oven to 350 degrees.

Beat eggs lightly in a bowl. Stir in milk and melted butter. Add caraway seeds. In a separate bowl, sift together flour, baking soda, salt and sugar. Gradually add dry ingredients to egg mixture. Stir in raisins. Pour batter into a greased 2-quart glass casserole dish, or 2 small loaf pans. Cut an "X" on the top. Bake 1¼ hours; reduce baking time for smaller loaves.

Kay De Nicola

RHUBARB BREAD

Batter

1½ cups chopped rhubarb	1 egg
(frozen works best)	2½ cups flour
1½ cups brown sugar	1 cup buttermilk
½ cup oil	1 teaspoon baking soda
1 teaspoon vanilla	¼ teaspoon salt

Topping

½ cup brown sugar	4 tablespoons butter
½ teaspoon cinnamon	

Preheat oven to 325 degrees.

Combine rhubarb, brown sugar, oil, vanilla and egg. Mix in flour, buttermilk, baking soda and salt. Pour batter into 2 greased and floured loaf pans.

Combine all topping ingredients and spread evenly over batter. Bake 1 hour.

Renee Booth

ZUCCHINI BREAD

3	cups chopped zucchini	2	teaspoons cinnamon
3	eggs	1	teaspoon baking soda
1	cup oil	¼	teaspoon baking powder
1¾	cups sugar	1	teaspoon salt
3	cups flour	1	teaspoon vanilla

Preheat oven to 350 degrees.

Combine zucchini, eggs, oil and sugar in a blender and process until smooth. In a bowl, combine flour, cinnamon, baking soda, baking powder and salt. Add zucchini mixture and mix with an electric mixer on medium speed for 3 minutes. Stir in vanilla. Pour batter into 2 greased and floured loaf pans. Bake 50 to 60 minutes.

Can add 1 cup chopped nuts and/or raisins with the vanilla.

Jennifer Norman

QUICK AND EASY BANANA NUT BREAD

½	(8-ounce) package cream cheese, softened	1	(18¼-ounce) package yellow cake mix
2	eggs	¾	cup chopped nuts
3	medium-size ripe bananas, mashed		

Preheat oven to 350 degrees.

Beat together cream cheese and eggs with an electric mixer on low until smooth. Add mashed bananas and mix well. Add cake mix and nuts and mix until blended. Divide batter evenly among 2 greased 7½x3-inch disposable loaf pans. Bake 45 minutes or until a toothpick inserted in the center comes out clean. Cool 20 minutes in pan. Remove from pans and cool on a rack.

Yield: 2 loaves

Susan Zarnowiec, daughter of E. "Mike" Clark

IMPROVED COCONUT BREAD

2¾ cups all-purpose flour	1 teaspoon salt
1¼ cups shredded coconut	1½ cups milk
1 cup sugar	2 tablespoons vegetable oil
1 tablespoon plus 1 teaspoon baking powder	1 egg
	1 teaspoon coconut extract

Preheat oven to 350 degrees.

Combine flour, coconut, sugar, baking powder and salt in a large bowl. In a separate bowl, mix milk, oil, egg and coconut extract. Add liquid mixture to dry ingredients and stir until moistened. Spoon batter into a greased and floured 9x5x3-inch loaf pan. Bake 1 hour or until a toothpick inserted in the center comes out clean. Cool in pan about 10 minutes. Remove from pan and cool completely on a wire rack.

Yield: 1 loaf

Recipe can be doubled and baked in three 8x3¾x2½-inch pans for a gift-giving size.

Sharyon Daigneau

FAVORITE PUMPKIN BREAD

3 cups sugar	2 teaspoons baking soda
1 cup salad oil	1 teaspoon cinnamon
4 eggs, beaten	1 teaspoon nutmeg
1 (16-ounce) can pumpkin	½ teaspoon ground cloves
3½ cups all-purpose flour	1 teaspoon ground allspice
1 teaspoon baking powder	¾ cup water
2 teaspoons salt	1-1½ cups chopped pecans (optional)

Preheat oven to 350 degrees.

Combine sugar, oil and eggs in a bowl and beat until light and fluffy. Stir in pumpkin. In a separate bowl, combine flour, baking powder, salt, baking sofa, cinnamon, nutmeg, cloves and allspice. Stir dry ingredients into pumpkin mixture. Add water and pecans and mix well. Spoon batter into 2 well greased 9x5x3-inch loaf pans. Bake 65 to 75 minutes or until a toothpick inserted into the center comes out clean.

Batter can also be divided between three 8x3¾x2½-inch pans.

Yield: 2 loaves

Sharyon Daigneau

LEMON BREAD

1¼ cups flour
1 teaspoon baking powder
1 stick butter, softened
1 cup sugar

2 eggs
⅓ cup whole milk
1½ tablespoons lemon zest
¾ cup chopped pecans

Lemon Syrup
⅓ cup fresh lemon juice

¼ cup sugar

Preheat oven to 350 degrees.

Sift together flour and baking powder in a medium bowl; set aside. In a separate bowl, beat butter and sugar with an electric mixer until blended. Add eggs, 1 at a time, and beat until incorporated. Reduce speed of mixer to low and mix in dry ingredients. Beat until blended. Add milk and lemon zest and beat until smooth. Scrape down sides of bowl. Stir in pecans by hand. Evenly divide batter between two 8x3¾x2½-inch greased loaf pans. Bake in center of oven for 45 minutes. Remove from oven and cool 15 minutes.

While loaves cool, prepare lemon syrup. Heat lemon juice in a small saucepan over medium heat. Add sugar and stir until slightly boiling. Use a fork to prick a few small holes in cooling loaves. Pour hot syrup over top. Wait about 5 minutes and remove loaves from pan. Cool completely on a rack. Slice and enjoy plain or with berries.

Lauren Palmero

 # COCONUT BREAD

½ cup shortening
2 eggs
2 cups milk
  Shredded meat of 1 coconut

1 cup sugar
2¼ cups flour
1 tablespoon baking powder

Preheat oven to 325 degrees.

Mix shortening, eggs, milk, coconut and sugar. Stir in flour and baking powder. Pour batter into a greased pan. Bake 40 minutes or until brown. Good served hot.

Mabel Witham

BLUEBERRY-ORANGE BREAD

1	(10-ounce) package frozen blueberries, thawed	4	tablespoons butter, melted
5	cups all-purpose flour	2	tablespoons baking powder
1½	cups orange juice	2	tablespoons orange zest
1	cup sugar	2	teaspoons salt
4	eggs	1	teaspoon baking soda

Preheat oven to 375 degrees.

Drain blueberries and pat dry; set aside. In a large bowl, mix flour, orange juice, sugar, eggs, melted butter, baking powder, orange zest, salt and baking soda with a spoon until dry ingredients are just moistened. Gently stir in blueberries. Pour batter into 2 well greased 1½-quart casserole dishes, or one 1½-quart casserole dish and one 9x5-inch loaf pan. Bake 50 minutes or until a toothpick inserted in the center comes out clean. Remove bread from dishes and serve warm, or cool on wire racks.

Yield: 2 loaves

Frank Pittman

SWEET POTATO BISCUITS

3	cups flour	2	cups cooked and mashed sweet potatoes
7	teaspoons baking powder		
1	teaspoon salt	½	cup vegetable shortening
¾	cup sugar		Melted butter

Preheat oven to 425 degrees.

Combine flour, baking powder, salt and sugar in a bowl. Add potatoes and shortening and mix. Roll out dough to about ½-inch thick. Cut into biscuits and place on a baking sheet. Brush top of biscuits with melted butter. Bake 10 minutes.

Leslie Warren

Florida is for amazement, wonder and delight and refreshment of the soul.

~ Ernest Lyons

BILL'S CINNAMON ROLLS / STICKY BUNS

½ cup granulated sugar	1 stick butter or margarine, divided
1 (¼-ounce) envelope active dry yeast	1 egg
½ teaspoon salt	½ cup light brown sugar
4 cups flour, divided	½ cup raisins
1 cup milk	1½ teaspoons cinnamon
	½ cup nuts (optional)

Preheat oven to 400 degrees.

Combine granulated sugar, yeast, salt and 1 cup flour. In a saucepan, heat milk and 4 tablespoons butter until warm (120 to 130 degrees). Blend dry ingredients into milk mixture with an electric mixer on low speed. Add egg. Increase to medium speed and mix 2 minutes. Stir in another 1½ cups flour. On a floured surface, knead dough about 10 minutes or until smooth, adding about ¼ cup more flour while kneading. Shape into a ball and place in a greased large bowl, turning dough to grease all sides. Cover and let rise in a warm place (80 to 85 degrees) for 1 hour or until doubled. Punch down dough and turn onto a floured surface. Cover and let rest 15 minutes.

Combine brown sugar, raisins, cinnamon and nuts. Melt remaining 4 tablespoons butter. Roll dough into an 18x12-inch rectangle. Brush with melted butter and sprinkle on brown sugar mixture. Starting with long side, roll jelly-roll style and pinch ends and seam to seal. With seam-side down, cut roll into 18 slices. Place slices, cut side down, in a greased 9x13-inch pan. Cover and let rise 40 minutes or until doubled.

Bake 20 minutes. Cool slightly and brush with glaze.

Glaze

1 cup powdered sugar	4 teaspoons water

For glaze, mix sugar and water until smooth.

For sticky buns, Combine 1 stick butter, 1 cup dark corn syrup and ¾ cup brown sugar in a saucepan and bring to a boil. Reduce heat and cook 2 minutes. Pour mixture into pan and arrange dough slices on top. Allow to rise 40 minutes. Bake as above, but turn out onto a pan when removed from the oven.

Serves: 18

Bill Reamer

POPPY SEED POUND CAKE MUFFINS

2 cups all-purpose flour	1 stick butter, softened
1 tablespoon poppy seeds	2 eggs
½ teaspoon salt	1 cup plain yogurt
¼ teaspoon baking soda	1 teaspoon vanilla
1 cup sugar	

Preheat oven to 400 degrees.

Combine flour, poppy seeds, salt and baking soda in a small bowl. In a large bowl, cream together sugar and butter. Beat in eggs, one at a time. Beat in yogurt and vanilla until well blended. Stir in dry ingredients until thoroughly moistened. Spoon batter into greased muffin cups. Bake 15 to 20 minutes or until a wooden toothpick inserted in the center comes out clean. Cool on a wire rack 5 minutes before serving.

Bonnie Brashear

SOUR CREAM COFFEE CAKE

Topping

1 cup brown sugar	½ cup chopped nuts, or more to
1 teaspoon cinnamon	taste

Batter

1 stick butter, softened	2 teaspoons baking powder
4 tablespoons margarine, softened	1 teaspoon baking soda
1 cup sugar	⅛ teaspoon salt
2 eggs	1 cup sour cream
2 cups sifted flour	1 teaspoon vanilla

Preheat oven to 350 degrees.

Combine all topping ingredients; set aside.

For batter, cream together butter, margarine, sugar and eggs in a bowl. In a separate bowl, sift together flour, baking powder, baking soda and salt. Add dry ingredients alternately with the sour cream to the creamed mixture. Stir in vanilla. Pour half the batter into a greased 9- or 10-inch tube pan. Add half of topping. Pour remainder of batter on top and marble in swirls. Sprinkle with remaining topping and repeat marbling. Bake 40 to 50 minutes. Leave in pan at least 2 hours or until completely cool before removing.

Leila Oughterson

BLUEBERRY BUCKLE

Berry Mixture

2 tablespoons all-purpose flour
2 tablespoons granulated sugar

2 cups blueberries

Topping

½ cup light brown sugar
⅓ cup all-purpose flour
½ teaspoon cinnamon

⅛ teaspoon nutmeg
4 tablespoons unsalted butter

Batter

2 cups all-purpose flour
2 teaspoons baking powder
½ teaspoon salt
4 tablespoons unsalted butter, softened

¾ cup granulated sugar
1 egg
1 teaspoon vanilla
½ cup milk

Preheat oven to 375 degrees.

For berry mixture, in a medium bowl, combine flour and sugar. Add blueberries and toss until coated; set aside.

For topping, combine brown sugar, flour, cinnamon and nutmeg. Cut in butter until crumbly; set aside.

To make batter, stir together flour, baking powder and salt in a bowl. In a medium bowl, cream butter on medium speed for 30 seconds. Add sugar and beat 4 minutes. Beat in egg and vanilla. Add dry ingredients alternately with milk, beating until combined. Fold in berry mixture. Spoon batter into a greased and floured 8- or 9-inch springform pan and spread evenly. Sprinkle evenly with topping. Bake 55 to 65 minutes. Cool at least 15 minutes before removing from pan. Serve warm with butter.

Susan Brock

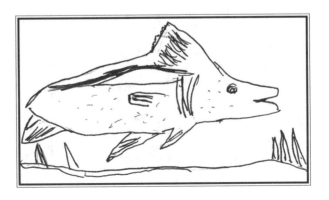

JEWISH COFFEE CAKE

Topping
¼ cup sugar
½ cup slivered almonds

1 teaspoon cinnamon

Batter
1 stick butter, softened
1 cup sugar
1 cup sour cream
2 eggs

2 cups flour
1 teaspoon baking powder
1 teaspoon baking soda
1 teaspoon vanilla

Preheat oven to 350 degrees.

Combine all topping ingredients; set aside.

To make batter, cream butter and sugar. Add sour cream, eggs, flour, baking powder, baking soda and vanilla in order listed. Mix well. Pour half of batter into a greased and floured 8-inch square pan. Sprinkle with half of topping. Pour remaining batter on top. Cut through batter with a knife. Sprinkle remaining topping over batter. Bake about 45 minutes.

Debbie Tranowski

OVERNIGHT BLUEBERRY COFFEE CAKE

Batter

2 cups all-purpose flour	½ teaspoon salt
1 cup granulated sugar	1 cup buttermilk
½ cup brown sugar	⅔ cup butter, melted
1 teaspoon baking powder	2 eggs, beaten
1 teaspoon baking soda	1 cup fresh or frozen blueberries
1 teaspoon cinnamon	

Topping

½ cup brown sugar	1 teaspoon cinnamon
½ cup chopped nuts	

Preheat oven to 350 degrees.

In a large bowl, combine flour, sugars, baking powder, baking soda, cinnamon and salt. In a separate bowl, combine buttermilk, melted butter and eggs. Add liquid mixture to dry ingredients and mix until well blended. Fold in blueberries. Pour batter into a greased 9x13-inch pan.

Combine all topping ingredients and sprinkle over batter. Cover and refrigerate several hours or overnight. Uncover and bake 45 to 50 minutes or until a toothpick inserted in the center comes out clean.

If using frozen berries, do not thaw first.

Denise Blanton

MANGO BREAD

2 cups flour	3 eggs
1½ cups sugar	¾ cup oil
2 teaspoons baking soda	½ cup raisins
1 teaspoon cinnamon	½ cup chopped nuts
½ teaspoon salt	2 cups chopped fresh ripe mango

Preheat oven to 325 degrees.

Combine flour, sugar, baking soda, cinnamon and salt in a large bowl. Add eggs, one at a time, and blend well. Add oil and blend well. Fold in raisins, nuts and mango. Pour batter into 2 greased and floured loaf pans. Bake 1 hour.

Jill Scanio

SMOKED SALMON OMELETS
WITH RED ONIONS AND CAPERS

12 eggs	4 tablespoons chopped red onion
1 teaspoon salt	4 teaspoons drained capers
½ teaspoon black pepper	8 tablespoons whipped cream
2 teaspoons butter	cheese
6 ounces smoked salmon, chopped	

Whisk together eggs, salt and pepper in a large bowl. Melt butter in an 8-inch diameter nonstick skillet over medium heat. Ladle ¾ cup of egg mixture into skillet. Cook until eggs are softly set, stirring often and lifting edges to allow uncooked portion to run under, covering skillet if necessary to help set top of eggs. Place one-fourth of salmon on half of omelet. Sprinkle with 1 tablespoon onion and 1 teaspoon capers. Top with 2 tablespoons cream cheese. Fold omelet in half over filling and slide onto a plate. Repeat with remaining ingredients to make 3 more omelets.

Serves: 4

Gretchen Hurchalla

BAKED SICILIAN FRITTATA

5 medium-size red potatoes, peeled and sliced	¾ cup Parmesan cheese
¼ cup olive oil	½ cup water
1 cup chopped onions	1 teaspoon dried basil
¼ cup chopped green bell peppers	½ teaspoon salt
3 cloves garlic, minced	½ teaspoon black pepper
4 cups frozen chopped broccoli	1½ cups shredded Monterey Jack cheese
12 eggs, beaten	

Preheat oven to 350 degrees.

Sauté potatoes in oil in a large skillet for 10 minutes. Add onions, bell peppers and garlic and sauté until tender. Add broccoli. Cover skillet and cook 5 minutes. Arrange mixture in an 11x7-inch baking dish. Combine eggs, Parmesan cheese, water, basil, salt and pepper and beat until blended. Pour mixture over vegetables in dish. Sprinkle with Monterey Jack cheese. Bake, uncovered, for 25 to 30 minutes or until set.

Serves: 8

Dagmar Bothwell

SAUSAGE BREAD

1	(8-ounce) package crescent rolls	8	ounces mozzarella cheese, shredded
3	eggs, beaten		
2	pounds pork sausage, browned and drained	2	teaspoons Parmesan cheese
		1	teaspoon garlic powder
8	ounces Cheddar cheese, shredded	1	teaspoon dried oregano
		1	teaspoon dried parsley

Preheat oven to 350 degrees.

Press together crescent rolls into one big square on a baking sheet. Reserve a small amount of beaten egg. Mix remaining beaten egg with cooked sausage, all cheeses, garlic powder, oregano and parsley. Spoon mixture into center of dough. Pull the sides of the dough over filling and pinch together on top. Brush with reserved beaten egg. Bake 35 to 40 minutes.

Vickie Carson

FRAN'S BREAKFAST SAUSAGE AND EGGS

2	tablespoons butter or margarine, softened	2	cups shredded Cheddar cheese
		6	eggs, beaten
8	slices bread, toasted, crusts removed	2	cups half-and-half
		1	teaspoon salt
1	pound pork sausage		

Preheat oven to 350 degrees.

Spread butter over toasted bread and arrange in a greased 9x13-inch pan; set aside. Brown sausage in a skillet; drain on paper towel. Spoon sausage over toast. Sprinkle cheese on top. Combine eggs, half-and-half and salt and pour over cheese. Cover pan with foil and refrigerate overnight. Remove from refrigerator 15 minutes prior to baking. Bake, uncovered, for 45 minutes or until center is set and a knife inserted in the center comes out clean. Serve immediately.

Fran Howard

CHRISTMAS BREAKFAST CASSEROLE

8   slices white or wheat bread, cubed
1   stick butter, cut into pats
1   (16-ounce) package mild breakfast sausage
2   zucchinis, diced
1   red bell pepper, diced
3   cups shredded Cheddar cheese
8   eggs
2½ cups whole milk
1   teaspoon salt
1   teaspoon dry mustard

Preheat oven to 350 degrees.

Spread bread cubes evenly in a greased large casserole dish. Place butter pats on bread cubes. Cook sausage, drain and spoon evenly over bread. Layer zucchini and bell peppers over sausage. Sprinkle cheese on top. Beat together eggs, milk, salt and mustard and pour over casserole. Refrigerate overnight. Bake 45 minutes or until bubbly.

Nicole Mader

EGGS FLORENTINE

1   (10-ounce) package frozen chopped spinach
1   cup shredded Cheddar cheese
1   pound bulk pork sausage
2   cups sliced fresh mushrooms
½   cup chopped scallions
2   tablespoons butter or margarine, melted
12 eggs, lightly beaten
2   cups whipping cream
1   cup shredded Swiss cheese
    Paprika

Preheat oven to 350 degrees.

Cook spinach according to package directions; drain well. Sprinkle Cheddar cheese over the bottom of a greased 9x13-inch baking dish. Spread spinach over cheese. Cook and crumble sausage in a skillet over medium heat until browned; drain. Spoon sausage over spinach. Sauté mushrooms and scallions in butter in a large skillet until tender. Sprinkle vegetables over sausage. Beat together eggs and cream with a whisk and pour over casserole. Top evenly with Swiss cheese and sprinkle with paprika. Bake, uncovered, for 40 to 45 minutes or until set.

Serves: 12

Dagmar Bothwell

CHILE EGG PUFF

10 eggs
½ cup flour
1 teaspoon baking powder
½ teaspoon salt
1 pint small curd creamed cottage
   cheese

1 pound Monterey Jack cheese,
   shredded
1 stick butter or margarine, melted
2 (4-ounce) cans diced green chiles

Preheat oven to 350 degrees.

Beat eggs until light. Add flour, baking powder, salt, cottage cheese, Monterey Jack cheese and melted butter. Mix until blended smoothly. Stir in chiles. Pour mixture into a greased 9x13-inch dish. Bake 35 minutes or until top is browned and center appears firm. Serve hot.

Recipe can be cut in half for fewer people. Use and 8- or 9-inch square pan.

Chiles can be replaced with fresh herbs, such as chives or parsley, or chopped green or red bell peppers.

Nancy Scott

DEMMA'S EGGS BAKE

9 slices white bread, crusts
   removed, quartered
¼ cup shredded Cheddar-Jack cheese
8 ounces bacon, cooked and
   crumbled

6 eggs
3 cups milk
½ teaspoon salt
1 (4-ounce) can mushrooms, drained

Preheat oven to 350 degrees.

Line a greased 9x13-inch pan with quartered bread slices. Top with cheese and crumbled bacon. Beat together eggs, milk and salt and pour over layers. Cover pan with foil or plastic and refrigerate overnight. In the morning, sprinkle mushrooms over top. Bake, uncovered, for 40 minutes. Remove from oven and let stand 5 minutes before cutting into squares.

Serves: 8 to 10

Demma Bailey

"BRUNCH" CASSEROLE

2   pounds breakfast sausage
2½ cups seasoned croutons
2   cups shredded Cheddar cheese
4   eggs, beaten

3   cups milk, divided
¾   teaspoon prepared mustard
1   (10¾-ounce) can condensed
    cream of mushroom soup

Preheat oven to 350 degrees.

Brown sausage and drain on paper towel; set aside. Spread croutons evenly in a greased 9x13-inch casserole dish. Add sausage. Top with cheese. Mix eggs, 2½ cups milk and mustard in a blender and pour over casserole. Cover pan and refrigerate overnight. In the morning, combine soup and remaining ½ cup milk. Spread mixture over top of casserole. Bake 1 hour.

Mary Marshall

POTATO BASIL FRITTATA

1   stick unsalted butter, divided
2   cups peeled and diced potatoes
8   eggs
1   (15-ounce) container ricotta
    cheese
¾   cup shredded Gruyère cheese

½   teaspoon salt
½   teaspoon black pepper
¾   cup chopped fresh basil
⅓   cup flour
¾   teaspoon baking powder

Preheat oven to 350 degrees.

Melt 3 tablespoons butter in a 10-inch ovenproof omelet pan over medium-low heat. Add potatoes and cook until tender. Melt remaining 5 tablespoons butter in a microwave. Whisk melted butter with eggs, ricotta cheese, Gruyère cheese, salt, pepper and basil. Mix flour and baking powder and sprinkle over egg mixture. Stir until blended. Pour egg mixture over potatoes and transfer pan to oven. Bake 50 to 60 minutes or until a knife comes out clean. Serve hot.

Denise Blanton

RICK'S CHEESE GRITS

2   cups water
½   cup quick grits
4   ounces cheese, shredded

Dash of garlic powder
Salt and white pepper to taste

Bring water to a boil in a saucepan. Slowly stir in grits. Reduce heat to medium-low. Cover and cook 5 to 7 minutes or until thickened, stirring occasionally. Add cheese, garlic powder and salt and pepper. Continue to cook and stir until cheese is melted.

Serves: 4

Rick Binder

FRENCH TOAST CASSEROLE

1   (1-pound) loaf French bread
8   eggs
2   cups half-and-half
1   cup milk
2   tablespoons sugar
1   teaspoon vanilla

¼   teaspoon cinnamon
¼   teaspoon nutmeg
    Dash of salt
    Praline topping (recipe below)
    Maple syrup

Preheat oven to 350 degrees.

Cut loaf of bread into 1-inch slices. Arrange bread in 2 rows, overlapping the slices, in a well greased 9x13-inch baking dish. In a large bowl, beat together eggs, half-and-half, milk, sugar, vanilla, cinnamon, nutmeg and salt until blended but not too bubbly. Pour mixture over bread, making sure all slices are covered evenly. Spoon some of egg mixture between slices. Cover with foil and refrigerate overnight.

In the morning, spread praline topping evenly over bread. Bake 40 minutes or until puffed and lightly golden. Serve with maple syrup.

Serves: 6 to 8

Praline Topping
2   sticks butter
1   cup light brown sugar
1   cup chopped pecans

2   tablespoons light corn syrup
½   teaspoon cinnamon
½   teaspoon nutmeg

Combine all topping ingredients in a medium bowl and blend well.

Janel Weigt

ORANGE FRENCH TOAST

4	eggs	1	loaf French bread, sliced 1-inch thick
⅔	cup freshly squeezed orange juice	5	tablespoons butter, melted
½	cup milk	½	cup chopped pecans
¼	cup sugar		Powdered sugar for garnish
½	teaspoon vanilla		Maple syrup
¼	teaspoon nutmeg		Fresh fruit (optional)

Preheat oven to 400 degrees.

In a mixing bowl, whisk together eggs, orange juice, milk, sugar, vanilla and nutmeg; set aside. Arrange bread in a single, tight-fitting layer in a greased 9x16-inch pan. Pour egg mixture over bread. Cover and refrigerate overnight, turning bread once.

In the morning, pour melted butter evenly over bread. Sprinkle with pecans. Bake 20 to 25 minutes or until golden brown. Sprinkle with powdered sugar. Serve with syrup and fresh fruit.

To increase the orange taste, melt orange marmalade in a microwave and brush over bread after removing from oven.

Serves: 4

Kiki Christina Shapero

 SUNDAY FRENCH TOAST

8	(¾-inch thick) slices French bread	½	teaspoon vanilla
4	eggs	¼	teaspoon salt
1	cup milk	2	tablespoons butter
3	tablespoons orange liqueur		Powdered sugar
1	tablespoon sugar		

Arrange bread in a 9x13-inch baking dish. Beat together eggs, milk, orange liqueur, sugar, vanilla and salt until well blended. Pour mixture over bread. Turn slices to coat evenly. Cover dish and refrigerate overnight.

In the morning, melt butter in a skillet. Cook bread in butter for 4 to 5 minutes on each side or until golden, flipping toast often to allow for even browning. Sprinkle with powdered sugar and serve.

Great served with Vermont maple syrup, but any pancake syrup will be delicious.

Christi Fuller

Salads and Soup

BOOK CLUB CHICKEN SALAD

2 cups coarsely chopped cooked chicken
1 small Granny Smith apple, chopped
½ cup chopped salted peanuts
1 (8-ounce) can crushed pineapple, drained
¾ cup mayonnaise
1 teaspoon lime zest
1 tablespoon fresh lime juice
1½ teaspoons lite soy sauce
½ teaspoon black pepper
1 head green leaf lettuce, washed and dried
1 fresh pineapple, peeled, cored and cut into 1-inch pieces
2 oranges, sectioned
2 kiwifruit, peeled and sliced
2 cups red or green seedless grapes
2 tablespoons chopped salted peanuts for garnish

Combine chicken, apples, ½ cup peanuts and pineapple in a large bowl. In a separate bowl, mix mayonnaise, lime zest and juice, soy sauce and pepper. Stir into chicken mixture. Arrange lettuce leaves on a serving platter. Heap chicken mixture in center of platter. Arrange pineapple pieces, oranges, kiwifruit and grapes around chicken salad. Sprinkle with 2 tablespoons peanuts for garnish.

Patty Henderson

CHICKEN AND CHERRY SALAD

2 cups dry gemelli, rotini or small macaroni pasta, cooked and drained
1½ cups cooked and cubed chicken
¾ cup Bing cherries, pitted and halved
¼ cup slivered almonds, toasted
1 stalk celery, thinly sliced
3-4 scallions, chopped
½ cup poppy seed dressing

Combine all ingredients except dressing in a large bowl. Pour dressing over top and toss until coated. Cover and chill at least 2 hours before serving.

Serves: 4

Seedless green grapes can be substituted for the cherries and packaged chicken strips used in place of the cubed chicken.

Michelle Wright

WENDY'S WARM CHICKEN SALAD

3	boneless, skinless chicken breasts Salt and pepper to taste	½	large red or green bell pepper, diced
3	tablespoons olive oil, divided	½	cup currants
½	cup chicken broth	2	tablespoons balsamic vinegar
1	large tart apple, cut into 1-inch chunks	½	teaspoon salt
⅓	small red onion or several scallions, chopped	1	(6-ounce) package long-grain and wild rice mix
		½	cup pecan or walnut pieces, toasted

Season chicken with salt and pepper to taste. Brown chicken in 1 tablespoon olive oil in a hot skillet. Add chicken broth and cook 4 minutes on each side over medium heat. Cut into bite-size pieces; set aside.

Combine apples, onions, bell peppers, currants, vinegar, remaining 2 tablespoons olive oil, ½ teaspoon salt and pepper to taste. Add chicken. Prepare rice mix according to package directions and add to chicken mixture while still hot. Add toasted nuts just before serving.

Serves: 6

Wendy Morgan

MRS. BREWER'S
VERY SPECIAL CHICKEN SALAD

5	cups cooked and finely cubed chicken	1	cup dry rice
2	tablespoons olive oil	1½	cups chopped small green grapes
2	tablespoons orange juice	1½	cups chopped celery
2	tablespoons plus 2 teaspoons cider or salad vinegar, divided	1	(13½-ounce) can pineapple tidbits, drained
1	teaspoon salt	1½	cups mayonnaise
			Lettuce for garnish

Combine chicken, olive oil, orange juice, 2 tablespoons vinegar and salt in a large bowl; set aside. Prepare rice according to package directions, adding 2 teaspoons vinegar to the cooking water; drain and separate kernels. Refrigerate chicken mixture, rice, grapes, celery and pineapple overnight. Just before serving, gently toss chicken mixture, rice, grapes, celery, pineapple and mayonnaise with a wooden spoon. Serve with a border of crisp lettuce on a serving platter.

Serves: 10 to 12

Carolyn Brovero

CHICKEN SALAD
WITH BACON AND ALMONDS

4-6 chicken breasts
1 medium onion
2 carrots
1 bay leaf
 Salt and pepper to taste
2 cups chopped celery
½ cup sliced almonds, toasted
4-5 slices bacon, cooked crisp and crumbled

1 cup mayonnaise
1 cup sour cream
1 teaspoon salt
2 tablespoons lemon juice
 Lettuce leaves or other greens
 Cherry tomatoes, olives or deviled
  eggs for garnish

Cook chicken in 6 quarts boiling water with onion, carrots, bay leaf and salt and pepper to taste until meat falls off the bone. Cool, debone and tear or cut chicken into small pieces to equal 4 cups. Combine chicken with celery, almonds and bacon in a bowl. In a separate bowl, combine mayonnaise, sour cream, 1 teaspoon salt and lemon juice. Toss chicken mixture with mayonnaise dressing and chill thoroughly. To serve, arrange chicken salad on a platter lined with lettuce. Garnish with cherry tomatoes, olives, deviled eggs or garnish of choice.

Serves: 8

Pat Parker

ORIENTAL COLESLAW

Salad

2 (3-ounce) packages Oriental ramen noodles, seasoning packets reserved
1 (16-ounce) packages coleslaw mix

2 bunches scallions, sliced
1 (3¼-ounce) package sunflower kernels
1 (2¼-ounce) package sliced almonds

Dressing

1 cup vegetable oil
¾ cup red wine vinegar
¾ cup sugar

2 reserved seasoning packets from ramen noodles

Crush noodles into a large bowl; reserve seasoning packets for dressing. Add coleslaw mix, scallions, sunflower kernels and almonds to bowl with noodles.

Mix all dressing ingredients well and pour over salad. Toss and serve immediately.

Mary Ann Hausenfus

ZIPPY COLESLAW

Salad

1 (16-ounce) package coleslaw mix
1 medium onion, chopped

½ cup chopped green or red bell peppers

Dressing

1 cup mayonnaise
1 tablespoon fresh horseradish
1 tablespoon distilled vinegar
1 teaspoon celery seed

¼ cup milk
Sea salt and freshly ground black pepper to taste
Paprika for garnish

Combine coleslaw mix, onions and bell peppers in a large bowl; cover and chill.

Mix all dressing ingredients except paprika and chill. Just before serving, pour dressing over salad. Sprinkle with paprika and serve.

The dressing ingredients can be increased or decreased according to your taste.

Pam Fogt

CABBAGE SLAW

¾ cup mayonnaise
2 tablespoons soy sauce
2 teaspoons sugar
1 teaspoon salt
1 medium head cabbage, shredded
   (about 8 cups)
½ cup chopped scallions

1 (6- or 8-ounce) can water
   chestnuts, drained and thinly
   sliced
1 (5- or 6-ounce) can bamboo
   shoots, drained and sliced
2 tablespoons chopped pimiento

About 30 minutes before serving, whisk together mayonnaise, soy sauce, sugar and salt. Add cabbage, scallions, water chestnuts, bamboo shoots and pimiento. Toss until well coated.

To make Chinese Cabbage Slaw, prepare as above, but substitute 1 medium head Chinese cabbage for the regular cabbage.

Serves: 8 to 10

Sharyon Daigneau

BROCCOLI SLAW

Salad
1 (3-ounce) package Oriental
   ramen noodles, seasoning
   packets reserved

1 (12-ounce) package broccoli slaw
   mix
1 bunch scallions, sliced
1 (2¼-ounce) package sliced almonds

Dressing
¼ cup water
½ cup vegetable oil
⅓ cup red wine vinegar

¼ cup sugar
1 reserved seasoning packet from
   ramen noodles

Crush noodles into a large bowl; reserve seasoning packet for dressing. Add broccoli slaw mix, scallions and almonds to bowl with noodles.

Mix all dressing ingredients well. Pour dressing over salad. Chill.

Denise Blanton

FROG-EYE SALAD

1 cup sugar
2 tablespoons flour
½ teaspoon salt
2 (20-ounce) cans pineapple chunks, juice reserved
1 (20-ounce) can crushed pineapple, juice reserved
2 eggs, beaten
1 tablespoon lemon juice

1 (1-pound) package acini di pepe pasta
1 tablespoon vegetable oil
3 (11-ounce) cans Mandarin oranges
1 (8-ounce) container frozen whipped topping, thawed
1 cup miniature marshmallows
1 cup coconut (optional)

Combine sugar, flour and salt in a medium saucepan. Drain juice from pineapple chunks and crushed pineapple, reserving 1¾ cups juice. Refrigerate drained pineapple in a covered container until the next day. Gradually stir reserved juice and beaten eggs into sugar mixture. Cook and stir over medium heat until thickened. Add lemon juice. Cool mixture to room temperature. Cook pasta in boiling water and vegetable oil until done; drain (in a colander with small holes), rinse with cold water and drain again. Cool to room temperature. Combine pasta with egg mixture and mix lightly but thoroughly. Refrigerate overnight in an airtight container.

The next day, add pineapple chunks, crushed pineapple, oranges, whipped topping, marshmallows and coconut. Mix lightly but thoroughly. Refrigerate until chilled. Salad keeps up to 1 week in refrigerator.

Serves: 24

Great for a large party or picnic.

Donna Banister

D.C. FRUIT PLATTER AND DIP

1 (6-ounce) can frozen orange juice concentrate, not thawed
1 cup milk
1 (3-ounce) package instant vanilla pudding mix
¼ cup sour cream

1 fresh pineapple
Nutmeg
Fruit of choice: apple slices, strawberries, melon balls, kiwi, etc.

Beat together frozen juice concentrate, milk and pudding mix. Stir in sour cream. Chill dip until firm and ready to serve. Cut pineapple lengthwise and hollow out to make a bowl for dip. Reserve pineapple pulp and cut into chunks. Place pineapple bowl on a serving tray and fill with dip. Arrange pineapple chunks and other fruit around dip.

To keep apples from browning after slicing, dip in lemon juice and soak in salt water.

Barbara Graunke

FRUIT SALAD

1 (20-ounce) can pineapple chunks, juice reserved	1 (20-ounce) can sliced peaches, well drained
1 (11-ounce) can Mandarin oranges, juice reserved	3-4 bananas, sliced
⅔ cup pineapple juice	1 bunch seedless grapes, halved
½ cup Mandarin orange juice	1 (10-ounce) jar maraschino cherries, halved
1 (3-ounce) package vanilla pudding and pie mix	

Drain pineapple chunks well, reserving ⅔ cup juice. Drain oranges well, reserving ½ cup juice. Combine reserved juices with pudding mix in a saucepan. Bring to a boil. Cook, stirring occasionally, until clear; cool. Add pineapple chunks, oranges and peaches. Refrigerate overnight. The next day, add banana slices and grapes. Just before serving, mix in cherries.

If strawberries are in season, substitute for grapes.

Jo Durham

CRANBERRY SALAD

1 (12-ounce) package cranberries	1 (3-ounce) package lemon gelatin
2 oranges, 1 peeled and 1 unpeeled	1 (¼-ounce) envelope unflavored gelatin
3-4 stalks celery	
1 cup sugar	1 cup finely chopped pecans
1 (8-ounce) can crushed pineapple, juice reserved	Red food coloring (optional)

Grind together cranberries, peeled and unpeeled orange and celery, or process in a food processor. Stir in sugar and let stand until sugar is dissolved. Drain ½ cup juice from the crushed pineapple (add water to equal ½ cup if needed) into a very small saucepan. Dissolve both gelatins in pineapple juice and heat until hot, but not boiling. Pour hot liquid over cranberry mixture. Add crushed pineapple, pecans and food coloring for desired color. Mix well and pour into molds. Refrigerate overnight.

This is a Thanksgiving and Christmas tradition.

Ann T. Combs

STRAWBERRY-WALNUT ARUGULA SALAD WITH BALSAMIC VINAIGRETTE DRESSING

½ cup chopped walnuts
6 cups arugula leaves
1 pint strawberries, thinly sliced

Balsamic Vinaigrette Dressing
(recipe below)

In a skillet over medium-low heat, gently roast walnuts, stirring often, for 4 minutes or until fragrant. Remove from heat and cool. In a bowl, toss arugula, strawberries and walnuts with Vinaigrette Dressing.

Serves: 6

Balsamic Vinaigrette Dressing
1 tablespoon balsamic vinegar
1 teaspoon Dijon mustard
1 teaspoon honey

Salt and pepper to taste
½ cup olive oil

Whisk together vinegar, mustard, honey and salt and pepper. While still whisking, drizzle in olive oil.

Yield: ½ cup

Emily Chapin

SPINACH AND RICE SALAD

2 cups cooked brown rice, cooled
1 (16-ounce) bag fresh spinach
½ red bell pepper, cut into thin strips
½ yellow bell pepper, cut into thin strips

¼ cup dried cranraisins or raisins
¼ cup sliced scallions
2 tablespoons sunflower kernels
Dressing (recipe below)

Combine all ingredients in a medium bowl. Toss lightly. Cover and refrigerate until serving.

Dressing
⅔ cup olive oil
2 tablespoons cider vinegar

2 teaspoons Cavender's all-purpose Greek seasoning

Combine all dressing ingredients.

Katie Preston

WATERMELON SALAD WITH FETA

6 cups torn mixed salad greens	½ cup Watermelon Vinaigrette
3 cups cubed seedless watermelon	(recipe below)
½ cup sliced onions	Cracked black pepper for garnish
⅓ cup crumbled feta cheese	

Just before serving, mix salad greens, watermelon, onions and cheese in a large bowl. Add Watermelon Vinaigrette and toss. Sprinkle with pepper to garnish.

Serves: 6

Watermelon Vinaigrette

2 tablespoons currant jelly	¼ teaspoon garlic pepper
¼ cup puréed seedless watermelon	1 teaspoon vegetable oil
2 tablespoons white wine vinegar	

Heat jelly in a small saucepan until just melted; cool. Add watermelon purée, vinegar, garlic pepper and vegetable oil. Stir until well blended. Store in refrigerator. Shake well before using.

Yield: ½ cup

Mary Hutchinson

PEA AND CORN SALAD

2 (16-ounce) cans white corn, drained	1 (2-ounce) jar diced pimiento
1 (16-ounce) can petite green peas, drained	1 bell pepper, diced
	2 tablespoons coarsely ground black pepper
1 bunch scallions, chopped	Dressing (recipe below)
1 cup chopped celery	

Combine all ingredients. Marinate in refrigerator overnight.

Serves: 15 to 20

Dressing

½ cup oil	½ cup sugar
½ cup red wine vinegar	

To make dressing, combine all ingredients and shake until sugar dissolves.

Jean Jacobs

SALAD GREENS WITH STRAWBERRIES

6-8 Romaine lettuce leaves, chopped	¼ cup chopped walnuts
1 small head Boston lettuce, chopped	1 cup sliced strawberries
½ cup shredded Monterey Jack cheese	Dressing to taste (recipe below)

Combine both lettuces, cheese, walnuts and strawberries in a bowl. Add desired amount of dressing and toss.

Dressing

1 cup vegetable oil	½ teaspoon salt
¾ cup sugar	½ teaspoon paprika
½ cup red wine vinegar	¼ teaspoon white pepper
2 cloves garlic, chopped	

Mix all dressing ingredients and shake well.

Mary Ann Hasenfus

CRUNCHY PEA SALAD

1 (10-ounce) package frozen peas, thawed	½ cup sliced scallions
1 (8-ounce) can sliced water chestnuts, drained	¼ cup mayonnaise
	¼ cup sour cream
1 cup thinly sliced celery	½ teaspoon seasoned salt

Combine peas, water chestnuts, celery and scallions in a bowl. In a separate, small bowl, mix mayonnaise, sour cream and seasoned salt. Add mayonnaise mixture to pea mixture and toss to coat. Chill until ready to serve.

Serves: 8

Bea Tranowski

ASPARAGUS FETA SALAD

2 pounds thin asparagus spears, cut into 1-inch pieces	½ pint halved cherry or grape tomatoes
1 (4-ounce) package feta cheese	Balsamic vinegar to taste
1 cup finely chopped basil	

Blanch asparagus and cool in ice water; drain. Mix asparagus with cheese, basil and tomatoes. Chill. Add vinegar and toss before serving.

Gimmee Cramer

APPLE WALNUT SALAD

1 cup walnuts	1 red apple
3 tablespoons butter	Lemon juice
½ cup sugar	2 heads lettuce or mixed greens
1 tablespoon black pepper	½ cup crumbled feta cheese
1 green apple	Poppy Seed Dressing to taste (recipe below)

Preheat oven to 350 degrees.

Mix walnuts and butter on a baking sheet and bake 15 minutes. Transfer hot nuts to a bowl with sugar and pepper.

Meanwhile, core and thinly slice green and red apples. Coat apple slices with lemon juice to prevent browning. Mix apples with walnuts, lettuce and feta. Toss and refrigerate 1 hour. Add Poppy Seed Dressing to salad just before serving.

Poppy Seed Dressing

¼-½ cup sugar	1 tablespoon lemon juice
1 teaspoon salt	1 cup salad oil
1 teaspoon dried mustard	1½ tablespoons poppy seeds
½ cup red wine vinegar	

For dressing, mix sugar, salt, mustard, vinegar and lemon juice and stir until sugar dissolves. Slowly whisk in oil. Add poppy seeds. Refrigerate any unused dressing. Dressing can be used on other salads, too.

To reduce fat and calories, decrease oil in dressing to ½ cup and add ½ cup water. Butter-flavored nonstick spray can be substituted for the butter used to toast the walnuts.

Charlene DeMarco

NOT JUST BROCCOLI (BROCCOLI SALAD)

1 large bunch broccoli, finely chopped	2 cups seedless red grapes, halved if large
2 cups chopped celery	Dressing (recipe below)
6 scallions, chopped	8 ounces bacon, cooked crisp and chopped
1 cup raisins	1 cup chopped pecans or almonds

Combine broccoli, celery, scallions, raisins and grapes. Chill. Just before serving, add dressing, bacon and nuts. Blend well.

Dressing

1 cup mayonnaise
½ cup milk

1 tablespoon white vinegar
½ cup sugar

Combine all dressing ingredients.

Mary Ann Hasenfus

FETA AND WALNUT SPINACH SALAD
WITH BASIL DRESSING

1 bunch fresh spinach, torn into bite-size pieces	½ cup crumbled feta cheese
1 small avocado, thinly sliced	½ cup coarsely chopped walnuts
½ medium-size red onion, thinly sliced	Basil Dressing (recipe below)

Toss together spinach, avocado, onions, feta and walnuts in a large bowl. Pour Basil Dressing over top and toss. Serve immediately.

Serves: 6

Basil Dressing

½ cup olive oil
¼ cup red wine vinegar
1 tablespoon dried basil, crumbled
2 teaspoons sugar

2 large cloves garlic, minced
½ teaspoon salt
½ teaspoon freshly ground black pepper

Combine all dressing ingredients in a blender or food processor and mix well. Store dressing in refrigerator in a jar with a tight-fitting lid. Shake well before using.

Yield: ¾ cup

Peggy C. Clute

CHICKPEA, GARLIC AND TOMATO TOSS

¼ cup extra virgin olive oil
4 teaspoons fresh lemon juice
1-3 cloves garlic, crushed
1 teaspoon fresh chopped basil, or
    more to taste
    Salt and pepper to taste

1 (15-ounce) can chickpeas, drained
3 scallions, thinly sliced
2 ripe tomatoes, diced
    Pita bread
    Leaf lettuce

Whisk oil, lemon juice, garlic, basil and salt and pepper in a bowl. Add chickpeas, scallions and tomatoes and toss until evenly coated. Serve in pita bread and lettuce, or serve over lettuce as a salad. Refrigerate if not serving immediately.

Bill Weaver

MIXED GREENS
WITH BLUEBERRIES AND FETA

1 tablespoon apple cider vinegar
¼ cup fat-free, reduced-sodium
    chicken broth
2 tablespoons extra virgin olive oil
1 teaspoon honey

1 cup fresh blueberries plus 10
    individual blueberries, divided
8 cups mixed salad greens
2 ounces reduced-fat feta cheese,
    crumbled

Combine vinegar, broth, olive oil, honey and 10 blueberries in a blender. Blend on low speed until smooth and well combined. Chill until needed. In a large bowl, toss salad greens with remaining 1 cup blueberries. Shake blueberry dressing until well blended and drizzle over salad. Toss slightly. Sprinkle feta cheese on top and serve.

Serves: 8

Karly Walker

TOFU POTATO SALAD

1 cauliflower, chopped
¼ cup chopped onions
2 large stalks celery, chopped
1 (16-ounce) tofu cake, cut into
    bite-size pieces

3-4 hard-boiled eggs, cut
    Low-fat mayonnaise to taste
    Salt and pepper to taste

Combine cauliflower, onions, celery, tofu and eggs in a bowl. Mix in mayonnaise to taste and season with salt and pepper.

Suzanne McGrenery

SPICED SHRIMP SALAD

20 cooked and deveined jumbo
    shrimp, each cut into 4 to
    5 pieces
2-3 stalks celery, chopped
2-3 scallions, chopped
1 (2¼-ounce) can sliced black olives
    with jalapeños
¼ cup capers (optional)
¼ cup pine nuts

2 tablespoons sun-dried tomatoes
    Finely chopped fresh parsley
1-2 teaspoons lemon juice
2-3 dashes Tabasco
½-1 cup mayonnaise to taste
½-1 cup sour cream to taste
    Salt and pepper to taste
    Freshly ground Parmesan cheese
    (optional)

Combine shrimp, celery, scallions, olives, capers, pine nuts, tomatoes, parsley, lemon juice and Tabasco in a bowl; set aside. Combine equal parts of mayonnaise and sour cream based on personal taste. Fold mayonnaise dressing into salad and season with salt and pepper. Serve hot on pasta or cold on mixed greens. Top with Parmesan cheese.

Jody Bond

POMPANO SALAD

2 pounds skinless Florida pompano
    fillets
¼ cup olive oil
¼ cup chopped scallions
3 tablespoons wine vinegar
2 tablespoons capers

3 cloves garlic, minced
2 teaspoons chopped fresh cilantro
½ teaspoon dried basil
½ teaspoon salt
½ teaspoon white pepper
    Salad greens

Cut fish fillets into 1-inch pieces. Broil fish 5 to 6 inches from a heat source for 3 to 5 minutes or until fish flakes easily with a fork. Remove from heat and transfer to a cool plate; set aside.

Combine olive oil, scallions, vinegar, capers, garlic, cilantro, basil, salt and white pepper. Mix well and pour into a flat-bottom storage container with a lid. Add fish in a single layer, cover tightly, and marinate in refrigerator for 2 hours. Remove fish from marinade and arrange on salad greens.

Serves: 6

Holly Whitney

WATERCRESS AND APPLE SALAD WITH SMOKED FISH

6 cups trimmed watercress sprigs (about 2 bunches)	Salt and pepper to taste
⅓ cup Cream Dressing (recipe below)	½ cup very thinly sliced red onions
2 tablespoons olive oil	2 red apples, thinly sliced
2 teaspoons apple cider vinegar	9 ounces smoked fish
	Fresh dill sprigs

Place watercress in a large bowl. Add dressing, olive oil and vinegar and toss to coat. Season with salt and pepper. Mount watercress in the center of 6 plates. Top with sliced onions. Fan apple slices over each salad and top with fish. Spoon extra dressing over each salad and garnish with dill.

Cream Dressing

1 cup whipping cream	2 teaspoons chopped fresh dill
⅓ cup prepared horseradish	⅛ teaspoon cayenne pepper
2 tablespoons olive oil	Salt and pepper to taste
2 tablespoons apple cider vinegar	

For dressing, whisk together cream, horseradish, olive oil, vinegar, dill and cayenne pepper in a small bowl. Season with salt and pepper.

Gretchen Hurchalla

STAR FRUIT SHRIMP SALAD

1 cup peeled and sliced Florida oranges	1 pound cooked shrimp or lobster
½ pound mixed salad greens, chilled	1 cup black beans, drained and rinsed
4 medium star fruit, sliced	

Combine all ingredients in a large bowl. Toss with dressing and serve.

Dressing

1 cup Florida orange juice	¼ cup canola oil
2 tablespoons honey	1 teaspoon salt

For dressing, pour orange juice into a saucepan and bring to a boil. Cook until liquid is reduced by half. Cool. Combine cooled orange juice, honey, oil and salt.

Serves: 5

Jill Myers

FLORIDA Classic FLAVORS CONCH SALAD

1 cup raw conch meat, finely diced	¼ cup chopped green bell peppers
½ cup chopped tomatoes	Lime juice
¼ cup chopped onions	Hot pepper sauce

Marinate conch, tomatoes, onions and bell peppers in lime juice to cover. Add hot sauce to taste.

Barb Hendry

FLORIDA Classic FLAVORS PERUVIAN CEVICHE

2 pounds skinned, boned grouper	6 cherry peppers or 3 jalapeño
2-3 cups lemon juice	peppers, chopped
1 onion, chopped	1 teaspoon salt

Cut grouper into bite-size pieces and place in a bowl. Add lemon juice, using enough to totally cover fish. Add onions, peppers and salt. Cover and marinate in refrigerator for several hours. Place fish on toothpicks and serve with ice cold beer.

If cutting peppers by hand, do so under running water. They can burn your skin.

Joan Hutchinson

CONCH CEVICHE

8 ounces fresh conch	1 yellow bell pepper, minced
Juice of 2 lemons, divided	¼ habanero pepper, seeded and
Juice of 2 limes, divided	minced
1 clove garlic, minced	1 bunch cilantro, stems removed,
1 tablespoon minced fresh ginger	chopped
½ red onion, minced	Salt and pepper to taste
1 red bell pepper, minced	

Dice conch into small pieces or cut into small, thin strips. If desired, cook conch in boiling seasoned water for 1 minute; drain and chill in ice water. Add half of the lemon and lime juices. Add garlic and ginger. Let stand 30 minutes. Add remaining juices, onions, peppers and cilantro. Season with salt and pepper. Serve with crackers or plantain chips.

Gretchen Hurchalla

CEVICHE

2 pounds raw white meat fish, cut into ¼-inch cubes	Olive oil
12 large lemons	Oregano to taste
8 tomatoes, diced	Salt to taste
1 large onion, diced	Chopped jalapeño pepper (optional)
1 bunch cilantro, stems removed, chopped	

Place fish in a bowl. Squeeze lemons over fish to cover. Marinate, covered, in refrigerator for 10 hours. Add tomatoes, onions and cilantro. Separate ceviche into small bowls. Add 1 teaspoon olive oil to each bowl. Season with oregano and salt. Add jalapeño pepper, if using. Serve cold.

Tom Kenny

TUNA AND AVOCADO PASTA SALAD

½ avocado, sliced ¾-inch thick	1 (6-ounce) can albacore tuna, drained
2 tomatoes, cut into ¾-inch cubes	
2 cups cooked shell macaroni	3 tablespoons light vinaigrette salad dressing
¼ cup sliced red onions	

Combine all ingredients and gently toss to mix.

Serves: 2

Karly Walker

 # V.V.'S BLUEFISH SALAD

1 cup chopped bluefish	Juice of 1 lemon
½ cup diced onion	Salt and pepper to taste
½ cup diced celery	Paprika to taste
1 teaspoon prepared mustard	Mayonnaise

Cook bluefish in boiling salted water; cool and flake. Add onion, celery, mustard and lemon juice. Season with salt and pepper and paprika. Mix in enough mayonnaise to reach desired consistency.

Jackie Wortham

PASTA SEAFOOD SALAD
WITH A CREAMY CITRUS DRESSING

½ pound dry shell pasta, or other
   short pasta
1 pound cooked, peeled and
   deveined medium shrimp
1 pound cooked bay scallops
1 pound imitation crabmeat
½ cup olive oil
1 cup tiny peas
1 cup kalamata olives
½ cup diced red bell peppers
½ cup minced red onions
   Salt and pepper to taste
1 cup Creamy Citrus Dressing
   (recipe below)

Cook pasta according to package directions; drain well, cool and transfer to a large mixing bowl. Add seafood and toss with pasta. In a small bowl, whisk together olive oil, peas, olives, bell peppers and onions. Pour mixture over salad. Season with salt and pepper. Add dressing and toss. Serve immediately. Can be served over salad greens.

Salad can be made in advance, covered, and refrigerated until ready to serve. Allow to return to room temperature. Add dressing just before serving.

Serves: 4 to 6

Creamy Citrus Dressing

3 tablespoons fresh orange juice
2 tablespoons fresh lime juice
2 eggs
2 tablespoons Dijon mustard
1 cup canola oil
1 cup olive oil
   Zest of 1 orange
   Salt and freshly ground black
   pepper to taste

Combine orange and lime juices, eggs and mustard in a food processor. Process 15 seconds. With motor running, gradually add both oils through the feed tube and process until the dressing is thickened. Transfer to a bowl, scraping down the sides, and fold in orange zest. Season with salt and pepper. Cover and refrigerate until ready to use.

Karen Cotler

The miracle of light upon a happy river in the morning is alchemy accepted, unexplained.

~ Ernest Lyons

SHRIMP SALAD WITH CAPER MARINADE

1 cup olive oil	1 teaspoon salt
1 cup rice vinegar	1 red bell pepper, sliced
1 (8-ounce) can tomato sauce	1 yellow bell pepper, sliced
¼ cup chopped fresh parsley	1 green bell pepper, sliced
3 tablespoons chopped capers	½ red onion, sliced
2 tablespoons hot pepper sauce	3 pounds shrimp, peeled and
2 tablespoons Worcestershire sauce	deveined
2 teaspoons dry mustard	

Combine all ingredients except shrimp; cover and chill. Cook shrimp in boiling salted water until shrimp turns pink; drain. Add shrimp to vinaigrette. Cover and chill 2 to 3 hours or overnight. Drain and serve. Can be served over lettuce with vinaigrette.

Serves: 8 to 10

Mary Hutchinson

 # CRAWFISH SALAD NASSAU STYLE

2-3 crawfish tails, cooked and diced	3 tablespoons lemon juice
1-2 tablespoons diced onions	3 tablespoons mayonnaise
1 tablespoon diced green bell peppers	2 tablespoons olive oil
3 hard-boiled eggs, diced	1 teaspoon hot pepper sauce
1 ripe tomato, diced	Salt and pepper to taste

Combine all ingredients and mix well. Chill at least 4 hours before serving.

Sue F. Hipson

FLAGLER GRILL POPPY SEED DRESSING

1 cup vegetable oil	1 tablespoon sugar
¼ cup rice wine vinegar	Salt and pepper to taste
3 tablespoons coconut crème	Chopped mango
1 tablespoon Dijon mustard	½ avocado
1 tablespoon poppy seeds	Shredded coconut

Combine oil, vinegar, crème, mustard, poppy seeds and sugar in a food processor or blender. Process 30 seconds. Season with salt and pepper. Serve over chopped mango and avocado half. Sprinkle coconut lightly on top.

Flagler Grill
Stuart, Florida

CHIPOLTE CAESAR DRESSING

3 cloves garlic, minced	2 teaspoons minced fresh parsley
Juice of ½ lemon	1 teaspoon Dijon mustard
¾ cup mayonnaise	1 teaspoon Worcestershire sauce
2-4 tablespoons anchovy paste, or to taste	1-2 teaspoons chipotle en adobe
2 tablespoons grated Parmesan cheese	Salt and pepper to taste

Purée all ingredients in a blender or food processor for 1 minute, scraping sides. Refrigerate 2 hours before serving.

Mary Hutchinson

CAYENNE-BUTTERMILK DRESSING

2 tablespoons sour cream, regular or low-fat	1 tablespoon fresh lime juice
½ cup buttermilk	1 teaspoon cayenne pepper
1 teaspoon minced garlic	Salt and freshly ground black pepper to taste
1 teaspoon minced red onions	

Combine all ingredients and mix well. May be prepared a day ahead and refrigerated in a squeeze bottle. Recipe can be doubled.

Makes: ½ cup

Karen Cotler

CITRUS DRESSING

½ cup sugar
1 teaspoon salt
1 teaspoon dry mustard
1 teaspoon celery salt

1 teaspoon paprika
1 teaspoon grated onion
¼ cup red wine vinegar

Combine all ingredients in a container and stir or shake until smooth. Serve over grapefruit and orange sections on lettuce.

Mary Ann Hasenfus

 GUACAMOLE DRESSING

1 cup mashed avocado
1 teaspoon lemon juice
2 tablespoons mayonnaise

½ teaspoon garlic powder
½ teaspoon salt
4-5 drops hot pepper sauce

Combine all ingredients in a bowl in order listed. Beat with an electric mixer until smooth. Place in an airtight container and refrigerate until needed.

Serves: 4 to 6

Carol Newman

GARLIC SALAD DRESSING

This recipe was inspired by **Florida's Finest**, a
1984 cookbook from The Junior League of South Brevard (Florida).
It was significantly modified by Gene Moore.

2 tablespoons water
2 cloves garlic, minced
½ tablespoon dried oregano
1 tablespoon Worcestershire sauce

¾ teaspoon salt
¾ teaspoon black pepper
1 cup sour cream
1 cup mayonnaise

Combine water, garlic, oregano, Worcestershire sauce, salt and pepper in a blender. Process for 3 to 4 seconds. Add sour cream and mayonnaise and blend about 5 seconds longer or until well blended. Refrigerate a few hours to allow flavors to blend.

Gene Moore

NINA'S FRENCH DRESSING

¼ teaspoon black pepper	½ teaspoon paprika
1 teaspoon salt	1 clove garlic, minced
½ teaspoon sugar	⅓ cup vinegar
¼ teaspoon dry mustard	⅔ cup vegetable oil

Combine pepper, salt, sugar, mustard, paprika, garlic and vinegar in a jar; shake well. Add oil and shake again.

Nina King, Pelican Hotel
Courtesy of Lillie Davis

ORANGE VINAIGRETTE DRESSING

2 tablespoons orange juice	2 tablespoons olive oil
2 tablespoons white wine vinegar	Freshly ground black pepper to
2 tablespoons orange zest	taste
¼ teaspoon salt	

Whisk together orange juice, vinegar, orange zest and salt in a small bowl until blended. Whisk in olive oil and season with pepper. Tastes great on a summer salad.

Colleen Hynes

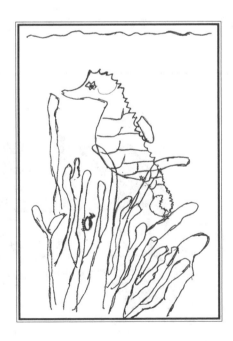

JIM AND JEN'S SEAFOOD CHILI

1	cup chopped onions	1	tablespoon cayenne pepper
6	cloves garlic, chopped	1	teaspoon dried thyme or other spices
2-3	tablespoons olive oil		
2	(14½-ounce) cans diced tomatoes	1	tablespoon cocoa powder
1	(10½-ounce) can clam juice	1	teaspoon allspice
1	(15-ounce) can black beans, rinsed	1	tablespoon sugar
		1	tablespoon lemon juice
1	(15-ounce) can pinto or small white beans, rinsed	¼	cup chopped fresh cilantro, stems removed
2	cups water	1	teaspoon ground cloves
1	(8-ounce) can tomato sauce	½	pound peeled shrimp
3	stalks celery, sliced	½	pound sliced calamari
4	bay leaves	½	pound salmon or other firm fish, cut into ½-inch cubes
2	tablespoons chili powder, or to taste	1	(10-ounce) package frozen corn

Sauté onions and garlic it olive oil. Add tomatoes, clam juice, black beans, pinto beans, water, tomato sauce, celery, bay leaves, chili powder, cayenne pepper, thyme, cocoa, allspice, sugar, lemon juice, cilantro and cloves. Cook over low heat for 45 to 60 minutes. When ready to serve, bring chili to a boil. Add shrimp, calamari, salmon and corn. Cook about 5 minutes, being careful to not overcook seafood.

You can vary the spices in the recipe to your taste. Use whatever beans or seafood you like best. Use vegetable or chicken broth for the clam juice if making regular chili.

Jim Wilbers

WHITE CHILI

1 onion, chopped
2 chicken breasts, cooked and
   chopped
1 clove garlic, chopped
1 teaspoon ground cumin
1 tablespoon salad oil
1 (15-ounce) can great Northern
   beans, undrained

1 (15-ounce) can garbanzo beans,
   undrained
1 (12-ounce) can white corn,
   undrained
2 cubes chicken bouillon
4 ounces Monterey Jack cheese,
   shredded, plus extra for garnish

Sauté onion, chicken, garlic and cumin in oil in a skillet. Transfer mixture to a crockpot. Add both beans, corn, chicken bouillon and cheese. Cook in crockpot at least until cheese melts; chili can be cooked in crockpot for hours, stirring frequently. Garnish individual servings with extra cheese. Serve with tortilla chips.

Serves: 8 to 10

Kim Bruder

SAUSAGE CHILI

10 links breakfast sausage, cut into
   small bites
2 pounds ground beef
1 green bell pepper, chopped
3 stalks celery, diced
1 large onion, diced
4 (15-ounce) cans kidney beans,
   drained
2 (10-ounce) cans tomato soup

2 (14½-ounce) cans diced tomatoes,
   undrained
2 tablespoons chili powder
1 teaspoon crushed red pepper
   flakes
1 cup sour cream for garnish
1 cup shredded Cheddar cheese for
   garnish

Brown sausage in a large skillet. Remove from pan; set aside. Add ground beef to same skillet and brown; drain and set aside. Add bell peppers, celery and onions to skillet and sauté. Return sausage and ground beef to skillet. Add beans, condensed tomato soup, tomatoes, chili powder and pepper flakes. Simmer on low heat for 1 hour. Garnish individual servings with sour cream and cheese, if desired.

Jackie Tucker

COUSIN CARL'S CHILI

2-3 cups dried pinto beans or other beans of choice	2½-3 pounds chuck roast
	Olive oil for browning
1-1½ bottles red table wine	3 heads garlic, coarsely chopped
1 tablespoon ground cumin	Salt and pepper to taste
1 tablespoon dried Mexican oregano	2 large onions, coarsely chopped
	1 bell pepper, chopped
6-18 tablespoons ground chiles (vary amount and mix mild and hot to taste)	1 cup grape tomatoes, whole

Soak beans overnight. Cook soaked beans for 1½ hours or until done; drain, reserving cooking liquid. Set beans aside. Pour wine into a large stockpot. Add cumin, oregano and ground chiles. Warm over low heat while meat is prepared. Slice chuck roast into bite-size strips; do not trim away fat. In a skillet, brown beef in olive oil with garlic in batches, adding oil as needed for each batch. Season each batch with salt and pepper before adding to stockpot. After last batch of meat, sauté onions in skillet in oil and pan drippings until translucent; add to stockpot. Increase heat and simmer chili, uncovered, for about 2 hours. As needed, add extra wine or reserved cooking liquid from beans to chili. Add bell peppers and tomatoes after first hour of cooking. Taste often and adjust seasonings as needed. Serve chili over beans.

Ground chiles are a must; chili powder from the grocery store just doesn't get it. Available online or at a Spanish market. You may vary the amount of ground chile to suit your desired degree of heat, but you are set once you start as it must cook from the beginning. Jalapeños or whole chiles may be added to raise the heat.

Have butcher grind your roast if you don't want to slice it yourself. Request the same blade as used for Italian sausage; a hamburger blade is too fine. However, sliced yourself is the preferred method for the best beef flavor.

Feel free to tamper with the recipe, just don't use tomato sauce or paste, or any form of ground chili powder that contains ingredients other than chile peppers.

Serves: 4 to 6 fanatics, or 20 lightweights

Carl Bice

> Don't bet against Mother Nature. She's been gambling since the hot rocks cooled. She won big with a little fish that crawled out on the mud, breathed air and learned to walk on land.
>
> ~ Ernest Lyons

 DEMMA'S CHILI

1½ medium onions, chopped	1 (14½-ounce) can stewed tomatoes
1 medium-size green bell pepper, chopped	2 (16-ounce) cans tomato sauce
1 stalk celery, chopped	1 (6-ounce) can tomato paste
1 clove garlic, minced	1 (12-ounce) can beer
3 tablespoons oil	½ teaspoon salt
4 pounds ground chuck, cooked and drained	½ teaspoon black pepper
½ cup chili powder	1¼ cups water
1 tablespoon ground cumin	1 (4-ounce) can chopped green chiles
2 teaspoons garlic salt	1 bay leaf
¼ teaspoon hot pepper sauce	2 (60-ounce) cans red kidney beans

Sauté onions, bell peppers, celery and garlic in oil. Add sautéed vegetables to cooked meat in a large pot; set aside. Combine chili powder, cumin, garlic salt, hot sauce, tomatoes, tomato sauce, tomato paste, beer, salt, pepper, water, chiles, bay leaf and kidney beans. Add bean mixture to cooked beef and vegetables. Simmer, uncovered, over low heat for 3 to 4 hours.

Serves: 20

Demma Bailey

CINCINNATI CHILI

2 pounds ground beef	¼ teaspoon ground nutmeg
1 quart water or chicken broth, or mixture of both	¼ teaspoon ground cloves
3 medium onions, finely chopped	¼ teaspoon oregano
1 clove garlic, chopped	¼ teaspoon celery seed
1 (6-ounce) can tomato paste	¼ teaspoon paprika
1 tablespoon cinnamon	1½ teaspoons chili powder
1 teaspoon dried hot pepper flakes	4 bay leaves
¼ teaspoon cumin seed	1 tablespoon vinegar or white wine, or both
¼ teaspoon ground allspice	

Combine all ingredients (do not brown meat) in a large pot. Cook 4 to 5 hours. Serve with spaghetti or white rice and top with chopped sweet onions or shredded cheese.

Kidney beans can be added.

Serves: 4 to 6

Elaine Clark

105

SEAFOOD CHOWDER

3 cups "good" water
3 cups puréed canned clams with juice
1 medium onion, diced
6 stalks celery, cut into ¼-inch pieces
3 medium carrots, diced
2 medium baking potatoes, diced
2 pounds any firm fish fillets, such as bluefish, grouper, dolphin, etc., cut into 1-inch pieces

1 pound shrimp, peeled and deveined, cut into 1-inch pieces
1 pound fresh bay or sea scallops
1 cup sherry wine
1 pint whipping cream or lactose-free milk
   Parsley to taste
   Salt to taste

Combine water, clams with juice, onions, celery and carrots in a large pot. Simmer about 30 minutes. Add potatoes and cook until tender. Add fish, shrimp and scallops and cook briefly until seafood is done; seafood will cook quickly. Remove from heat and add wine and cream. Season with parsley and salt.

Manhattan-Style Chowder: Add one (8-ounce) can diced tomatoes or 1 cup diced fresh tomatoes before bringing to a simmer. Add ½ teaspoon thyme before adding seafood. Delete cream.

Floyd De Nicola

SUSAN JOHNSON'S GROUPER CHOWDER

2 fish bouillon cubes
4 cups boiling water
1 onion, diced
1 green bell pepper, diced
8-10 small red potatoes, chopped

4 (14½-ounce) cans stewed tomatoes
½ head garlic, chopped
1 pound flaked baked grouper
2 bay leaves
   Black pepper to taste

Dissolve bouillon cubes in boiling water. Add onions, bell peppers and potatoes and cook until potatoes are tender. Add tomatoes, garlic, grouper, bay leaves and pepper. Simmer until chowder smells good. Enjoy! Great with a fresh loaf of French bread.

To bake grouper, cook 10 minutes per inch of thickness at 350 to 400 degrees.

Jennifer Strauss

BAHAMIAN CONCH CHOWDER

¼ pound bacon, diced
½ cup olive oil
2 jalapeño peppers, seeded and diced
1 large Spanish onion, diced
½ bunch celery, diced
2 carrots, diced
1 green bell pepper, diced
1 yellow bell pepper, diced
2 banana peppers, seeded and diced
1 tablespoon dried hot pepper flakes
10 small new potatoes, peeled and diced, reserved in water

1 quart peeled plum tomatoes, thoroughly crushed
1 quart tomato purée
3 bay leaves
1 bunch fresh thyme
1 bunch fresh oregano
1 bunch fresh marjoram
1 bunch fresh basil
3¼ quarts fish stock
2⅔ quarts bottled clam juice
2½ pounds cleaned and ground conch meat
Tabasco sauce to taste

In a very large soup pot or Dutch oven, sauté bacon in olive oil until done. Stir in jalapeños, onions, celery, carrots and all peppers and sauté briskly. Add pepper flakes. Add potatoes, tomatoes and tomato purée. Reduce heat and add bay leaves. Combine thyme, oregano, marjoram and basil in a cheesecloth and tie shut. Add cheesecloth to pot.

In a separate large pot, bring fish stock and clam juice to a boil. Whisk in conch meat. Bring to a boil, then strain quickly into pot with vegetables; reserving conch. When potatoes are tender, whisk in reserved conch. Season with Tabasco. Bring to a boil and serve immediately, or chill for later use.

Serves: 12

Holly Whitney

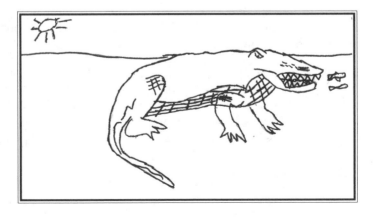

FISH CHOWDER

2	cups water	2	quarts milk
1	bay leaf	1	(14-ounce) can evaporated milk
1½	pounds boneless white fish fillets		Dash of white wine or sherry
2	strips bacon, chopped		(optional)
4	medium onions, chopped		Tabasco sauce to taste
1½	tablespoons flour		Salt and pepper to taste
2	medium potatoes, peeled and chopped		

Combine water and bay leaf in a heavy skillet with a lid and bring to a boil. Add fish. Reduce heat to medium and cook until fish flakes. Use a slotted spoon to remove fish; set aside. Remove bay leaf and reserve cooking liquid; set aside. Cook bacon until crisp; drain. Sauté onions in bacon until browned. Add flour and brown 2 to 3 minutes. Cook potatoes in reserved fish cooking liquid in a large stockpot until tender. Add fish to potatoes. Stir in onion mixture. Add both milks. Heat over medium-high heat until thick and creamy but do not boil. Add wine, if using. Season with Tabasco and salt and pepper.

Serves: 6

Hermance Dupuis

SANTA FE CORN CHOWDER

½	pound hot Italian sausage, casings removed and sausage crumbled	1	bay leaf
		1	teaspoon dried thyme
1	tablespoon vegetable oil	6	cups chicken broth
1	cup chopped onion	2	boiling potatoes, peeled and cut into ½-inch cubes
½	cup chopped celery	¾	cup whipping cream
1	cup chopped red bell pepper		Salt and pepper to taste
½	cup chopped green bell pepper	2	tablespoons finely chopped fresh coriander for garnish
3	cups frozen corn, thawed		

Brown sausage in oil in a kettle over medium heat, stirring occasionally; drain. Add onions, celery and all bell peppers and sauté until vegetables are softened. Add corn, bay leaf and thyme and cook and stir 1 minute. Stir in broth and simmer, stirring occasionally, for 30 minutes. Add potatoes and cream and simmer 25 minutes longer, stirring occasionally. Discard bay leaf and season with salt and pepper. Garnish with fresh coriander.

Serves: 8 to 10, makes about 12 cups

Becky Arnold

HEARTY CHEDDAR CHOWDER

3 cups water
3 chicken or vegetable bouillon cubes
4 medium potatoes, peeled and diced
1 medium onion, sliced
1 cup thinly sliced carrots
½ cup diced green bell peppers
5 tablespoons butter or margarine

⅓ cup all-purpose flour
3½ cups milk
4 cups shredded sharp Cheddar cheese
1 (2-ounce) jar diced pimientos, drained
¼ teaspoon hot pepper sauce, or to taste
Salt and pepper to taste

Combine water and bouillon cubes in a Dutch oven and bring to a boil. Add potatoes, onions, carrots and bell peppers. Cover and simmer 12 minutes or until vegetables are tender. Melt butter in a heavy saucepan. Blend in flour and cook 1 minute. Gradually stir in milk. Cook, stirring constantly, over medium heat until thickened. Add cheese and stir until melted. Stir cheese sauce and pimiento into Dutch oven. Season with hot sauce and salt and pepper. Cook over low heat until thoroughly heated; do not boil.

May add cooked chicken or sausage for a heartier meal.

Serves: 8 to 10

Sharyon Daigneau

THE SAWDUSTMAKER'S CORN AND SAUSAGE CHOWDER

1 pound mild bulk ground sausage
1 large onion, chopped
3 large potatoes, peeled and cubed
2 teaspoons salt, or to taste
½ teaspoon black pepper
1 teaspoon dried basil

2 cups water
1 (17-ounce) can cream-style corn
1 (16½-ounce) can whole kernel corn, drained
1 (12-ounce) can evaporated milk

Shape sausage into a large patty. Brown patty for 5 minutes on each side in a large skillet; drain, reserving 2 tablespoons pan drippings in skillet. Break sausage into pieces into a soup kettle. Sauté onions in reserved drippings in skillet. Add sautéed onions to kettle along with potatoes, salt, pepper, basil and water. Cover and simmer 15 minutes. Stir in both cans of corn and milk. Cover and heat thoroughly.

Carl Bice

SOUTHWESTERN CHICKEN AND CORN CHOWDER

½   red bell pepper, chopped
1-2 cloves garlic, chopped
½   onion, finely chopped
2   stalks celery, finely chopped
1   teaspoon olive oil
1   stick butter
6-8 tablespoons flour
2   cups chicken broth, or as needed
2   cups half-and-half

½   pound cooked boneless chicken breast, diced
2   cups fresh or frozen white corn
1   teaspoon ground cumin
⅛   teaspoon cayenne pepper, or dash of hot pepper sauce
    Salt and pepper to taste
1   (14½-ounce) can black beans, drained and rinsed
¼   cup chopped fresh cilantro for garnish

Sauté bell peppers, garlic, onions and celery in olive oil in a small skillet over medium heat until tender and browned; set aside. Melt butter in a large, heavy stockpot. Add flour, a little at a time, and stir with a wire whisk over medium heat until cooked and starting to brown. Gradually whisk in broth. Whisk in half-and-half until blended. Heat until mixture is thickened. Add sautéed vegetables, chicken and corn. Season with cumin, cayenne pepper and salt and pepper. Add black beans. Simmer on low heat until flavors blend. Serve immediately garnished with cilantro.

Serves: 6 to 8

Holly Whitney

LOBSTER BISQUE

1½	pounds fresh Florida lobster	¼	cup finely chopped celery
1¼	cups water	3	tablespoons flour
1	(8-ounce) bottle clam juice	2	cups milk
1	whole clove	3	tablespoons tomato paste
2	bay leaves	¼	teaspoon salt
1	tablespoon butter		Black pepper to taste
1	small onion, finely chopped	2	tablespoons dry sherry

Cook lobster; pick meat from shell, head and claws, reserving shell. Chop tail meat; set all meat aside. Place shell in a large pot with water, clam juice, whole clove and bay leaves. Cook over medium heat for 30 minutes. Strain; reserving broth. Melt butter in a large saucepan. Add onions and celery and sauté 3 minutes. Sprinkle flour over sautéed vegetables and cook 1 minute longer, stirring frequently. Add reserved broth, milk, tomato paste, salt and pepper. Cook, stirring constantly, for 10 minutes or until thickened. Add lobster meat. Remove from heat and stir in sherry. Serve hot.

Jane Hurchalla

JIM'S HEARTY CHICKEN NOODLE SOUP

2-2½	pounds chicken parts, skinned	1½	tablespoons instant chicken bouillon
6	cups water		
1	large onion, chopped	1	tablespoon dried parsley
6	carrots, cut into ½-inch pieces	1	teaspoon salt
5	stalks celery, cut into ½-inch pieces	½	teaspoon dried rosemary
		½	teaspoon black pepper
1	(14½-ounce) can whole tomatoes, undrained, cut up	1	cup dry fine egg noodles

Combine all ingredients, except noodles, in a crockpot. Cover and cook on low for 8 to 10 hours or high for 5 to 6 hours or until chicken and vegetables are tender. Remove chicken pieces and set aside to cool slightly. Set control on high and stir in noodles. Cover and cook 30 minutes. Meanwhile, remove chicken bones and cut meat into bite-size pieces. Return meat to crockpot. Cook until noodles are tender.

Serves: 6 to 8

Lloyd Wescoat

CHICKEN ANDOUILLE GUMBO

1½ gallons water	1¼ cups vegetable oil
1 (4-pound) chicken, cut up	1½ cups all-purpose flour
5 bay leaves	1 tablespoon salt
5 fresh parsley sprigs	1 teaspoon black pepper
3 cloves garlic, whole	1 teaspoon cayenne pepper
1 pound andouille or smoked sausage, diced	1 bunch scallions, chopped
2 medium onions, chopped	½ cup chopped fresh parsley
1 large green bell pepper, chopped	½ teaspoon filé powder
1 large stalk celery, chopped	Hot cooked rice
3 tablespoons minced garlic	Hot pepper sauce of choice (optional)
4 cubes chicken bouillon	

Combine water, chicken, bay leaves, parsley sprigs and whole garlic cloves in a large stockpot and bring to a boil. Reduce heat, cover and simmer 1 hour. Remove chicken, reserving broth. Skin and bone chicken and coarsely chop meat; set meat aside. Pour broth through a wire-mesh strainer into a large bowl, discarding solids. Measure 1 gallon of broth and return to stockpot. Add sausage, onions, bell peppers, celery, minced garlic and chicken bouillon. Simmer, stirring occasionally, for 1 hour.

Heat oil in a heavy skillet over medium heat. Gradually whisk in flour. Cook, whisking constantly, for 20 minutes or until flour is a dark caramel color. (The smooth, dark mahogany roux mixture imparts a smoky, nutty flavor to the gumbo.)

Stir roux into sausage mixture and simmer, stirring occasionally, for 1 hour. Stir in chicken, salt, black pepper and cayenne pepper. Simmer, stirring occasionally, for 45 minutes. Skim off fat. Stir in scallions and chopped parsley. Simmer 10 minutes, stirring occasionally. Remove from heat and stir in filé powder. Serve over hot cooked rice with hot sauce.

Yield: 4½ quarts

Susan Brock

Wild places, inhabited by legions of wild creatures, with the beauty of the woods, the wonder of the wind and the sunlight, remind us that there is more on our marvelous plant Earth than mankind's cities, inventions, rivalries - and importance.

~ Ernest Lyons

RICE FLORENTINE SOUP

Florentine is a garnish of spinach.

½ cup julienne onion
½ cup sliced carrots (cut in half lengthwise, then cut on bias)
½ cup diagonally sliced celery
2 cloves garlic, chopped
2 tablespoons butter
1 cup dry long-grain rice

1 quart chicken broth
1 teaspoon soy sauce
  Salt and white pepper to taste
10 ounces spinach
  Diced cooked chicken (optional)
1 egg, beaten

Lightly sauté onions, carrots, celery and garlic in butter. Add rice, broth and soy sauce. Bring to a boil. Reduce heat and simmer 25 minutes. Season with salt and white pepper. Add spinach and lightly simmer 5 minutes. Add chicken, if using. Slowly add beaten egg in a thin stream around the edge of pot. Allow egg to cook before stirring.

Serves: 4, makes about 1 ½ quarts

Fred C. Martin
Owner/Chef
Uncle Freddie's Hometown Grille
Gradualte Culinary Institute of America
Hyde Park, New York

SAUSAGE AND SWEET POTATO SOUP

1 cup smoked sausage, cubed (may use andouille)
7 slices bacon, chopped
1 large onion, chopped
3 quarts chicken broth
6 large sweet potatoes, peeled and cubed

2 teaspoons dried oregano
2 bay leaves
1 teaspoon salt
½ teaspoon black pepper
1 teaspoon liquid smoke
1 cup whipping cream
1 cup sour cream

Cook sausage and bacon in a large skillet over medium-high heat for 3 to 4 minutes. Add onions and cook until translucent. Transfer mixture to a large soup pot. Add chicken broth, sweet potatoes, oregano, bay leaves, salt, pepper and liquid smoke. Bring to a boil and cook until potatoes are tender. Remove bay leaves and remove from heat. Add cream. Purée mixture in small batches in a food processor. Return soup to pot and gently reheat, if needed. Garnish individual servings with a dollop of sour cream.

Anna Taylor

CREAM OF MUENSTER AND BROCCOLI SOUP

3 tablespoons butter	¼ teaspoon nutmeg
¼ cup unsifted all-purpose flour	2 cups fresh broccoli florets, cut
1 quart milk	into ½-inch pieces
2 cubes chicken bouillon, or	1 (8-ounce) package Muenster
2 teaspoons granules	cheese, shredded

Melt butter in a large saucepan. Blend in flour. Cook and stir over low heat for 1 minute. Gradually add milk, bouillon and nutmeg. Cook and whisk over medium heat for 5 minutes or until mixture thickens. In a small saucepan or steamer, steam broccoli until just tender. Add steamed broccoli to soup. Reduce heat and cook 3 to 5 minutes longer. Add cheese and stir gently until melted and smooth. Serve hot.

Shelley Evans

 MRS. PETERS' SMOKED FISH SOUP

1 onion, chopped	2 stalks celery, chopped
2 tablespoons butter or margarine	1 teaspoon Worcestershire sauce
2 tablespoons flour	Dash of hot pepper sauce
4 cups milk, scalded	2 tablespoons dry sherry
2 cups Mrs. Peters' smoked fish,	Salt and pepper to taste
flaked	1 cup cream

Sauté onions in butter until brown. Stir in flour and gradually add milk. Simmer gently. Add fish, celery, Worcestershire sauce, hot sauce and sherry. Season with salt and pepper. Add cream. Heat thoroughly; do not boil.

Serves: 4 to 6

Florence Werle

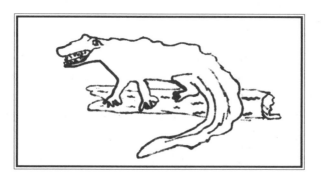

PLANTAIN SOUP WITH AVOCADO CREAM

1	large plantain	1	avocado, peeled and pitted
1	medium-size sweet onion	2	tablespoons sour cream
4	cups chicken broth	2	tablespoons chopped fresh cilantro
	Salt and pepper to taste	1	tablespoon lime juice

Grate plantain with a medium-size grater into a medium saucepan, then grate in onion. Add broth to saucepan and cook over medium heat, stirring frequently, for about 25 minutes. Soup will thicken as it simmers. Season with salt and pepper.

Meanwhile, prepare avocado cream by combining avocado, sour cream and cilantro in a blender. Purée. Add lime juice and season to taste with salt and pepper. Serve soup in bowls and float or swirl avocado cream on top.

Dagmar Bothwell

MEXICAN CHICKEN SOUP

4	boneless, skinless chicken breast halves, cut into bite-size pieces	1	(15¼-ounce) can whole kernel corn, drained
1	large onion, chopped	2	(14½-ounce) cans chicken broth
1	tablespoon vegetable oil	1-1½	tablespoons chili powder
2	(10-ounce) cans diced tomatoes and green chiles	1	teaspoon sugar
1	(10-ounce) can Mexican diced tomatoes and green chiles	½	teaspoon salt
1	(19-ounce) can red kidney beans, rinsed and drained	⅓	cup chopped fresh cilantro (optional)
1	(15-ounce) can black beans, rinsed and drained		Chopped avocado, fresh cilantro sprigs and fried tortilla strips for garnish

Sauté chicken and onions in oil in a Dutch oven over medium-high heat until chicken is lightly browned. Stir in all tomatoes and chiles, both beans, corn, broth, chili powder, sugar and salt. Bring to a boil over medium-high heat, stirring often. Cover, reduce heat and simmer 30 minutes. Sprinkle with cilantro and garnish as desired.

Serves: 14

Carol Davis

TOSCANA SOUP

½ pound Italian sausage links
¾ cup diced onions
1½ teaspoons minced garlic
4 slices bacon, chopped
4 cups chicken broth

2 baking potatoes, peeled, halved lengthwise, and cut into ¼-inch slices
2 cups chopped kale
⅓ cup whipping cream
Salt and pepper

Preheat oven to 300 degrees.

Place sausage links on a baking pan and bake 15 to 20 minutes. Halve links lengthwise, then cut diagonally into ½-inch slices; set aside. Place onions, garlic and bacon in a 4-quart saucepan and cook over medium heat for 3 to 4 minutes or until onions are almost translucent. Add broth and potatoes and bring to a boil. Reduce heat and simmer 15 minutes. Add kale, cream and sausage pieces. Season with salt and pepper. Simmer 5 minutes longer.

Lisa Meadows

FETA SHRIMP SOUP

1 tablespoon butter
2 tablespoons olive oil
1 medium onion, chopped
2 cloves garlic, minced
5 Roma tomatoes, peeled and chopped
1 (8-ounce) bottle clam juice
1 cup dry white wine

¾ teaspoon dried oregano
Pinch of salt
½ teaspoon black pepper
4 ounces crumbled feta cheese
1 pound medium shrimp, peeled and deveined
¼ cup chopped fresh parsley

Heat butter and oil in a large pot over medium heat. Stir in onions and garlic and cook until tender. Mix in tomatoes, clam juice and wine. Season with oregano, salt and pepper. Bring to a boil. Reduce heat to low and simmer 10 minutes.

Purée soup until smooth in batches in a blender. Return to pot and stir in cheese. Cook 10 minutes longer. Stir in shrimp and cook 3 minutes or until shrimp is opaque. Mix in parsley just before serving.

Serves: 4

Gretchen Hurchalla

ROASTED TOMATO AND BARLEY SOUP

6 cups peeled, seeded and coarsely chopped tomatoes, or 3 (28-ounce) cans whole tomatoes, drained and chopped	2 carrots, diced (1½ cups)
	3 tablespoons olive oil
	¾ cup pearl barley
	7-8 cups chicken broth
1 Spanish onion, diced (2 cups)	Salt and pepper to taste
3 cloves garlic, minced	3 tablespoons chopped fresh parsley

Preheat oven to 450 degrees.

Combine tomatoes, onions, garlic, carrots and oil and turn into a shallow roasting pan. Bake 40 to 45 minutes, turning occasionally. Transfer roasted vegetables to a soup pot. Add barley and broth and bring to a boil. Reduce heat and simmer, uncovered, for 40 to 45 minutes or until barley is tender. Season with salt and pepper. Add parsley just before serving. Serve with garlic knots or focaccia bread.

Serves: 6 to 7

Lena Kasliner

CILANTRO-LIME SOUP

2 tablespoons olive oil	1 cup seeded and chopped tomatoes
1 onion, chopped	
2 cloves garlic, minced	½ bunch fresh cilantro, tied together with kitchen string
1 tablespoon chili powder	
2 boneless, skinless chicken breast halves, cut into ¾-inch pieces	¼ cup chopped fresh cilantro
	¼ cup fresh lime juice
5 cups canned low-salt chicken broth	Salt and pepper to taste
	Sour cream for garnish
1 cup fresh or frozen corn	

Heat oil in a large heavy saucepan over medium-high heat. Add onions and garlic and sauté 3 minutes or until slightly softened. Add chili powder and cook and stir 1 minute. Add chicken and stir 2 minutes. Add broth, corn, tomatoes and tied cilantro to saucepan. Bring to a boil. Reduce heat and simmer 10 minutes or until chicken in cooked through. Discard tied cilantro. Soup can be made a day ahead up to this point and chilled. Bring to a simmer before continuing. Add chopped cilantro and lime juice. Season with salt and pepper. Garnish with sour cream.

Lauren Palmero

TORTELLINI SOUP

3	cloves garlic, minced	2	(9-ounce) packages spinach-cheese tortellini
1	medium onion, finely chopped		
2	tablespoons olive oil	1	(28-ounce) can crushed tomatoes
3	(14-ounce) cans chicken broth	8	ounces fresh spinach, chopped
2	teaspoons dried basil	½	cup freshly grated Parmesan cheese
2	teaspoons dried oregano		

Brown garlic and onions in olive oil. Add broth, basil and oregano. Stir in tortellini and simmer 10 to 12 minutes. Stir in tomatoes and spinach. Sprinkle with cheese.

Dorothy Dicks

PASTA FAGIOLI (FAZOOL)

This recipe is perfect for a quick last-minute supper.
We like it with a Caesar salad.

2	small onions, finely chopped	2	tablespoons oregano, or to taste
2	cloves garlic, crushed	2	tablespoons basil, or to taste
	Olive oil		Salt and pepper to taste
2	(8-ounce) cans tomato sauce	8	ounces dry elbow macaroni pasta
2	(15-ounce) cans cannellini beans		Freshly grated Parmesan cheese

In a large pot, sauté onions and garlic in enough olive oil to coat until tender. Stir in tomato sauce, beans and 2 bean cans of water. Add oregano, basil and salt and pepper. Cover and cook over low heat for about 20 minutes, stirring often. Uncover and bring to a boil. Add pasta and cook, stirring often, for 8 minutes or until tender. Serve with Parmesan cheese.

Serves: 4

Marie Servinsky

CARROT AND CELERY SOUP

1	small onion, minced	½	teaspoon dried tarragon
2	tablespoons butter	2	cups chicken broth
1	small carrot, thinly sliced	½	cup white wine or chicken broth
1	stalk celery, thinly sliced, leaves reserved		

Cook onions in butter in a saucepan until tender. Stir in carrots, celery and tarragon. Add broth and wine. Bring to a boil. Reduce heat and simmer 15 minutes. Garnish individual servings with reserved celery leaves.

Serves: 2

Tippy Greenleaf

SPLIT PEA SOUP

1	(16-ounce) package dry split green peas	1	pound kielbasa, diagonally sliced
6	cups water	2	medium potatoes, peeled and diced
1	large leek or onion, chopped	2	cups chopped celery with leaves
2	teaspoons salt	½	teaspoon black pepper

Pick over peas and rinse; drain. Combine peas and water in a large heavy kettle. Bring to a boil. Stir in leeks and salt. Reduce heat, cover and simmer 30 minutes. Add kielbasa and simmer 1 hour. Add potatoes, celery and pepper. Simmer 45 minutes or until soup is thick and rich and potatoes are tender.

If red potatoes are used, leave skins on.

Serves: 8

Jean Jacobs

CREAM OF MUSHROOM SOUP

5 cups sliced fresh mushrooms	3 tablespoons all-purpose flour
1 large onion, chopped	1 cup whipping cream
1 tablespoon chopped garlic	3 tablespoons butter
½ teaspoon ground thyme	1 teaspoon sherry
1½ cups chicken broth	Salt and pepper to taste

Cook mushrooms, onions, garlic and thyme in broth in a saucepan over medium heat for 10 minutes or until mushrooms are tender. Place half of mushroom mixture in a blender. Add flour to blender and purée. Return to saucepan. Add cream, butter and sherry to saucepan. Simmer, stirring constantly, over medium-low heat until thickened. Season with salt and pepper.

Serves: 4

Louise Lueders

SOUTHWEST PECAN SOUP

½ cup minced onions	6 cups chicken broth
1 tablespoon minced garlic	8 ounces pecan pieces
2 tablespoons butter	2 tablespoons chopped chipotles in
2 cups whipping cream	adobo sauce, or to taste
¼ cup tomato paste	Salt to taste

Sauté onions and garlic in butter; do not brown. Add cream, tomato paste and broth and bring to a simmer. Meanwhile, in a blender, purée some of the pecans. Add puréed and remaining pecans to soup. Stir in chipotles, adding more if a spicier flavor is desired. Season with salt.

Serves: 6 to 8

Peggy Clute

STRAWBERRY SOUP

1 (16-ounce) package frozen whole	1 cup half-and-half
strawberries, thawed, or 1 pint	¼ cup sugar
fresh	2 tablespoons white wine
1 cup sour cream	

Process strawberries in a blender. Mix in sour cream, half-and-half, sugar and wine. Chill several hours or overnight.

Sharyon Daigneau

CHILLED CANTALOUPE SOUP WITH MINT

4   cups cubed cantaloupe
      (about 1 large)
2   tablespoons honey, or to taste
3   tablespoons freshly squeezed
      lime juice, or to taste

⅛   teaspoon ground cardamom, or
      to taste (optional)
    Sliced fresh strawberries for
      garnish
¼   cup fresh whole mint leaves for
      garnish

Place cantaloupe in a wide, shallow microwave-safe container. Microwave at 50 percent power for 2 minutes or just until melon softens slightly. Transfer cantaloupe to a blender or food processor. Add honey, lime juice and cardamom. Blend until smooth. Transfer to a bowl and cover. Refrigerate 1 to 2 hours or until chilled. Taste before serving, adding more honey, lime juice or cardamom as needed. Garnish individual servings with strawberry slices and mint leaves.

Serves: 4

Cecilia Wright

COLD TOMATO-ORANGE SOUP

1   tablespoon butter
½   cup minced onions
2½ cups canned plum tomatoes,
      undrained
1   cup chicken broth
¾   cup orange juice
2   tablespoons thinly sliced basil
      leaves

Salt and freshly ground black
  pepper to taste
Thin orange slices for garnish
  (optional)
Sour cream for garnish (optional)

Melt butter in a wide saucepan. Add onions and cook until soft. Add undrained tomatoes and chicken broth. Cover and simmer 15 minutes. Remove from heat and purée with a hand-held blender or in a food processor or blender. Stir in orange juice and basil. Season with salt and pepper. Cover and chill 3 hours or overnight. Garnish individual servings with orange slices and a dollop of sour cream.

Dagmar Bothwell

JAMAICAN BLACK BEAN STEW

2 pounds sweet potatoes, peeled and cut into ¾-inch chunks
3 pounds butternut squash, peeled and cut into ¾-inch chunks
1 large onion, chopped
1 (14-ounce) can vegetable broth
3 cloves garlic, minced
1 tablespoon curry powder
1½ teaspoons allspice
½ teaspoon cayenne pepper
¼ teaspoon salt
2 (15-ounce) cans black beans, rinsed and drained
½ cup raisins
3 tablespoons fresh lime juice
2 cups dry brown rice, prepared according to package
Fresh or canned diced tomato
Diced cucumber

Combine potatoes, squash, onions, broth, garlic, curry powder, allspice, cayenne pepper and salt in a Dutch oven. Bring to a boil. Reduce heat to low and simmer, covered, for 5 minutes. Add beans and raisins. Simmer 5 minutes. Remove from heat and stir in lime juice. Serve over cooked rice. Top with diced tomato and cucumber.

Serves: 8

Lloyd Wescoat

SEAFOOD STEW

2½ cups chicken broth
½ cup dry long-grain rice
2 teaspoons chili powder
2 cloves garlic, minced
1 (14½-ounce) can diced tomatoes, undrained
¾ cup julienned green bell peppers
¾ cup julienned red or yellow bell peppers
½ cup thinly sliced onions
½ pound snapper fillets, cut into 1-inch pieces
4 ounces raw medium shrimp, peeled and deveined
¾ cup orange juice concentrate

Bring broth to a boil in a saucepan. Add rice, chili powder and garlic and return to a boil. Reduce heat and simmer, covered, for 15 to 20 minutes or until rice is tender. Add tomatoes, bell peppers and onions. Cover and cook over medium heat until vegetables are tender. Add fish, shrimp and orange juice concentrate. Cover and simmer 2 to 4 minutes or until fish flakes easily with a fork and shrimp turn pink.

Serves: 6

Gretchen Hurchalla

BEEF STEW WITH CHORIZO

2 tablespoons vegetable oil
2 pounds sirloin tip roast or stew meat, cut into 1-inch cubes
½ cup flour
½ pound chorizo or other spicy sausage, cut into ¼-inch slices
2 large onions, chopped
2 teaspoons minced garlic
1 cup Burgundy or other dry red wine
2 cups water
4 teaspoons beef bouillon granules
1 (14½-ounce) can stewed tomatoes
2 tablespoons Dijon mustard

¼ teaspoon cayenne pepper
1 teaspoon dried oregano
½ teaspoon dried thyme
2 bay leaves
¼ teaspoon black pepper
⅛ teaspoon ground cloves
½ teaspoon dried basil
1 tablespoon Worcestershire sauce
2 cups sliced carrots, ½-inch thick
2 cups peeled and cubed potatoes, ¾-inch
1 (10-ounce) package frozen peas
½ cup sliced pimiento-stuffed green olives, drained

Heat oil in a large pot over medium-high heat. Dredge beef in flour, shaking off excess. Sauté beef and chorizo in oil until brown. Add onions and garlic and sauté 5 minutes, stirring occasionally. Add wine, water, bouillon, tomatoes, mustard, cayenne, oregano, thyme, bay leaves, black pepper, cloves, basil and Worcestershire sauce. Bring to a boil. Reduce heat to a simmer and cook, covered, for 1 hour or until beef is fork-tender, stirring occasionally. Add carrots, potatoes, peas and olives. Bring to a boil. Reduce heat to a simmer and cook 30 to 40 minutes longer or until potatoes are tender. Part, or all of this time, you may wish too uncover to allow juice to thicken. Remove bay leaves before serving.

Gene Moore

Watching the stars appear is a contemplative luxury which cannot be done in a hurry. That is probably why so few indulge in it any more. It takes spare time, that precious stuff which might otherwise be better spent motoring, watching TV, eating or even worrying.

~ Ernest Lyons

Entrées

BEEF TENDERLOIN WITH PEBRE SAUCE

½ cup soy sauce	½ tablespoon garlic powder
⅓ cup vegetable oil	1 (4-pound) beef tenderloin,
1½ tablespoons Dijon mustard	trimmed

Preheat oven to 450 degrees.

Combine soy sauce, oil, mustard and garlic powder in a bowl. Pour mixture over beef in a zip-top bag, turning beef until coated. Seal bag and marinate in refrigerator 8 hours, turning occasionally.

Remove tenderloin from marinade and place on a lightly greased roasting rack in a shallow roasting pan. Bake 35 to 45 minutes or until desired degrees of doneness. Let stand 10 minutes before slicing. Serve with Pebre Sauce.

Serves: 6 to 8

Pebre Sauce

4 jalapeño chiles, seeded and minced	2 tablespoons chopped fresh chives
¼ cup fresh lemon juice	2 tablespoons chopped fresh cilantro
1 tablespoon salt	2 tablespoons chopped fresh parsley
¼ cup vegetable oil	3 tablespoons white wine vinegar

Combine jalapeños, lemon juice and salt in a bowl. Cover and let stand 30 minutes. Drain jalapeños and discard liquid. Add oil, chives, cilantro, parsley and vinegar to jalapeños and mix well.

Colleen Hynes

MARINATED FLANK STEAK

1 flank steak	1 teaspoon sugar or sugar substitute
½ cup vegetable oil	
¼ cup red wine vinegar	1 teaspoon teriyaki sauce
1 envelope dry onion soup mix	

Score steak and place in a non-metallic dish or a large zip-top plastic bag. Combine oil, vinegar, soup mix, sugar and teriyaki sauce and pour over steak. Cover or seal and marinate in refrigerator for at least 5 hours or overnight. Remove steak from marinade and place on a boiler pan. Broil 4 minutes on each side for rare meat. Slice on an angle to serve.

Serves: 4

Donna Dolan

CHEESE ROULADES

8   slices lean beef round, thinly
      sliced
    Salt and freshly ground black
      pepper
8   slices bacon
8   slices Swiss cheese
1   tablespoon olive oil
1   tablespoon butter

3   large onions, coarsely chopped
3   tomatoes, peeled and chopped
½   cup red wine
2   cups sliced fresh mushrooms
2   teaspoons herbes de Provence
1   small bunch fresh parsley,
      chopped

Lay slices of beef flat and sprinkle with salt and pepper. Top each with a slice of bacon and a slice of cheese. Roll up and secure with toothpicks. Heat olive oil and butter over high heat in a large pot. Add beef rolls and brown well on all sides. Add onions, tomatoes and wine. Cover pot and simmer over low heat for about 1 hour, 20 minutes, turning roulades occasionally. Add water or wine if too much liquid evaporates. Add mushrooms and herbes de Provence during the last 15 minutes of cooking. Season with salt and pepper as needed. Serve over noodles and sprinkle with parsley.

Serves: 4 to 6

Dagmar Bothwell

STUFFED AND ROLLED STEAK

6   thin-cut sirloin steaks
    Meat tenderizer
2   cups cooked rice
1   teaspoon adobo seasoning

1   teaspoon crushed dried basil
2   tablespoons vegetable oil
1   (16-ounce) can tomato sauce
2   (12-ounce) cans beef gravy

Pound steaks and sprinkle with meat tenderizer. Mix rice with adobo seasoning and basil. Spread rice mixture thinly over steak. Roll up and secure with toothpicks. Brown meat rolls in vegetable oil in a Dutch oven on the stove. Reduce heat and add tomato sauce and gravy. Simmer 45 to 60 minutes. Serve over the remainder of the seasoned rice.

Serves: 6

Jeannie Pessolano

SHREDDED BEEF SALAD

Beef

1	(1-pound) flank steak	4	whole black peppercorns
1	white onion, quartered	1	bay leaf
1	tablespoon fine sea salt	1	teaspoon dried oregano
2	cloves garlic, crushed	2	tablespoons chopped fresh cilantro

Vinaigrette

3	tablespoons white wine vinegar	1½	teaspoons fine sea salt
1½	tablespoons fresh lime juice	½	teaspoon black pepper
1	tablespoon dried oregano	½	cup extra virgin olive oil

Salad

2	tomatoes, quartered	2	hearts romaine lettuce, cored, leaves quartered crosswise
½	cup finely sliced red onions		
	Salt and pepper to taste	6	radishes, thinly sliced
		2	tablespoons chopped fresh cilantro

Place steak in a large pot and add enough water to cover steak by 2 inches. Add onion, salt, garlic, peppercorns, bay leaf, oregano and cilantro. Bring to a boil over high heat, skimming any foam from top of liquid. Reduce heat to medium-low. Simmer, uncovered, for 1½ hours or until steak is tender. Add more water as needed while cooking to keep meat covered. Refrigerate, uncovered, until the meat and liquid are cold, at least 3 hours or up to 1 day. Remove steak from liquid, reserving liquid. Trim excess fat. Cut steak crosswise into 3 pieces, then shred coarsely. Transfer to a large bowl and add enough reserved cooking liquid to cover beef completely.

To make vinaigrette, whisk together vinegar, lime juice, oregano, salt and pepper in a small bowl. Gradually whisk in olive oil.

To assemble salad, combine tomatoes, onions and 3 tablespoons vinaigrette in a medium bowl and toss to coat. Season with salt and pepper. Drain liquid from shredded beef. Add lettuce, radishes and cilantro to beef. Mix in enough of remaining vinaigrette to coat beef and vegetables. Divide beef mixture onto individual salad plates. Serve with tomato mixture.

The beef alone may be warmed and served with tortillas and salsa. Or, rolled in tortillas with cheese, covered with enchilada sauce and baked at 350 degrees for 20 to 30 minutes or until heated through.

Serves: 6

Mary Hutchinson

LONDON BROIL WITH
RED WINE AND MUSHROOMS SAUCE

2	pounds London broil	1	tablespoon fresh lemon juice
	Unseasoned meat tenderizer	3	tablespoons minced garlic
⅓	cup olive oil	2	teaspoons red wine vinegar
¼	cup chopped fresh parsley	½	teaspoon black pepper

Sprinkle both sides of meat with meat tenderizer. Score meat diagonally in a criss-cross pattern on both sides. Cover meat with plastic wrap and let stand at room temperature for 1 hour. Combine olive oil, parsley, lemon juice, garlic, vinegar and pepper in a zip-top bag. Add meat to bag and turn to coat. Seal bag and refrigerate 4 to 8 hours, turning often.

When ready to cook, remove meat from marinade, discarding marinade. Grill to desired degree of doneness. Cut into ⅑- to ¼-inch slices. Spoon Red Wine and Mushroom Sauce over meat slices and serve.

Serves: 6

Red Wine and Mushroom Sauce

2	cups sliced fresh mushrooms	¼	teaspoon rosemary
1	tablespoon olive oil	¼	teaspoon black pepper
1	cup red wine	¼	teaspoon dried thyme
2	cups beef broth		Salt to taste
1	tablespoon cornstarch		

Sauté mushrooms in olive oil in a skillet until done; remove from heat. In a saucepan, combine wine, broth and cornstarch. Add rosemary, black pepper and thyme. Cook over medium heat, stirring constantly. When sauce thickens, add sautéed mushrooms. Season with salt. Reduce heat to low and keep warm until ready to serve.

Louise Lueders

> **B**ird-watching and nature-watching in general have been increasing in popularity but it is a distinctly new trend when the animals start watching the people.
>
> ~ Ernest Lyons

RIB-EYE ROAST WITH VEGETABLES

2⅔	cups balsamic vinegar	4	cloves garlic, minced
1	cup dry red wine	6	tablespoons olive oil
1	tablespoon dark brown sugar		Salt and pepper to taste
2	pounds red-skin baby potatoes	1	(5-pound) boneless rib-eye roast,
1½	pounds carrots, cut into 2-inch		trimmed and tied
	pieces	⅓	cup chopped fresh parsley
2	medium onions, quartered		

Preheat oven to 325 degrees.

Combine vinegar, wine and brown sugar in a saucepan. Bring to a boil over medium heat, stirring until sugar is dissolved. Continue to boil 25 to 30 minutes or until mixture is syrupy and reduced to ¾ cup. Remove from heat.

Place one oven rack in the center of the oven and a second rack in the bottom third of the oven. In a large bowl, toss potatoes, carrots, onions and garlic with olive oil until coated. Scatter vegetables on a large, rimmed baking sheet. Season with salt and pepper. Bake on lower rack in oven for 35 minutes, stirring occasionally. Place roast on a rack set in a roasting pan. Season with salt and pepper. Place on center rack in oven. Roast meat and vegetables for about 1 hour, 45 minutes longer. Transfer meat to a cutting board and tent with foil. Let stand 10 minutes before cutting. Mix parsley with roasted vegetables in a large bowl. Arrange meat slices and vegetables on individual plates and drizzle with balsamic glaze.

Serves: 8

Ev Roarke

EASY BEEF STROGANOFF

4	pounds stir-fry beef	2	soup cans Burgundy wine
2	envelopes dry onion soup mix	1	pint reduced-fat sour cream
2	(10¾-ounce) cans condensed	8	ounces fresh mushrooms, sliced
	cream of mushroom soup		

Preheat oven to 325 degrees.

Place beef, soup mix, condensed soup and burgundy in a casserole dish; do not stir. Bake, covered, for 3 hours. Mix in sour cream and mushrooms. Reduce temperature to 300 degrees and bake 1 hour longer. Serve over egg noodles.

Heather Arnold

 # CORNED BEEF DINNER

Preheat oven to 350 degrees.

Put corned beef in a Dutch oven. Cover with water and simmer 1 hour per pound of meat, or until tender. Remove meat from water and place in a roasting pan; reserve cooking liquid. Cover with Sweet Mustard Sauce. Bake while you cook your vegetables in reserved cooking liquid. The vegetables, potatoes, carrots, onions and cabbage, will take about 20 minutes to cook. For crisper cabbage, add a little after other vegetables are added.

Sweet Mustard Sauce
½ cup yellow mustard
¼ cup brown sugar
½ teaspoon ground cloves

Combine all ingredients. Warm any extra sauce and serve it with your dinner. It "makes" the meal!

Sandy Thurlow

MEXICAN PIE

2 (9-inch) refrigerated pie crusts, divided
1 pound ground beef
1 tablespoon fajita seasoning
½ cup dry quick-cooking rice
1 (15-ounce) can black beans, drained
1 (11-ounce) can Mexican corn, drained
1 (2¼-ounce) can sliced black olives, drained
1 teaspoon garlic powder
½ teaspoon ground cumin
½ teaspoon salt
1 cup sour cream
1 cup salsa
2 cups shredded Cheddar or Monterey-Jack cheese
1 egg, beaten
1 teaspoon parsley

Preheat oven to 400 degrees.

Place 1 pie crust in a 9-inch deep dish pie pan. Brown ground beef with fajita seasoning in a skillet. Mix browned beef with dry rice, beans, corn, olives, garlic powder, cumin, salt, sour cream, salsa and cheese. Pour mixture into unbaked pie crust, mounding high in the center. Place second pie crust over top and crimp edges together. Cut a few small slits on top. Brush with egg and sprinkle with parsley. Cover edges with foil. Bake 15 minutes. Remove foil and bake 25 to 35 minutes longer or until crust is browned.

Serves: 6 adults or 3 teenagers

Amanda Tilton Martin

 BEEF

APPLE BARBECUE FLANK STEAK

½ cup apple jelly
1 (8-ounce) can no-salt-added
 tomato sauce
¼ cup vinegar
2 tablespoons light brown sugar

2 tablespoons water
1 teaspoon hot pepper sauce, or to
 taste
¼ teaspoon salt
1½ pounds flank steak

Combine all ingredients except steak in a saucepan. Bring to a boil and stir until smooth. Reduce heat to a simmer and cook 20 to 25 minutes, stirring occasionally; cool. Place steak in a zip-top bag. Pour ½ cup cooled sauce over steak. Seal bag and marinate in refrigerator for 8 hours. Remove steak from marinade, discarding marinade. Grill on a hot grill for 7 to 10 minutes on each side or to desired degree of doneness. Cut steak in thin slices across the grain and serve with remaining sauce.

John Austin

JAPANESE STEAK ROLLS

1 pound flank steak
 Salt and pepper to taste
16 asparagus spears, trimmed and
 cut into 8-inch pieces
16 scallions, cut into 8-inch pieces

6 tablespoons seasoned rice vinegar
6 tablespoons low-sodium soy sauce
4 teaspoons sugar
1 tablespoon sesame oil

Slice steak across the grain into 16 strips, each ¼- to ½-inch thick. Pound each strip to about ⅑-inch thick and season with salt and pepper. Place 1 asparagus spear and 1 scallion across the short end of each beef strip. Roll beef around vegetables and secure with a wooden toothpick. Repeat to make 16 rolls. Place rolls in a single layer in a shallow baking pan. Combine vinegar, soy sauce, sugar and sesame oil and pour over steak rolls. Marinate 10 minutes. Broil steak rolls on high heat for 5 minutes. Remove from pan and tent to keep warm. Strain marinade into a small saucepan and bring to a boil. Cook 5 minutes or until syrupy. Spoon glaze over each serving.

Serves: 4 to 5

Brenda Matthews

TEXAS HASH

1	pound ground beef	½	cup dry rice
3	large onions, chopped	2	teaspoons chili powder
1	large green bell pepper, chopped	2	teaspoons salt
1	(14½-ounce) can tomatoes, undrained	⅛	teaspoon black pepper

Preheat oven to 350 degrees.

Brown beef in a large skillet; drain off fat. Add onions and bell peppers to beef and cook until onions are tender. Stir in tomatoes, rice, chili powder, salt and pepper. Cook until heated through. Pour into an ungreased 2-quart casserole dish. Cover and bake 1 hour.

Serves: 4 to 6

Frank Pittman

CLASSIC ROAST BEEF DINNER

1	(2- to 3-pound) boneless beef roast	8	ounces fresh mushrooms, sliced (optional)
	Seasoned salt and pepper to taste	4-5	potatoes, peeled and cut into wedges
1	(10-ounce) can condensed French onion soup	4-5	carrots, cut into 1-inch pieces

Preheat oven to 350 degrees.

Place roast in a large baking dish and sprinkle with seasoned salt and pepper. Pour condensed soup over roast and surround with mushrooms. Bake about 1 hour. Meanwhile, cook potatoes and carrots in a small amount of water until tender. Reserve ½ cup of vegetable cooking liquid. Add vegetables and reserved ½ cup cooking liquid to roast. Bake 20 to 30 minutes longer or to desired degree of doneness. Transfer roast to a serving platter and surround with vegetables. Pour pan juices into a gravy boat or bowl and serve on the side.

Serves: 6 to 8

Michelle Fowler

FLANK STEAK IN BEER

½ cup beer
½ cup vegetable oil
1 teaspoon garlic powder
1 teaspoon seasoned salt

1 teaspoon coarsely ground black
   pepper
1 bunch scallions, sliced
1 flank steak

Combine all ingredients except steak. Pour mixture over steak in a plastic zip-top bag. Marinate in refrigerator overnight or longer, turning occasionally. Remove steak from marinade. Grill on a hot grill to desired degree of doneness. Remove from heat and let stand 5 minutes before slicing on the diagonal.

Serves: 2 to 3

Lisa Massing

CHEESE AND BEEF ROLL-UPS SANDWICHES

1 (8-ounce) package cream
   cheese, softened
2 tablespoons prepared
   horseradish
5 (8-inch) flour tortillas

25-30 spinach leaves, stems removed
10   thin slices deli Italian roast
      beef
8   ounces American or Cheddar
      cheese, shredded

Beat cream cheese and horseradish together until smooth in a small bowl with an electric mixer on medium speed, scraping bowl often. Spread about 3 tablespoons of mixture evenly on each tortilla. Arrange 5 to 6 spinach leaves over cream cheese. Place 2 slices roast beef over spinach and sprinkle with about ⅓ cup American cheese. Roll tortilla up tightly and wrap with plastic wrap. Repeat with remaining tortillas. Refrigerate at least 4 hours or overnight. To serve, cut into serving sizes.

Sue Hammock

ITALIAN SANDWICHES
WITH MARJORAM-CAPER DRESSING

½ cup olive oil
¼ cup chopped fresh Italian parsley
¼ cup drained capers
4 tablespoons chopped fresh marjoram, divided
2 tablespoons red wine vinegar
Salt and pepper to taste

1 sourdough baguette, halved lengthwise
12 ounces assorted deli meats and cheeses, such as mortadella, salami and provolone
1 cup thinly sliced Vidalia onions

Blend olive oil, parsley, capers, 3 tablespoons marjoram and vinegar in a food processor until herbs are finely chopped. Season with salt and pepper. Transfer dressing to a bowl and let stand 30 minutes. Mix in remaining 1 tablespoon marjoram. Spoon dressing mixture evenly over cut sides of bread. Arrange meats, cheeses and onions on bottom half of bread. Cover with top half of bread. Cut diagonally into individual servings.

Serves: 4

Peter Lueders

CAJUN MEAT LOAF

2	tablespoons butter	¼	teaspoon ground cumin
½	large onion, chopped	1	pound lean ground beef
½	cup chopped green bell peppers	1	egg, beaten
1	teaspoon salt	½	cup dry fine bread crumbs
¾	teaspoon cayenne pepper	½	cup ketchup, divided
½	teaspoon dried thyme	1	teaspoon Worcestershire sauce
½	teaspoon black pepper		

Preheat oven to 375 degrees.

Melt butter in a heavy skillet over medium to low heat. Add onions, bell peppers, salt, cayenne pepper, thyme, black pepper and cumin and cook 10 minutes or until vegetables are very tender. Combine beef, egg, bread crumbs, ¼ cup ketchup and Worcestershire sauce in a medium bowl. Blend in sautéed vegetables. Form mixture into a loaf in a baking dish. Bake 20 minutes. Spread remaining ¼ cup ketchup on top. Bake 40 minutes longer.

Serves: 4 to 6

Jim Wilbers

MAMA'S BEST COUNTRY MEAT LOAF

1	cup cracker or bread crumbs	½	cup ketchup
	Milk	3	tablespoons soy sauce
1	cup chopped onions	¾	cup chopped green bell peppers
1	pound ground beef		(optional)
1	pound ground turkey		Salt and pepper to taste
1	pound hot sausage		Celery salt to taste
2	eggs		

Preheat oven to 325 to 350 degrees.

Soak crumbs in enough milk to moisten all crumbs; set aside. Sauté onions until softened. Mix together all meats. Combine soaked crumbs, sautéed onions, eggs, ketchup, soy sauce and bell peppers. Add to meat mixture and blend. Season with salt and pepper and celery salt. Form mixture into 3 loaves and place in pans. Bake 1 to 1½ hours.

This recipe is also great to use in stuffed peppers or as meatballs. The meatloaf freezes well, raw or cooked.

Yield: 3 loaves

Barbara Oehlbeck

SPICY MEAT LOAF WITH TOMATO GRAVY

2 pounds ground beef	⅓ cup ketchup
1 (1¼-ounce) envelope taco seasoning	1 (10-ounce) can Rotel tomatoes and green chiles
½ cup seasoned bread crumbs	½ cup shredded Monterey Jack cheese
1 cup diced Vidalia onions	
2 eggs, beaten	

Preheat oven to 425 degrees.

Combine ground beef, taco seasoning, bread crumbs, onions, eggs and ketchup. Shape into a loaf and place in a 9x13-inch baking pan. Pour tomatoes and chiles over the top. Bake 50 minutes. Drain off juices and top with cheese. Let stand while making gravy.

Tomato Gravy

3 tablespoons butter	2 (10-ounce) cans tomatoes and green chiles
3 tablespoons flour	¼ cup chopped fresh cilantro
1 (16-ounce) can tomato sauce	1½ teaspoons sugar

Melt butter in a large saucepan over medium-high heat. Whisk in flour until smooth and cook and stir 1 to 2 minutes. Stir in tomato sauce, tomatoes and chiles, cilantro and sugar. Cook over medium heat 5 to 10 minutes or until hot. Serve with Spicy Meat Loaf.

Amanda Tilton Martin

CITRUS-SEARED CHICKEN
WITH ORANGE OLIVE SAUCE

1	cup orange juice	4	boneless chicken breast halves
¼	cup red grapefruit juice	½	cup chopped red bell peppers
3	teaspoons jerk seasoning, divided	¼	cup chopped pimiento-stuffed
¾	teaspoon ground cumin		green olives
¼	cup flour	¼	cup chopped kalamata olives
2	tablespoons olive oil	1	tablespoon honey

Combine citrus juices, 2 teaspoons jerk seasoning and cumin in a glass bowl. In a shallow bowl, combine flour and remaining 1 teaspoon jerk seasoning. Heat oil in a large nonstick skillet over medium heat. Dip chicken in juice mixture, then dredge in seasoned flour. Cook in oil for 5 minutes on each side or until golden brown and cooked through. Transfer to a serving plate and keep warm. Stir remaining seasoned flour into skillet drippings. Add remaining juice mixture, bell peppers, both olives and honey. Cook 2 to 3 minutes or until thickened. Serve sauce with chicken.

Eileen Geiger

BANANA LEAF-LEMON GRASS CHICKEN

1	banana leaf	4	long lemon grass leaves
	Olive oil		Orange zest
2	chicken breasts	4	slices star fruit (optional)
	Salt and pepper to taste		

Preheat oven to 375 degrees.

Wash banana leaf and cut on both sides of the central spine, discarding spine. Brush olive oil on the shiny side of the leaf and place oil-side up on surface; set aside.

Season chicken with salt and pepper. Wrap each breast around 2 lemon grass leaves. Place each chicken breast at the end of one of the banana leaf halves. Sprinkle chicken with orange zest and add 2 slices star fruit to each. Roll up chicken breasts in the banana leaves and place in a glass or metal baking dish. Bake 40 minutes.

Eric Buetens

PALM CITY STYLE CHICKEN CASSEROLE

4	cooked chicken breasts, coarsely chopped	4	scallions, chopped
½	head broccoli, coarsely chopped and slightly cooked	1	bunch parsley, chopped
			Juice of ½ lemon
1	(1-pound) package raw baby carrots, slightly cooked	½	clove garlic, smashed well
		1	pint mayonnaise, or less if desired
			Coarsely ground black pepper

Combine chicken, broccoli, carrots and scallions in a large casserole dish. In a separate bowl, mix parsley, lemon juice, garlic, mayonnaise and pepper. Add mayonnaise mixture to casserole and blend well. Serve chilled or warm in the oven at 350 degrees for 20 minutes.

Serves: 4 to 6

Jody Bond

CHICKEN ASPARAGUS CASSEROLE

2	teaspoons vegetable oil	2	eggs
1	cup seeded and chopped green and/or red bell peppers	1½	cups chopped cooked chicken
1	medium onion, chopped	1	(10-ounce) package frozen chopped asparagus, thawed and drained
2	cloves garlic, minced		
1	(10¾-ounce) can condensed cream of asparagus soup	8	ounces dry egg noodles, cooked and drained
1	(8-ounce) container ricotta cheese		Black pepper (optional)
2	cups shredded Cheddar cheese, divided		

Preheat oven to 350 degrees.

Heat oil in a small skillet over medium heat. Add bell peppers, onions and garlic and cook and stir until vegetables are crisp-tender. In a large bowl, mix condensed soup, ricotta cheese, 1 cup Cheddar cheese and eggs until well blended. Add onion mixture, chicken, asparagus and cooked noodles and mix well. Season with black pepper. Spread mixture evenly in a greased 9x13-inch casserole dish. Top with remaining 1 cup Cheddar cheese. Bake 30 minutes or until center is set and cheese is bubbly. Let stand 5 minutes before serving.

Serves: 10

Karen Parker

CURRIED COCONUT CHICKEN

2	pounds boneless, skinless chicken breasts, cut into ½-inch cubes	2	tablespoons chopped garlic
1	teaspoon salt	1	(14-ounce) can coconut milk
1	teaspoon white pepper	1	(14½-ounce) can diced tomatoes
1½	tablespoons vegetable oil	1	(8-ounce) can tomato sauce
2	tablespoons curry powder	3	tablespoons sugar
1	small onion, chopped	1	tablespoon dried basil

Season chicken with salt and pepper. In a large skillet, heat oil with curry powder over medium-high for 2 minutes. Stir in onions and garlic and cook 1 minute. Add chicken and brown on all sides. Reduce heat to medium and cook 7 to 10 minutes. Pour coconut milk, tomatoes, tomato sauce, sugar and basil into pan and stir to combine. Simmer 30 to 40 minutes, stirring occasionally.

Serves: 6 to 8

Joan Hutchinson

CARIBBEAN PAPAYA CHICKEN

½	cup orange marmalade	4	medium boneless, skinless chicken breast halves, cut into 1-inch cubes
½	cup fresh lime juice		
1	teaspoon chopped fresh ginger		
1	teaspoon ground nutmeg	2	medium papayas, peeled, seeded and cut into 1-inch cubes
	Pinch cayenne pepper		
2	tablespoons vegetable oil	½	cup chopped fresh cilantro
			Salt and pepper to taste

Combine marmalade, lime juice, ginger, nutmeg and cayenne pepper in a saucepan. Heat until marmalade is melted and all ingredients are well blended. Heat oil in a nonstick skillet. Add chicken and cook until browned. Add papaya and toss several minutes. Stir in marmalade sauce and sauté 3 to 4 minutes or until chicken is cooked through. Spoon into a serving dish and sprinkle with cilantro. Serve with basmati or long-grain white rice.

Ken Stegina

GORGONZOLA CHICKEN

6	boneless, skinless chicken breast halves, cubed	2	tablespoons chopped garlic
¼	teaspoon salt	½	cup chicken broth
⅛	teaspoon black pepper	¼	cup whipping cream
2	tablespoons butter	4	ounces Gorgonzola cheese
1	tablespoon olive oil	2	tablespoons chopped fresh basil

Season chicken with salt and pepper. Melt butter with olive oil in a large skillet over medium heat. Add chicken and cook until just browned on all sides. Add garlic and sauté about 3 minutes. Stir in broth and cook until chicken is done. Reduce heat to low and stir in cream. Add cheese and stir until sauce is smooth. Continue to cook until sauce reaches desired consistency. Add basil. Serve over rice.

Serves: 8

Colleen Hynes

BAKED CHICKEN AND ARTICHOKES

4	boneless, skinless chicken breasts	1	(8-ounce) jar sliced mushrooms, drained
½	teaspoon paprika		
1	teaspoon salt	2	tablespoons flour
¼	teaspoon black pepper	⅔	cup chicken broth
6	tablespoons butter, divided	3	tablespoons white wine (optional)
1	(15-ounce) can artichoke hearts, drained and quartered		

Preheat oven to 375 degrees.

Sprinkle chicken with paprika, salt and pepper. Melt 4 tablespoons butter in a large skillet. Add chicken and brown on both sides. Transfer to a greased 2-quart casserole dish, reserving drippings in skillet. Arrange artichokes around chicken. Add remaining 2 tablespoons butter to skillet drippings. Add mushrooms and sauté 4 to 5 minutes. Stir flour into skillet. Gradually add broth and wine and mix well. Cook over medium heat, stirring constantly, for 5 minutes or until thick and bubbly. Pour sauce over chicken and cover dish. Bake 40 minutes.

Serves: 4 to 6

Pat Cook

CHICKEN WITH LEMON CAPER SAUCE

6	boneless, skinless chicken breast halves, thinly sliced	6	tablespoons lemon juice
	Salt and pepper to taste	2	tablespoons capers
1	tablespoon olive oil	⅔	cup extra dry vermouth
		1	tablespoon chopped fresh parsley

Season chicken with salt and pepper. Heat olive oil in a skillet. Add chicken and cook until brown. Remove chicken from pan and keep warm, reserving drippings in skillet. Add lemon juice, capers and vermouth and cook about 2 minutes. Stir in parsley and spoon over chicken. Serve over couscous or cooked pasta.

Serves: 6

Dr. James Gray, Palm City

CHICKEN WITH SHRIMP, SUN-DRIED TOMATOES AND ARTICHOKES

4	boneless, skinless chicken breasts, cut into large chunks	1	large fresh tomato, cut into chunks
2	tablespoons olive oil, divided	¼	cup dry white wine
1	tablespoon butter		Salt and pepper to taste
½	pound raw large shrimp, peeled and deveined with tails intact	1	(6½-ounce) jar marinated artichoke hearts, drained
1	small onion, chopped	1	cup whipping cream
1	clove garlic, minced		Fettuccini or linguine pasta, cooked al dente
½	cup sun-dried tomatoes, oil-packed, cut into strips		Parmesan cheese
			Chopped fresh parsley

Sauté chicken in 1 tablespoon olive oil and butter in a skillet until brown on all sides. Remove from skillet; set aside and keep warm. Wash and pat dry shrimp. Sauté shrimp in same skillet for 2 minutes or until they just turn opaque. Remove from skillet; set aside and keep warm. Add remaining 1 tablespoon olive oil to pan. Add onions and garlic and sauté about 1 minute. Stir in sun-dried tomatoes and fresh tomatoes and cook about 1 minute. Return chicken and shrimp to skillet. Add wine and stir to deglaze pan, scraping up browned bits from the bottom. Season lightly with salt and pepper. Gently fold in artichokes, then whipping cream. Stir quickly to coat. Combine in a large serving bowl with cooked pasta and toss lightly. Sprinkle cheese and parsley on top.

Serves: 4 to 6

Barbara Blaydon

SWEET AND SOUR CASSEROLE

¼	cup flour	½	cup sugar
	Salt and pepper to taste	¾	cup water
3	pounds stew meat or chicken	3	green bell peppers, cut into chunks
2	tablespoons vegetable oil		
2	tablespoons Worcestershire sauce	2	cups chopped onions
2	tablespoons vinegar	1	(20-ounce) can pineapple chunks, drained
¼	cup soy sauce		
¾	cup ketchup		

Preheat oven to 300 degrees.

Season flour with salt and pepper. Roll meat in seasoned flour. Heat oil in a large skillet. Add meat and cook until browned. In a small pan, combine Worcestershire sauce, vinegar and soy sauce. Cook until heated. In a 4-quart casserole dish, mix together browned meat, ketchup, sugar, water, bell peppers, onions and pineapple. Pour heated sauce over the top. Mix well and cover dish. Bake 2½ hours. Uncover and bake 30 minutes longer. Serve with white rice.

Serves: 6 to 7

Marie Carlton

MEXICAN CHICKEN PASTA

½	green bell pepper, chopped	1	(16-ounce) jar picante sauce
½	yellow bell pepper, chopped	2	tablespoons chopped fresh parsley, or 1 teaspoon dried
1	large onion, chopped		
3	stalks celery, chopped	½	teaspoon salt
3	cloves garlic, minced	½	teaspoon hot pepper sauce, or to taste
3	tablespoons olive oil		
1	pound boneless, skinless chicken breasts, cubed	8	ounces dry penne pasta, cooked and drained

Sauté all bell peppers, onions, celery and garlic in olive oil over medium-high heat for 3 to 4 minutes or until crisp-tender. Add chicken and cook 4 to 5 minutes or until chicken is done. Stir in picante sauce and bring to a boil. Reduce heat and add parsley, salt and pepper sauce. Cook 3 minutes or until heated. Serve over pasta.

Patty Henderson

GRILLED JERK CHICKEN

3 scallions, chopped	1 tablespoon brown sugar
5 large cloves garlic, chopped	1 tablespoon chopped fresh thyme
1 small Vidalia onion, chopped	2 teaspoons ground allspice
4 Scotch Bonnet or habanero peppers, seeded and stemmed	2 teaspoons black pepper
¼ cup fresh lime juice	¾ teaspoon nutmeg
2 tablespoons soy sauce	½ teaspoon cinnamon
3 tablespoons olive oil	6 pounds chicken breasts, thighs and/or drumsticks
1½ tablespoons salt	

Blend all ingredients except chicken in a food processor or blender until smooth. Divide chicken pieces and marinade mixture equally between 2 zip-top bags. Press out excess air from bags and seal. Turn bags several times to coat all chicken. Place bags in a shallow pan and marinate in refrigerator all day or overnight.

When ready to cook, heat grill on high heat, then reduce to medium heat. Remove chicken from marinade and place on grill. Cook 15 to 20 minutes or until brown on all sides. Reduce heat to low and cook 25 minutes longer or until chicken is done.

Serves: 8

Mary Hutchinson

FETA CHEESE BAKE

6 boneless, skinless chicken breast halves	1 (4-ounce) package feta cheese with basil and tomato
2 tablespoons lemon juice, divided	¼ cup finely chopped red bell peppers
¼ teaspoon salt	
¼ teaspoon black pepper	¼ cup finely chopped fresh parsley

Preheat oven to 350 degrees.

Arrange chicken breasts in a 9x13-inch baking dish. Drizzle chicken with 1 tablespoon lemon juice and season with salt and pepper. Top with feta cheese and drizzle with remaining 1 tablespoon lemon juice. Bake 35 to 40 minutes. Sprinkle with bell peppers and parsley.

Serves: 6

Cecilia Wright

PECAN CHICKEN

4	boneless, skinless chicken breast halves	¼	cup Dijon mustard
¼	cup honey	1	cup chopped pecans

Preheat oven to 350 degrees.

Place each chicken breast between wax paper and flatten to ¼-inch thick. Combine honey and mustard and spread over both sides of chicken. Dredge in pecans and arrange chicken on a lightly greased baking dish. Bake 30 minutes.

Serves: 4

Sharyon Daigneau

CHICKEN TETRAZZINI

1	(2- to 4-pound) chicken	12	ounces sharp cheese, shredded
½	cup chopped celery	1-2	tablespoons chopped jalapeño peppers
1	medium onion, chopped		
1	medium bell pepper, chopped	1	(4-ounce) can mushrooms, drained
4	tablespoons margarine		
1	(8-ounce) package dry spaghetti, broken into 2- to 3-inch pieces, cooked and drained	1	(10¾-ounce) can condensed cream of mushroom soup
			Parmesan cheese
1	(2-ounce) jar pimientos, drained		

Preheat oven to 350 degrees.

Cook chicken in 2 quarts boiling water; cool. Skin chicken and remove meat from bones; reserving cooking broth. Chop meat and set aside. Sauté celery, onions and bell peppers in margarine until tender. Combine chicken and sautéed vegetables with cooked spaghetti, pimientos, sharp cheese, jalapeño peppers, mushrooms and condensed soup. Add a soup can full of reserved broth. Mix well and pour into a shallow 9x13-inch baking pan. Sprinkle with Parmesan cheese. Bake about 40 minutes.

Kris Kerr

SHRIMP, CHICKEN AND SAUSAGE JAMBALAYA

1	pound boneless, skinless chicken breasts, cubed	8	stalks celery, chopped
2-3	tablespoons olive oil	3-4	cloves garlic, minced
	Tony Chachere's Creole seasoning	2	bay leaves
1	(16-ounce) package smoked hot sausage, cut diagonally into ¼-inch slices	1	(6-ounce) can tomato paste
		1	(28-ounce) can diced tomatoes
		3	(14-ounce) cans chicken broth, divided
1	pound peeled and deveined raw large shrimp		Hot pepper sauce
			Cayenne pepper
	Zatarain's shrimp boil	2	teaspoons butter
1	large onion, chopped	1¾	cups dry white long-grain rice
1	large bell pepper, chopped		

In a large skillet, cook chicken in olive oil over medium heat for 5 to 8 minutes. Season with Creole seasoning; set aside. Brown sausage in skillet 3 to 5 minutes; set aside, reserving drippings in skillet. Cook shrimp with shrimp boil in boiling water according to directions; drain and set aside. Add onions, bell peppers, celery and garlic in skillet drippings and cook 5 to 8 minutes or until brown. Add bay leaves and tomato paste and cook and stir 5 minutes or until browned. Stir in diced tomatoes and 1 can broth and simmer over medium heat. Season to taste with pepper sauce and cayenne pepper.

Meanwhile, bring remaining 2 cans of broth and butter to a boil in a heavy pot with a lid. Stir in rice. Cover and reduce heat to low. Cook 20 minutes or until liquid is absorbed or rice is cooked; set aside.

Add chicken, sausage and shrimp to tomato mixture. Simmer over low heat until blended. Stir in rice and simmer 10 minutes longer. Adjust seasonings and serve.

Serves: 6 to 8

Gretchen Hurchalla

What has happened to awe? Where has wonder gone? I suspect that too much has been "explained" by the ignorant to the stupid. Modern man's greatest loss of spirit may be that he has ceased to be amazed at the wonders all around him.

~ Ernest Lyons

CHICKEN RUBY

4	boneless, skinless chicken breast halves	¾	cup orange juice
⅓	cup flour	1½	cups fresh or frozen cranberries (rinse in cold water if frozen)
4	tablespoons butter	¼	teaspoon ground ginger
¼	cup chopped onions	¼	teaspoon black pepper
¾	cup sugar	¼	teaspoon cinnamon
1	teaspoon orange zest		

Coat chicken with flour. Melt butter in a hot skillet. Add chicken to skillet and brown. Add onions and cook until softened. Stir in sugar, orange zest and juice, cranberries, ginger, pepper and cinnamon. Cover and simmer over low heat for 45 minutes or until chicken is tender, basting occasionally while cooking. Serve over white rice.

Chicken can be left whole, or cut into strips or chunks. Chicken will cook faster if cut into pieces.

Serves: 4

Suzanne Stanton

CHICKEN ENCHILADAS

1	yellow onion, diced	1	teaspoon dried oregano
1	teaspoon minced garlic	½	teaspoon dried basil
2	tablespoons butter	8	flour tortillas
1	(16-ounce) can crushed tomatoes	1	cup diced cooked chicken
1	(4-ounce) can chopped green chiles	1	cup shredded Cheddar cheese
1	(8-ounce) can tomato sauce	2	cups shredded Monterey Jack cheese
1	teaspoon sugar	¾	cup sour cream

Preheat oven to 350 degrees.

Sauté onions and garlic in butter. Add tomatoes, chiles, tomato sauce, sugar, oregano and basil and bring to a boil. Reduce heat and simmer 20 minutes. Spoon some of sauce over tortillas, one at a time, to soften slightly. Top each tortilla with a few pieces of chicken and both cheeses, reserving 1 cup of a mixture of cheeses for topping. Roll up enchiladas and place, seam-side down, in a greased baking dish. Blend sour cream with remaining sauce and pour over top. Sprinkle with reserved cheese. Bake 40 minutes.

Serves: 4 to 6

Michelle Fowler

CITRUS BARBECUED CHICKEN BREASTS

1½ cups bottled barbecue sauce	6 boneless, skinless large chicken
1 tablespoon orange zest	breast halves
⅓ cup orange juice	Orange slices for garnish (optional)

Mix barbecue sauce, orange zest and juice. Reserve and refrigerate about ½ cup of mixture. Place chicken in a baking dish. Pour remaining sauce over chicken, turning to coat both sides. Cover and refrigerate 3 to 4 hours.

If using a grill, drain chicken and discard marinade. Cook on a greased and preheated grill over medium heat for 15 to 20 minutes or until cooked through. Brush chicken occasionally while grilling with reserved sauce. Transfer to a serving plate and garnish with orange slices.

If baking, drain some of marinade, leaving some sauce in baking dish. Bake at 350 degrees for 40 to 45 minutes or until chicken is cooked through. Heat reserved sauce in a saucepan. When cooked, transfer chicken to a serving dish. Drizzle heated sauce over chicken and garnish with orange slices.

Serves: 6

Sharyon Daigneau

SHERRY CHICKEN

4 boneless, skinless chicken breasts	1 onion, sliced
1 egg, beaten	1½ cups cream sherry (not cooking
Seasoned bread crumbs	sherry)
Oil for frying	½ cup water
1 pound mushrooms, sliced	

Dip chicken in egg, then dredge in bread crumbs. Cook chicken in just enough oil to fry in a large skillet; remove chicken and set aside. Remove any excess oil from skillet, leaving bread crumbs and pan juices. Add mushrooms and onions to skillet and sauté until tender. Return chicken to skillet along with cream sherry and water. Cover and simmer about 30 minutes. If too much liquid evaporates, add more sherry so there is enough gravy to serve over chicken.

Strips of red and yellow bell peppers can be added with the mushrooms and onions.

Serves: 4

Dolores Smith

 # CHICKEN SUPREME

4 chicken breasts	1 cup sliced onions
4 chicken legs	1 cup sliced celery
¼ cup vermouth	1 cup sliced mushrooms
Salt and pepper to taste	1 pint sour cream
1 cup sliced carrots	

Arrange chicken breasts and legs in a skillet with a tight-fitting lid. Add vermouth and season with salt and pepper. Add carrots, onions, celery and mushrooms over chicken. Simmer until chicken is done and vegetables are tender. Remove chicken and drain all liquid from vegetables. Blend sour cream into vegetables. Cook until heated, but do not boil. Serve vegetables over chicken with noodles or dumplings.

Chee Chee Ricou Gunsolus

CHICKEN BREAST IN PECAN CRUST

1 cup low-fat milk	1 teaspoon freshly ground black pepper
1½ teaspoons cayenne pepper	3 egg whites, lightly beaten
4 medium boneless, skinless chicken breast halves	½ cup chopped pecans
1 cup cornmeal	1 tablespoon butter or margarine
½ teaspoon salt	

Preheat oven to 400 degrees.

Mix milk and cayenne together. Pound chicken to about 1-inch thick with a mallet or the bottom of a heavy skillet. Add chicken to milk mixture and marinate 10 minutes. Season cornmeal with salt and pepper. Remove chicken from marinade and roll in seasoned cornmeal until completely coated. Dip chicken in egg whites, then roll in pecans. Melt butter in a nonstick skillet. When hot, add chicken and cook 3 minutes on each side or until golden browned. Transfer to a baking sheet. Bake 5 minutes or until done. Chicken will be nice and juicy on the inside and crunchy on the outside.

Serves: 4

Dagmar Bothwell

CREOLE CHICKEN CAKES
WITH SPICY MUSTARD SAUCE

2	tablespoons butter	1	cup soft bread crumbs
4	scallions, thinly sliced	1	egg, beaten
½	cup finely diced red bell peppers	2	tablespoons mayonnaise
1	clove garlic, crushed	2	teaspoons Creole seasoning
3	cups cooked chicken, finely chopped	1	tablespoon Creole mustard
		½	cup vegetable oil

Melt butter in a large skillet over medium heat. Add scallions, bell peppers and garlic and sauté 5 minutes or until just tender. Transfer sautéed vegetables to a bowl. Add chicken, bread crumbs, egg, mayonnaise, Creole seasoning and mustard. Form mixture into 8 patties. Fry patties in hot oil over medium heat for 3 minutes on each side or until just browned; do not overcrowd skillet. Drain on paper towel and keep warm until serving.

Spicy Mustard Sauce

2	tablespoons Creole mustard	4	scallions, sliced
1	cup mayonnaise	½	tablespoon chopped fresh parsley
2	cloves garlic, crushed	¼	teaspoon cayenne pepper

Combine all sauce ingredients. Serve over chicken cakes.

Amanda Tilton Martin

LEMON BARBECUE CHICKEN

3	(2 to 2½-pound) broiler/fryer chickens	2	teaspoons crushed dried basil
		2	teaspoons onion powder
3	cups salad oil	½	teaspoon crushed dried thyme
½	cup lemon juice	1	clove garlic, crushed
1	tablespoon salt	1	lemon, sliced
1	teaspoon paprika		

Wash chickens, split in half and place in a large bowl. Combine oil, lemon juice, salt, paprika, basil, onion powder, thyme, garlic and lemon slices and mix well. Pour mixture over chicken and cover tightly. Refrigerate 6 to 8 hours or overnight. Remove chicken from refrigerator 1 hour before grilling. Place on hot grill, skin-side up; reserve marinade. Grill 20 to 25 minutes, brushing often with marinade. Turn chicken and cook 20 minutes longer.

Serves: 6 to 12

Sharyon Daigneau

CHINESE LEMON CHICKEN

½ cup plus 2 tablespoons cornstarch, divided	3 tablespoons light brown sugar
¾ cup water, divided	1 tablespoon minced fresh ginger
2 egg yolks	1 cup low-sodium chicken broth
4 boneless chicken breasts	⅓ cup fresh lemon juice
2 cups corn oil	½ cup sliced scallions, cut diagonally into 1-inch pieces for garnish

In a medium bowl, combine ½ cup cornstarch, ¼ cup water and egg yolks and whisk until batter is smooth. Add chicken and coat thoroughly. In a large skillet, heat oil until sizzling. Add chicken in batches and fry until chicken is tender and golden on both sides; drain on paper towel and keep warm.

In a medium saucepan, mix remaining 2 tablespoons cornstarch, brown sugar and ginger. Stir in remaining ½ cup water and broth. Cook over medium heat, stirring frequently, until mixture comes to a boil. Boil 1 minute. Remove from heat and stir in lemon juice. Cut each chicken breast on a diagonal into 4 pieces. Arrange on a serving platter. Pour lemon sauce over chicken and sprinkle with scallions for garnish.

Serves: 4

Patty Henderson

MAGGY'S FRIED CHICKEN

1 fryer chicken	Flour for coating
Vegetable shortening for frying	Salt to taste

Cut chicken into pieces: wings, shortjoints, drumsticks, breasts, front and rear backs. Smaller chickens are best; small pieces work best. Heat enough shortening to 375 degrees to cover ½-inch in the bottom of an electric skillet. Sift ¼ cup flour into a heavy brown paper grocery bag. Season flour with salt. Add 2 to 3 chicken pieces to bag, shut bag and shake hard. Place coated chicken in hot fat. Repeat until all chicken is coated and skillet is full, sifting a little flour into bag between each batch. Cook chicken until bottom is nicely browned and turn. Browning time will vary from piece to piece. Drain on paper towel.

Maggy Hurchalla

GORGONZOLA AND MUSHROOMS
STUFFED CHICKEN BREASTS

4	chicken breast halves	1	clove garlic, minced
½	teaspoon garlic powder	¼	cup sherry
¼	teaspoon salt	6	ounces Gorgonzola cheese, crumbled
¼	teaspoon black pepper	1	tablespoon chopped fresh parsley
1	tablespoon butter	½	red bell pepper, chopped
3	cups thinly sliced fresh mushrooms		

Preheat oven to 400 degrees.

Cut a pocket into each breast by inserting a knife into the thickest part of the meat and cutting into the inside close to all the edges. Season chicken with garlic powder, salt and pepper; set aside. Melt butter in a skillet over medium heat. Add mushrooms and garlic and sauté until tender. Add sherry and cook 3 minutes. Cool, then drain off any liquid from mushrooms. Combine mushrooms with cheese, parsley and bell peppers. Fill each chicken breast with mushroom stuffing and secure with a toothpick. Place chicken breasts in a baking dish. Bake 25 minutes or until cheese starts to run out of breasts. Serve topped with any leftover stuffing.

Patty Henderson

CHICKEN WINGS
WITH JALAPEÑO PEPPER SAUCE

1	(12-ounce) bottle chili sauce	1	medium onion, sliced
½	cup dark brown sugar	4	jalapeño peppers, seeded
½	cup vegetable oil	2	tablespoons Worcestershire sauce
½	cup distilled vinegar	2	teaspoons salt
¼	cup ketchup	36	chicken wings (about 6 pounds)

Preheat oven to 375 degrees.

Combine all ingredients except chicken in a blender and process 30 seconds or until mixture is well blended; set sauce aside.

Remove and discard chicken wing tips. Cut wings in half at the joint and place in a greased roasting pan. Pour half of sauce over wings. Bake 30 minutes. Turn wings and top with remaining sauce. Bake 30 minutes longer or until done. Serve warm.

Serves: 6 to 8

Ken Stegina

CRUNCHY CHICKEN

2	cups Ritz cracker crumbs (about 1 sleeve)	2	teaspoons salt (optional)
¾	cup Parmesan cheese	⅛	teaspoon black pepper
¼	cup chopped fresh parsley	2	fryer chickens, cut into pieces, or substitute all breasts
1	clove garlic, pressed	2	sticks butter, melted

Preheat oven to 350 degrees.

Combine cracker crumbs, cheese, parsley, garlic, salt and pepper in a plastic zip-top bag. Dip chicken in melted butter, then dredge in cracker mixture. Arrange coated chicken in a 9x13-inch baking dish. Drizzle remaining butter over chicken. Bake 1 hour or until fully cooked; do not turn chicken.

Teresita Smith

PATRICE'S CHICKEN AND DUMPLINGS

1	cup flour	1	stick butter
2	tablespoons poultry seasoning	4	chicken bouillon cubes
1	tablespoon garlic powder (NOT garlic salt)	8	cups water
2	teaspoons paprika	1	stalk celery heart, coarsely chopped
1	teaspoon salt	1	(16-ounce) package raw baby carrots
1	teaspoon black pepper		
2	onions, coarsely chopped	2	(8-ounce) cans refrigerated biscuit dough
4	pounds skinless, bone-in chicken thighs		Cooked yellow rice (optional)

Blend flour, poultry seasoning, garlic powder, paprika, salt and pepper in a large mixing bowl. Separate onions into 2 equal piles. Wash chicken thighs, and while still moist, dredge in flour mixture. Melt butter in a large Dutch oven. Add coated chicken, all remaining flour mixture and 1 pile of onions. Cook about 10 minutes over medium heat, stirring constantly; you are par-cooking the chicken and making a roux. Add bouillon cubes and water. Increase to high and bring to a boil while stirring. Reduce heat to low and cover pan half-way. Simmer 1 hour, stirring frequently. Add remaining chopped onions, celery and carrots. Simmer over medium heat for 15 minutes longer, stirring frequently. Stir carefully one last time, then arrange biscuits so they are floating on top. Sprinkle with extra paprika for color. Reduce to low heat and cover pot. Simmer until biscuits are cooked through. If desired, serve with rice.

Patrice Florio

CHICKEN MARSALA

6	boneless, skinless chicken breasts	¾	cup Marsala wine
2	egg whites, beaten	¾	cup chicken broth
1	cup seasoned bread crumbs		Salt and pepper to taste
½	cup olive oil	¾	cup shredded Monterey Jack or
8	ounces fresh mushrooms, sliced		mozzarella cheese

Preheat oven to 350 degrees.

Pound chicken between sheets of wax paper to ½-inch thick. Dip chicken in egg whites, then dredge in bread crumbs. Heat oil in a skillet over medium-high heat. Sauté chicken in oil until golden brown. Transfer to a 9x13-inch casserole dish, overlapping breasts. Sprinkle mushroom slices around breasts. Pour wine and broth over the top and season with salt and pepper. Bake 20 minutes. Top with cheese and return to oven until cheese begins to brown. Serve immediately.

Linda Gannon

 # CHICKEN BREAST PARMESAN

½	cup seasoned fine bread crumbs	2	tablespoons olive oil
¼	cup Parmesan cheese, plus extra	1	cup shredded mozzarella cheese
	for topping	1	(15-ounce) can tomato sauce
1½	pounds boneless chicken breast	¼	teaspoon dried oregano
1	egg, well beaten		Pinch of sugar

Combine bread crumbs and ¼ cup Parmesan cheese on wax paper. Dip chicken in egg, then coat with bread crumb mixture. Heat oil over high heat in a skillet. Add chicken to skillet and brown on both sides. Transfer chicken to a glass baking dish and sprinkle mozzarella cheese on top. In a small bowl, mix tomato sauce, oregano and sugar. Spoon mixture over chicken and cheese. Cover dish and microwave 5 to 6 minutes or until sauce is bubbly and meat is done. Or, bake at 350 degrees for about 30 minutes. Sprinkle with extra Parmesan cheese and heat, uncovered, until cheese is melted.

Nancy Dillard

PEACHY CHICKEN

4	(4-ounce) boneless, skinless chicken breast halves	1	(15¼-ounce) can sliced peaches, undrained
1	tablespoon vegetable oil	½	cup brown sugar
1	tablespoon butter	½	cup orange juice
		1	envelope dry onion soup mix

Brown chicken in oil and butter in a large skillet over medium heat; set aside and keep warm. Add undrained peaches, brown sugar, orange juice and soup mix to skillet and stir to combine. Bring to a boil. Cook and stir 2 minutes. Reduce heat and return chicken to skillet. Simmer, uncovered, for 15 to 20 minutes or until chicken juices run clear. Serve over rice, if desired.

Serves: 4

Karen Parker

GRILLED ASIAN CHICKEN KEBABS WITH PEANUT SAUCE

½	cup cream of coconut	2	cloves garlic, crushed
3	tablespoons lime juice	¼	teaspoon cayenne pepper
1	tablespoon vegetable oil	4	boneless, skinless chicken breast halves
2	teaspoons soy sauce		

Combine all ingredients except chicken and mix well; set marinade aside. Cut each chicken breast into 4 pieces. Add chicken to marinade and toss gently to coat. Cover and marinate in refrigerator at least 4 hours.

Soak four 10-inch wooden skewers in water for at least 30 minutes. Remove chicken from marinade, discarding marinade. Thread chicken onto skewers. Grill over medium heat for 2 to 3 minutes on each side or until chicken is done. Serve with Peanut Sauce.

Serves: 4

Peanut Sauce

⅓	cup chunky peanut butter	1	tablespoon cider vinegar
⅓	cup water	2	cloves garlic, crushed
2	tablespoons soy sauce		Pinch of cayenne pepper

Combine all sauce ingredients and mix well.

Yield: ¾ cup

Dagmar Bothwell

CHICKEN AVOCADO SANDWICH WRAP

½ cup balsamic vinegar
⅓ cup olive oil
1 tablespoon sugar
2 cloves garlic, pressed
½ teaspoon salt
¼ teaspoon black pepper
6 boneless, skinless chicken breasts

1 large green bell pepper, quartered
1 large red bell pepper, quartered
1 large red onion, cut into ¾-inch thick slices
2 large avocados, peeled and sliced
8 (10-inch) tortillas
Avocado Mayonnaise (recipe below)

Whisk together vinegar, olive oil, sugar, garlic, salt and pepper in a bowl. Place chicken in a plastic zip-top bag. Pour half of marinade mixture over chicken. In a second bag, combine remaining marinade with all bell peppers, onions and avocados. Seal and toss both bags to coat contents. Refrigerate at least 1 hour, tossing occasionally.

Grill chicken and vegetables over medium-high heat, turning once or so, for 20 minutes or until done. Vegetables may be done and need to be removed from grill before chicken. Cool chicken and vegetables and cut all into strips.

Spread Avocado Mayonnaise over tortillas. Place chicken and vegetables on top. Roll up and cut diagonally. Enjoy.

Avocado Mayonnaise
2 ripe small avocados
½ cup mayonnaise
1 clove garlic, pressed

1 tablespoon lemon juice
2 tablespoons chopped fresh basil

Peel and mash avocados in a small bowl. Stir in mayonnaise, garlic, lemon juice and basil and blend well. Cover and chill.

Colleen Hynes

156

VEAL SCALLOPS WITH LEEKS AND CREAM

2 tablespoons unsalted butter, divided
2 large leeks, chopped, white and pale green parts only (about 2 cups)
1 teaspoon chopped fresh thyme
6 veal scallops
½ teaspoon salt
¼ teaspoon freshly ground black pepper
½ cup whipping cream
2 scallions, sliced for garnish

Melt 1 tablespoon butter in a large skillet over medium heat. Add leeks and thyme and sauté 8 minutes or until leeks are tender and just beginning to brown. Transfer to a small bowl; set aside. Increase heat to medium high and add remaining 1 tablespoon butter to same skillet. Season veal with salt and pepper. Add veal to skillet and cook 2 minutes per side or until browned and tender. Transfer veal to a serving platter and cover with foil to keep warm. Add sautéed leeks and cream to skillet. Boil, scraping up any browned bits, about 2 minutes or until reduced to a sauce consistency. Adjust seasoning as needed. Pour sauce over veal and garnish with scallions.

Serves: 4 to 6

Dagmar Bothwell

FRENCH LAMB SHANKS

1 cup flour, plus extra for gravy
1 teaspoon salt
½ teaspoon black pepper
1 lamb shank per person
2 tablespoons olive oil
1 (14-ounce) can chicken broth
2 cloves garlic, minced
1 cup red wine
2 bay leaves
2 teaspoons chopped fresh parsley
1 onion, sliced
1 (1-pound) bag raw baby carrots

Season 1 cup flour with salt and pepper. Roll each lamb shank in seasoned flour and brown in hot olive oil in a skillet. Drain off oil, leaving shanks in skillet. Combine broth, garlic, wine, bay leaves, parsley, onions and carrots and pour over shanks. Cover and simmer very gently for 2 to 3 hours or until shanks are fork-tender. Remove shanks to a serving platter. Mix extra flour with cold water and add to skillet. Cook and stir until mixture thickens into a gravy.

Marjorie Sayers

TRINIDAD VEAL

1⅓ pounds veal stew meat, gristle
  trimmed, cubed
1 tomato, skinned and chopped
2 slices onion, or more, finely
  chopped
½ cup chopped celery with tops
1 clove garlic, chopped
  Salt and pepper to taste
2 dashes Worcestershire sauce, or
  more

½ teaspoon cinnamon, or to taste
1-2 tablespoons canola oil
1-1½ tablespoons sugar
1 (10-ounce) package frozen
  julienned green beans,
  partially thawed
1-2 tablespoons butter
1 tablespoon ketchup

Combine veal, tomatoes, onions, celery, garlic, salt and pepper, Worcestershire sauce and cinnamon in a bowl and marinate at least 15 minutes. Add just enough oil to a heavy saucepan or Dutch oven to cover the bottom. Add a heaping tablespoon sugar all at once in a clump in the center of the pan. Increase heat to high and watch sugar carefully. When sugar caramelizes, and before it starts to burn, quickly add marinated mixture and stir to disperse sugar. Reduce heat to a simmer and cover. Add beans, unless you like them crisp-tender, in which case, add them a little later. After about 10 minutes, add butter and ketchup. Cook 30 to 60 minutes or until fork-tender, depending on the quantity and size of the veal cubes. Add hot water, as needed, while cooking to be sure to have enough gravy. Serve over hot rice.

Serves: 4

Louise Carnevale

TURKEY AND HAM TETRAZZINI

7 ounces dry spaghetti	½ cup chopped green bell pepper, sautéed, or one (4-ounce) can diced pimientos
4 tablespoons butter or margarine	
¼ cup flour	
1 teaspoon salt	¼-½ cup coarsely chopped black olives
¼ teaspoon white pepper	
¼ teaspoon nutmeg	8 ounces mushrooms, sliced, sautéed in margarine
2 cups chicken or turkey broth, or 1 (14-ounce) can	
1 cup half-and-half	1 egg yolk
3 tablespoons dry sherry wine	½ cup Parmesan cheese
2 cups chopped cooked turkey	½ cup slivered almonds, toasted (optional)
½ cup cubed cooked ham	

Preheat oven to 350 degrees.

Break spaghetti into 2-inch pieces and drop into 6 cups boiling water to which 4 teaspoons salt has been added. Return to a boil. Cook, stirring constantly, for 3 minutes. Cover with a tight-fitting lid, remove from heat and let stand 10 minutes. Rinse with hot water and drain; place in a bowl and set aside. Melt butter in a saucepan over low heat. Blend in flour, salt, white pepper and nutmeg. Cook and stir over low heat until smooth. Remove from heat and stir in broth and half-and-half. Bring to a boil. Boil 1 minute, stirring constantly. Blend in sherry. Pour sauce over spaghetti and mix until blended. Add turkey, ham, bell peppers, olives, mushrooms and egg yolk. Pour mixture into a 2-quart casserole dish. Sprinkle with cheese and almonds. Bake, uncovered, for 25 to 30 minutes. Remove from oven and tent with foil. Let stand 10 minutes before serving.

Serves: 6 to 8

Mrs. Vaughn Monroe

A characteristic of the Florida spruce woods is that they are very still. While their trunks are bent by the wind, you rarely feel more than a breath of air close to the ground. They are especially quiet early in the morning.

~ Ernest Lyons

GRILLED TURKEY BREAST
WITH CRANBERRY SALSA

1	(6-pound) turkey breast	2	tablespoons fresh lime juice
¼	cup orange juice	2	jalapeño chiles, seeded and
1	cup cranberry juice		chopped
¼	cup olive oil	½	cup honey
1	teaspoon salt	½	cup chopped red onions
1	teaspoon black pepper	½	cup chopped dried apricots
¾	cup chopped fresh cilantro, divided	2	large oranges, peeled, seeded
3	cups frozen cranberries		and chopped

Place turkey in a large plastic zip-top bag. Combine orange juice, cranberry juice, olive oil, salt, pepper and ¼ cup cilantro in a bowl. Cover tightly and shake marinade vigorously. Reserve ½ cup of marinade in refrigerator. Pour remaining marinade over turkey and seal bag. Marinate in refrigerator for 8 hours, turning occasionally.

Chop cranberries in a food processor. Add remaining ½ cup cilantro, lime juice, jalapeño, honey, onions, apricots and oranges. Pulse until chopped. Chill until serving.

Remove turkey from marinade, discarding marinade. Cook turkey on a grill for about 15 minutes on each side or until a meat thermometer reaches 170 degrees. Baste with reserved marinade while cooking. Let stand 10 minutes before slicing. Serve with cranberry salsa.

Cindy Doney

SAUSAGE AND PEPPERS

¼	cup cooking oil	1	medium onion, sliced
1	clove garlic, minced		Salt and pepper to taste
4	large green bell peppers, sliced	2	pounds sweet or hot Italian
1	large red or yellow bell pepper,		sausage
	sliced		

Preheat oven to 350 degrees.

Heat oil in a large skillet. Add garlic and brown slightly. Add all bell peppers and onions and cook, stirring frequently, until peppers soften. Bake sausage in a baking pan for 45 minutes or until browned. Slice sausage and combine with vegetable mixture. Bake 15 minutes longer.

Serves: 6

Johanna Florio

VEGGIE BURGERS

2 cups cooked lentils	1 tablespoon steak sauce
1 cup minced portobella mushrooms	2 tablespoons liquid smoke
1 cup bulgur wheat	¼ teaspoon minced tarragon
2 cloves garlic, roasted and puréed	Salt and pepper to taste
1 cup whole wheat bread crumbs	2 tablespoons olive oil

Mash lentils until smooth in a large bowl. Add mushrooms, bulgur wheat, garlic, bread crumbs, steak sauce, liquid smoke, and tarragon. Season with salt and pepper. Refrigerate at least 2 hours. Form mixture into 6 patties. Brush patties with olive oil. Grill 6 minutes on each side or until done.

Top burgers with your favorite cheese.

Karly Walker

EGGPLANT ROLLS WITH GARLIC HERB

1 eggplant	1 (14-ounce) jar spaghetti sauce
½ cup dry seasoned bread crumbs	Hot cooked pasta
3 tablespoons olive oil	½ cup Parmesan cheese
1 (6½-ounce) package cream cheese with garlic and herbs	

Preheat oven to 350 degrees.

Cut eggplant into lengthwise slices and trim both ends. Soak slices in salt water for 10 minutes; drain. Coat both sides of eggplant with bread crumbs. Heat oil in a skillet. Add eggplant to skillet and cook 3 minutes on each side. Spread each slice evenly with cheese and roll up. Secure with a toothpick and place rolls in a baking dish. Pour spaghetti sauce over rolls. Bake 15 minutes. Serve sauce and eggplant rolls over hot pasta. Sprinkle Parmesan cheese on top.

Serves: 4

K.K. Walker

TOFU MEATBALLS

1	pound tofu	½	teaspoon garlic powder
¼	cup Italian bread crumbs, plus more for coating	1	teaspoon dried oregano
		¼	teaspoon onion powder
1	egg	½	teaspoon fennel seeds (optional)
¼	cup Parmesan cheese	¼	teaspoon salt

Preheat oven to 350 degrees.

Mash tofu with an electric mixer until tofu has no flat edges. Add ¼ cup bread crumbs, egg, cheese, garlic powder, oregano, onion powder, fennel seeds and salt. Mix well. Shape mixture into tiny balls about the diameter of a quarter and roll in extra bread crumbs. Bake 20 to 30 minutes, turning once or twice. Adjust seasonings as needed to taste.

These are best, especially for new tofu eaters, if simmered in spaghetti sauce for an hour.

Janet Church

STROMBOLI

1	loaf frozen bread dough, thawed	½	pound mozzarella cheese, shredded
1	teaspoon cornmeal		
½	pound deli ham, thinly sliced	1	small or ½ medium-size sweet onion, thinly sliced (optional)
½	pound pepperoni, thinly sliced		
½	pound provolone cheese, thinly sliced	½	cup sliced mushrooms, sautéed (optional)
		2	tablespoons Parmesan cheese

Preheat oven to 350 degrees.

Roll dough into a 10x16-inch rectangle on a floured surface. Sprinkle a baking sheet with cornmeal to prevent sticking. Place dough rectangle on prepared baking sheet. Add layers of ham, pepperoni, provolone and mozzarella cheeses, onions and mushrooms on one side of rectangle, leaving a 1-inch border around dough. Fold top over, sealing ends and edges by pressing with fingers. Sprinkle with Parmesan cheese. Bake 30 minutes.

Pat Cook

TORTELLINI SAUSAGE ALFREDO

1 (9-ounce) package refrigerated cheese or spinach tortellini	½ cup chopped onions
1 teaspoon olive oil	¼ cup chopped green bell peppers
¼ teaspoon salt	¼ cup sliced fresh mushrooms
¼ teaspoon white pepper	2 tablespoons all-purpose flour
⅛ teaspoon garlic powder	1¼ cups milk
Dash of ground nutmeg	¼ cup Parmesan cheese
4 ounces bulk Italian sausage	⅛ teaspoon Worcestershire sauce

Cook tortellini with olive oil, salt, white pepper, garlic powder and nutmeg in a large saucepan of boiling water until pasta is tender. Meanwhile, in a large skillet, cook sausage, onions, bell peppers and mushrooms over medium heat until sausage is no longer pink. Drain and stir in flour until blended. Gradually add milk and bring to a boil. Cook and stir 2 minutes or until thickened. Drain tortellini and add to sausage mixture. Stir in cheese and Worcestershire sauce.

Serves: 2

Janel Weigt

SAUSAGE AND PEPPERS PASTA

1 pound Italian sausage	1 (16-ounce) package dry penne pasta, cooked and drained
2 large onions, chopped	
2-3 large green bell peppers	8 ounces Parmesan cheese
1 (32-ounce) jar spaghetti sauce, divided	1 pound mozzarella cheese, shredded
½ cup water	

Preheat oven to 350 degrees.

Brown sausage in a large skillet; remove sausage to drain. Add onions and bell peppers to drippings in skillet and sauté until tender. Return sausage to pan. Add 1½ cups spaghetti sauce and water. Cook over medium heat for 1 minute. In a greased 9x13-inch baking pan, spread a layer of spaghetti sauce. Add a layer of pasta, a thin layer of Parmesan cheese and a thin layer of mozzarella cheese. Repeat layers. Top with remaining spaghetti sauce and sprinkle with remaining cheese. Bake, covered, for 1 hour.

Susie Fogarty

CHICKEN LASAGNA PARMESAN

4 tablespoons olive oil, divided	12 lasagna noodles
1 small onion, chopped	1 pound boneless, skinless chicken
1 clove garlic, minced	breast
1 (16-ounce) can diced tomatoes, undrained	1 (16-ounce) container ricotta cheese
1 (6-ounce) can tomato paste	12 ounces mozzarella cheese,
¼ cup water	shredded, plus 1 cup for topping
½ teaspoon salt, divided	½ cup Parmesan cheese
1 teaspoon crushed dried oregano	Fresh parsley for garnish

Preheat oven to 350 degrees.

Heat 2 tablespoons olive oil in a large saucepan. Add onions and garlic and cook 5 to 7 minutes or until tender, stirring occasionally. Add undrained tomatoes, tomato paste, water, ¼ teaspoon salt and oregano. Bring to a boil. Reduce heat to low and cover. Simmer, stirring occasionally, for about 1 hour.

Cook lasagna noodles according to package directions; drain. Meanwhile, cut chicken into thin slices. In a large skillet, heat remaining 2 tablespoons olive oil. Add chicken slices and sauté until chicken loses its pink color. Remove from heat and sprinkle with remaining ¼ teaspoon salt

To assemble lasagna, spoon ½ cup tomato sauce into a 9x13-inch baking dish. Top with 4 lasagna noodles. Using one-third of each, layer with ricotta cheese, chicken, mozzarella cheese and Parmesan cheese. Repeat layers and top with ½ cup sauce. Bake 30 minutes or until heated through. Top with 1 cup mozzarella cheese. Bake 5 minutes longer or until cheese melts. Remove from oven and let stand 10 minutes before serving. Garnish with parsley. Heat remaining tomato sauce and serve with lasagna.

Leroy and Ella Fay Jackson

SPINACH LASAGNA

1	cup chopped fresh mushrooms	1	teaspoon salt
1	cup chopped onions	½	teaspoon black pepper
1	tablespoon minced garlic	1	egg
2	tablespoons olive oil	20	lasagna noodles, cooked according to package directions and drained
2	cups fresh spinach		
3	cups ricotta cheese		
⅔	cup Romano cheese	3	cups shredded mozzarella cheese
1	teaspoon dried oregano	1	cup Parmesan cheese
1	teaspoon dried basil	3	cups spaghetti sauce

Preheat oven to 350 degrees.

Cook mushrooms, onions and garlic in olive oil over medium heat until onions are tender. Drain excess liquid; set aside to cool. Cook spinach in boiling water for 5 minutes. Drain and squeeze out excess liquid. Chop spinach. Mix spinach with ricotta cheese, Romano cheese, oregano, basil, salt, pepper and egg. Beat in cooled mushroom mixture; set aside.

Arrange 5 lasagna noodles in the bottom of a lightly greased baking dish. Spread 2 cups spinach mixture over noodles. Sprinkle 1 cup mozzarella cheese and ⅓ cup Parmesan cheese on top. Spread 1 cup spaghetti sauce over cheeses. Repeat layers twice. Cover dish with foil and bake 1 hour. Let stand at room temperature 15 minutes before serving.

Serves: 10

Louise Lueders

 FETTUCCINE

1	pound dry fettuccine noodles	1	pint sour cream
1	stick butter	¼	cup lemon zest
1	egg yolk	¼	cup dried parsley
½	cup Parmesan or Romano cheese		

Cook fettuccini noodles according to directions on package. Meanwhile, melt butter in a skillet and cook 1 minute. Gently stir in egg yolk. Add cheese, sour cream, lemon zest and parsley. Mix until blended. Drain cooked fettuccine and mix with cheese sauce. Serve hot.

For a variation, add cooked peas, sliced mushrooms and ½ cup chopped prosciutto ham.

Steve Bartholomew

STUFFED SHELLS

1 pound ground beef	2 eggs, beaten
2 tablespoons minced garlic	1 (10-ounce) package frozen
Salt and pepper to taste	chopped spinach, cooked and
2 tablespoons olive oil	well drained
1 (32-ounce) container ricotta	1 (12-ounce) package jumbo pasta
cheese	shells, cooked and drained
1 pound mozzarella cheese,	1 (32-ounce) jar bottled marinara
shredded, divided	sauce
2 tablespoons Parmesan cheese	

Preheat oven to 350 degrees.

Brown beef with garlic and salt and pepper in olive oil; drain. In a large bowl, combine beef, ricotta cheese, three-fourths of mozzarella cheese, Parmesan cheese and eggs. Add spinach and mix well. Stuff about 2 teaspoons of mixture into each cooked shell. Pour a small amount of marinara sauce into the bottom of a large baking pan. Arrange stuffed shells in pan. Pour remaining sauce over the top. Top with remaining mozzarella cheese. Bake 30 minutes or until bubbly.

Serves: 6

Marjorie Sayers

BOW TIES AND SAUSAGE

8 ounces dry bow-tie pasta	½ cup beef or vegetable broth, or
12 ounces cooked smoked sausage,	use bouillon
cut into ½-inch pieces	¼ teaspoon black pepper
2 medium-size red bell peppers, cut	¼ cup chopped fresh Italian flat-leaf
into strips	parsley
1 (14½-ounce) can diced tomatoes	

Cook pasta according to package directions. Meanwhile, cook sausage and bell peppers in a large skillet over medium heat until peppers are crisp-tender and sausage is heated through. Stir in tomatoes, broth and black pepper and bring to a boil. Reduce heat and simmer 5 minutes. Drain pasta and place in a serving bowl. Pour sausage mixture over pasta. Sprinkle with parsley and toss gently to coat.

Serves: 4

Michelle Wright

BAKED ZITI WITH VEGETABLES

2 tablespoons olive oil, divided	1 teaspoon crumbled dried basil
1 medium-size green bell pepper, diced	½ teaspoon salt
1 medium-size red bell pepper, diced	½ teaspoon black pepper
2 large onions, coarsely chopped	¼ teaspoon crumbled dried oregano
2 cloves garlic, finely chopped	½ pound yellow squash, diced
1 (16-ounce) can whole tomatoes, undrained	½ cup frozen corn
1 (8-ounce) can tomato sauce	1 (8-ounce) package dry ziti pasta, cooked according to package
¼ cup dry red wine	1 (8-ounce) container part-skim ricotta cheese
	1 cup Parmesan cheese

Preheat oven to 375 degrees.

Heat 1 tablespoon olive oil in a large skillet over medium heat. Add all bell peppers and sauté 5 minutes or until barely tender. Remove peppers with a slotted spoon; set aside. In same skillet, heat remaining 1 tablespoon olive oil. Add onions and sauté 4 to 5 minutes or until softened. Add garlic and sauté 2 minutes longer. Break up tomatoes with a fork and add with liquid to skillet. Stir in tomato sauce, wine, basil, salt, black pepper and oregano. Bring to a boil. Reduce heat and simmer, uncovered, for 20 minutes or until slightly thickened. Add squash and corn and cook and stir until tender.

Combine ziti, tomato mixture, ricotta cheese and bell peppers in a large bowl. Spoon ziti mixture into a greased 2½-quart casserole dish. Sprinkle evenly with Parmesan cheese. Bake 25 minutes.

Becky Arnold

PORK TENDERLOIN
WITH ORANGE-CHIPOTLE SAUCE

3½ pounds pork tenderloins
6   cups orange juice, preferably freshly squeezed, divided
2   teaspoons salt
2   tablespoons butter
3   large shallots, finely chopped
1   cup dry white wine

2¾ cups low-salt chicken broth
2   tablespoons chopped fresh cilantro
1   tablespoon chopped fresh chives
1   tablespoon minced canned chipotle chiles

Divide pork into 2 plastic zip-top bags. Pour 1 cup orange juice and 1 teaspoon salt into each bag and seal. Turn to coat and refrigerate at least 3 hours or overnight. Melt butter in a large saucepan over medium-high heat. Add shallots and sauté 2 minutes or until softened but not browned. Add wine and boil 10 minutes or until reduced to a glaze. Stir in remaining 4 cups orange juice and broth and boil 45 minutes or until reduced to 1¾ cups; set aside. Drain pork and pat dry, discarding marinade. Grill pork 20 to 25 minutes or to desired degree of doneness, turning often. Transfer to a work surface and tent with foil. Let stand 5 minutes. Meanwhile, bring orange sauce to a simmer. Mix in cilantro, chives and chipotles. Slice pork and serve with sauce.

Serves: 10

Mary Hutchinson

CLAUDE MONET PORK CHOPS

1   tablespoon butter
4   medium onions, sliced
4   pork chops
    Salt and pepper to taste

½   cup bread crumbs
½   cup Parmesan cheese
½   cup dry white wine

Preheat oven to 325 degrees.

Melt butter in a hot skillet. Add onions and sauté until golden. Season pork chops with salt and pepper and place in an ovenproof dish. Pile sautéed onions on top and sprinkle with bread crumbs and cheese. Pour wine over the top. Bake, uncovered, for 45 to 60 minutes or until golden brown.

Serves: 4

Lorraine Nehls

FRENCH COUNTRY DISH

4 slices bacon, cut into small pieces	8 cloves garlic, finely chopped or crushed, divided
1 tablespoon olive oil	Salt and pepper to taste
1 pound sweet Italian sausage links	1 cup white wine
4 boneless, skinless chicken thighs, cut into bite-size pieces	2 (16-ounce) cans white beans, undrained
1 small pork tenderloin, or 2 loin chops, cut into bite-size pieces	1 (14½-ounce) can diced tomatoes, undrained
1 teaspoon dried thyme	1 loaf crusty French bread
2 bay leaves	1 tablespoon olive oil

Fry bacon in olive oil in a large pot. At the same time, pierce sausage and broil, turning to brown on all sides. Add chicken to bacon. Stir in pork. Add thyme and bay leaves. Stir and add 7 cloves garlic and salt and pepper. Cut sausage into small pieces and add to pot. Stir in wine and bring to a boil. Add undrained beans and tomatoes and bring to a boil again. Cook 5 to 10 minutes.

Split loaf of bread lengthwise. Spread olive oil and remaining crushed clove garlic over split sides of bread. Broil until golden brown. Cut bread into 4- or 5-inch sections.

Remove bay leaves and transfer contents of pot into a large bowl. Place toasted pieces of bread in a circular pattern around the outside of the bowl. Serve with a green salad on the side. The bread can be used to soak up the broth.

Serves: 4 to 6

Dick Dungey

PORK ROAST IN GIN

½ cup frozen orange juice
    concentrate, thawed
⅓ cup gin
3 tablespoons sugar
1 tablespoon soy sauce
¼ teaspoon ground ginger
1 clove minced garlic

⅛ teaspoon black pepper
4 small onions, quartered, or
    1 pound pearl onions
1½ pounds boneless pork roast
    Orange slices and scallions for
    garnish (optional)

Preheat oven to 350 degrees.

Combine orange juice concentrate, gin, sugar, soy sauce, ginger, garlic and black pepper in a baking dish. Pierce pork in several places and add to liquid mixture along with onions. Turn pork to coat well with marinade. Let stand 1 hour, turning occasionally. Roast, basting occasionally, for 1 hour or until a meat thermometer registers 160 degrees. If needed, add water to dish while cooking to prevent sauce from drying out. Remove from oven and let stand 10 minutes before slicing. Garnish with orange slices and scallions.

Serves: 6

Ella Fay Jackson

PEACHY PORK

1 (12-ounce) pork tenderloin,
    trimmed
1 (16-ounce) can sliced peaches in
    light syrup
¼ cup cold water

1½ teaspoons cornstarch
¼ teaspoon salt
⅛ teaspoon ground allspice or
    nutmeg

Cut tenderloin into sixteen ½-inch slices. Place each slice between plastic wrap and pound lightly with a meat mallet to ¼-inch thickness. Coat a large skillet with cooking spray and heat over medium heat. Cook pork for 3 to 4 minutes, turning once. Remove from skillet and cover to keep warm. Wipe out skillet with paper towel. Drain peaches, reserving ½ cup syrup; set peaches aside. Pour reserved syrup into a small bowl. Stir in water, cornstarch, salt and allspice. Add mixture to skillet and cook and stir until thickened and bubbly. Add meat and peaches to skillet and cook until heated through. Serve over hot rice.

Serves: 4

Michelle Wright

PORK TENDERLOIN ISLAND BARBECUE

1	(16-ounce) bottle barbecue sauce	1	tablespoon hot pepper sauce
1	teaspoon brown sugar	¼	cup dark rum
¼	cup orange juice	2	pounds pork tenderloin

Combine all ingredients except pork in a medium bowl. Add pork and marinate in refrigerator for 2 to 10 hours. Remove pork from marinade, reserving marinade. Grill pork over indirect medium heat for 15 to 20 minutes, turning occasionally. Meanwhile, heat reserved marinade in a saucepan. Baste pork with marinade while grilling. When done, let stand 5 to 10 minutes before slicing.

Serves: 4 to 6

Kathy Walker

PAN-ROASTED PORK WITH
APPLE CHUTNEY AND PEPPER RELISH

3½	tablespoons extra-virgin olive oil, divided	2	jalapeño chiles, seeded and finely chopped
1	large Granny Smith apple, quartered	1	large red bell pepper, quartered
½	cup white wine vinegar	1	large yellow bell pepper, quartered
½	cup light brown sugar	1	small red onion, cut into ¼-inch dice
½	tablespoon mustard seeds	1	large clove garlic, minced
¼	teaspoon whole allspice berries	¼	cup minced fresh ginger
	Pinch of cayenne pepper	2	(12-ounce) pork tenderloins
	Salt and pepper to taste		

Heat ½ tablespoon olive oil in a skillet. Add apples and cook over high heat for 3 minutes or until brown on the bottom. Add vinegar, brown sugar, mustard seeds, allspice and cayenne and simmer over medium heat for 5 minutes or until thickened. Season with salt and pepper; set aside. In a large skillet, heat 2 tablespoons olive oil. Add jalapeños, all bell peppers, onions, garlic and ginger. Cover and cook relish over low heat, stirring occasionally, for 10 minutes or until softened. Season with salt and pepper and transfer to a bowl.

In the same skillet, heat remaining 1 tablespoon olive oil. Season pork with salt and pepper and add to skillet. Cook over medium heat until browned on all sides. Cover and cook, turning once, until done. Transfer tenderloins to a carving board and cover loosely with foil. Let stand 10 minutes. Slice pork and serve with chutney and pepper relish.

Serves: 4

Virginia Lueders

MARIA'S SHREDDED PORK

4	pounds boneless country-style pork ribs	2	teaspoons fine sea salt
2	cups plus 2 tablespoons water, divided	1	teaspoon ground cumin
		1	habanero chile, halved and seeded
1½	cups freshly squeezed orange juice	1	teaspoon orange zest
6	cloves garlic, peeled	¼	cup brandy

Cut pork ribs crosswise into thirds, trimming off large pieces of fat. Combine pork with 2 cups water, orange juice, garlic, salt, cumin, habanero and orange zest in a deep 12-inch skillet. Bring to a boil. Reduce heat and cover. Simmer 1 hour, 45 minutes or until pork is tender, stirring occasionally. Add extra water, ¼ cup at a time, if needed to keep meat submerged. Uncover and boil until liquid is reduced in half. Stir in brandy and boil until liquid evaporates. Cool meat slightly and tear into strips; meat may have already fallen apart during cooking. Return meat to skillet and add 2 tablespoons water to reheat meat. Serve with tortillas, guacamole and salsa.

Serves: 8

Mary Hutchinson

Seafood Entrées

FLORIDA ORIENTAL GRILLED FISH

¼ cup Key lime juice
1 clove garlic, finely chopped
1 teaspoon grated ginger root
1 tablespoon soy sauce
2 tablespoons olive oil

1 teaspoon Dijon mustard
Black pepper to taste
Tuna steaks or cut up Blue
Runner fillets

Combine all ingredients except fish in a bowl. Add fish, turning steaks with a fork until well coated. Grill fish, turning once, until a fish flakes when tested with a fork.

Jane Hurchalla

PARMESAN FISH

⅔ cup freshly grated Parmesan
cheese
¼ cup flour
½ teaspoon salt
¼ teaspoon black pepper
1 teaspoon paprika

1 egg, beaten
¼ cup milk
2 pounds catfish or tilapia fish
fillets
4 tablespoons butter, melted
⅓ cup sliced almonds

Preheat oven to 350 degrees.

Combine cheese, flour, salt, pepper and paprika in a shallow dish. In a separate dish, combine egg and milk. Dip fillets in egg mixture, then dredge in flour mixture. Arrange fillets in a greased 9x13-inch baking dish. Drizzle with melted butter and sprinkle with almonds. Bake 35 to 40 minutes or until fish flakes easily.

Kevin Henderson

SMOKED FISH

The fish that I smoke is fresh caught in Florida. Use Blue Fish, Spanish Mackerel, King Mackerel, Amber Jack or any legal fish. Clean fish and fillet; no bones, no skin, no red matter—just white fish.

Marinade
1   cup brown sugar
½   cup soy sauce
¼   cup sea or Kosher salt
4   cups pure water (no chlorine)

Combine all marinade ingredients and stir until sugar and salt dissolves. Place fish fillets in a 2-gallon plastic pail or bucket. Pour marinade over fish, making sure fish is completely covered. Cover container and refrigerate at least overnight.

To smoke fish, rinse marinated fillets lightly. Drain and pat fish dry with paper towel. Place fish on a cloth towel and let dry about 2 hours. Transfer fish to the shelves of a preheated smoker. Add a small pan on the burner filled with small pieces of citrus, apple, alder, cherry or hickory wood. Smoke until done.

Marinade can be used for turkey breasts, shrimp, scallops, beef jerky, venison and wild pig.

Floyd De Nicola

GRILLED COBIA STEAKS

¼   cup virgin olive oil
2   tablespoons minced fresh garlic
    Salt and freshly ground black
      pepper to taste
2   tablespoons Dijon mustard
2   teaspoons dried herbes de
      Provence, or to taste
4   fresh cobia fillets

Combine olive oil, garlic, salt and pepper, mustard and herbes de Provence for a marinade. Place fillets in a large bowl and pour marinade over fish. Marinate in refrigerator at least 30 minutes.

Grill fish on a preheated and greased grill over medium heat. Brown on both sides until fish flakes with a fork; do not overcook.

This marinade is also great on fresh dolphin, pork loin or chicken breasts.

Serves: 4

Gretchen Hurchalla

SAVORY POACHED FISH

1	teaspoon butter	¼	teaspoon dried thyme
1	onion, about half the size of the tomato, sliced	¼	teaspoon dried basil
1	large tomato, diced	3	generous splashes good white wine
1	large clove garlic, minced	1	large bay leaf, preferably fresh from a Red Bay
2	square inches orange peel, very thin, no white, cut into ¼-inch long strips		Any non-oily fish, such as snook, snapper, redfish, gag or sheepshead

Melt butter in a large skillet. Add onions and cook over low heat for a while. Add tomatoes, garlic, orange peel, thyme, basil, wine and bay leaf. Cook over low heat a while longer. Arrange fish in liquid in skillet. Cook over low heat until a fork sticks easily through the thickest part of the fish.

Bob Hurchalla

 # FRIED OKEECHOBEE CATFISH

	Small Okeechobee catfish	Salt and pepper to taste
2	eggs	Milk or cream, chilled
2	cups white cornmeal	Oil for deep frying

Skin fish and trim off head. Beat eggs in a bowl. In a separate bowl, mix cornmeal with salt and pepper. Pour milk into a third bowl. Dip fish in milk, then in eggs and then coat with seasoned cornmeal. Deep fry in 375 degree oil until brown and crispy. Season with salt and pepper to taste. Serve piping hot with hush puppies.

This recipe can be adapted to any fish you would want to pan fry such as small catfish, speckled perch and the salt water species such as croakers and mangrove snappers. Clean and dress fish by gutting, rinsing well and chilling fish.

Jan Fogt

 HEAVENLY BROILED FISH

2 pounds skinless fish fillets, fresh or frozen, thawed	3 tablespoons mayonnaise or salad dressing
2 tablespoons lemon juice	3 tablespoons chopped scallions
½ cup grated Parmesan cheese	¼ teaspoon salt
4 tablespoons butter or margarine, softened	Dash of hot pepper sauce

Place fillets in a single layer on a well greased ovenproof 16x10-inch platter. Brush fillets with lemon juice and let stand 10 minutes. Meanwhile, combine cheese, butter, mayonnaise, scallions, salt and hot sauce. Broil fish about 4 inches from heat source for 6 to 8 minutes or until fillets flake easily when tested with a fork. Spread cheese mixture over fillets. Broil 2 to 3 minutes longer or until brown.

Tilda Lorraine

POACHED FISH IN CURRY SAUCE

¼ cup olive oil	2 tablespoons turmeric
1 medium onion, chopped	2 teaspoons salt
4 cloves garlic, chopped	1 cup apple or orange juice, divided
2 tablespoons ground cumin	
2 tablespoons chili powder	2 tablespoons arrowroot
1 tablespoon ground ginger	1½-2 pounds fish fillet of choice
1 tablespoon garlic powder	

Heat oil in a skillet. Add onions, garlic, cumin, chili powder, ginger, garlic powder, turmeric and salt and sauté. Add ½ cup juice. Thicken remaining ½ cup juice with arrowroot and stir into skillet. Add fish fillets to skillet and poach about 20 minutes, depending on thickness of fillets.

Bonnie Cornell

> The mullet is a happy fish, one of the few that has fun just for the sake of fun. In the cool of the day on the broad rivers it leaps lazily just for the joy of jumping, its popeyes surveying the sunset.
>
> ~ Ernest Lyons

BRAISED FISH

1½	pounds fish fillets	½	tablespoon soy sauce
2	tablespoons flour	2	tablespoons sherry
¼	cup oil		Black pepper
½	teaspoon sugar		Chopped chives or scallions
1	teaspoon ground ginger	1	tablespoon chopped fresh parsley
¼	teaspoon garlic powder	2	medium tomatoes, chopped

Dust fish with flour. Heat oil in a skillet. Brown fish in hot oil on both sides. Combine sugar, ginger, garlic powder, soy sauce and sherry in a measuring cup. Add water to equal 1 cup. Pour mixture over fish. Cover skillet and cook 10 minutes. Add black pepper, chives, parsley and tomatoes. Cook, uncovered, 5 minutes longer.

Serves: 4

Michelle Villa

 **FISH SAUCE**

2	cloves garlic, minced		Fresh parsley to taste
2	large onions, chopped	1	tablespoon oregano
2	tablespoons olive oil		Salt and pepper to taste
2	(28-ounce) cans Italian tomatoes, chopped	1	pound grouper fillet, lobster, shrimp or scallops
	Fresh basil to taste		

Sauté garlic and onions in olive oil until tender. Add tomatoes, basil, parsley, oregano and salt and pepper. Simmer gently for 2 hours. Add fish that has been cut into small pieces, if needed. Cook 3 to 4 minutes for fish, 5 minutes for shellfish. Serve over noodles.

Bess Masi

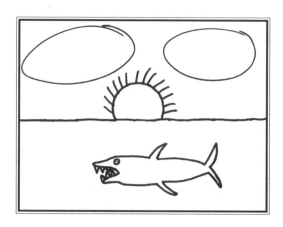

FABULOUS FISH

1	pound orange roughy, tilapia or cod	½	teaspoon black pepper, or to taste
1	stick butter, melted		Dash of cayenne pepper
¼	cup soy-based steak marinade	1	lemon, quartered
1	teaspoon salt, or to taste	2	small tomatoes, thinly sliced

Preheat oven to 375 degrees.

Place fish in a 9x13-inch baking dish or pan. Mix melted butter, steak marinade, salt, black pepper and cayenne pepper and pour over fish. Squeeze lemon on fish. Lay tomato slices on top. Bake 25 to 30 minutes or until fish is flaky.

Karen Parker

GRILLED FISH TACOS

3	pounds boneless white fish fillets		Salt and freshly ground black pepper
5	limes, divided		Olive oil
1	cup mayonnaise	3	cups finely shredded red cabbage
	Pinch of sugar	2	cups pico de gallo
12	corn tortillas		Lime wedges for garnish

Preheat oven to 250 degrees.

Place fish fillets in a large glass or stainless steel bowl. Cut 3 limes in half and squeeze juice of limes over fish. Marinate fish in lime juice in refrigerator for 1 hour.

Meanwhile, squeeze juice of remaining 2 limes into a separate bowl. Add mayonnaise and sugar; set aside.

When ready to cook, heat a charcoal or gas grill to high. Wrap stack of tortillas in foil and warm in oven. Remove fish from the refrigerator and pat dry with paper towel. Season both sides with salt and pepper. Brush grill liberally with olive oil. Place fillets on grill and cook until fish flakes easily or has almost no pink flesh in the center. Place fillets on a cutting board and shred with 2 forks.

Remove tortillas from oven. For each serving, arrange 2 tortillas, partially overlapping, on a large plate. Place 4 heaping tablespoons of shredded fish in center of tortillas. Top with some of cabbage, pico de gallo and mayonnaise sauce. Serve with lime wedges on the side.

Serves: 6

Kim Bruder

GRILLED MARGARITA GROUPER

1½ pounds grouper fillets	1 medium onion, finely chopped
⅓ cup white or gold tequila	1 tablespoon minced jalapeño or
½ cup triple sec	serrano chiles, or more to taste
¾ cup fresh lime juice	2-4 tablespoons chopped fresh
1 teaspoon salt, or more to taste	cilantro
2-3 large cloves garlic, crushed	Pinch of sugar
1 tablespoon vegetable oil, divided	Freshly ground black pepper
3 medium tomatoes, diced	

Place fish in a dish large enough to hold fillets in a single layer. Combine tequila, triple sec, lime juice, salt, garlic and 2 teaspoons oil. Pour mixture over fish, rubbing marinade over fillets. Cover and marinate 30 minutes at room temperature, or up to 3 hours in the refrigerator, turning occasionally.

Just before serving, combine tomatoes, onions, chiles, cilantro, sugar and salt to taste; set aside. Heat a grill to very hot. Drain fish, reserving marinade. Pat fillets dry and brush lightly with remaining 1 teaspoon oil. Season with black pepper. Cook on greased grill for 4 minutes on each side or until flesh is opaque.

Meanwhile, boil reserved marinade in a saucepan for 2 minutes. Discard garlic. Spoon some of marinade over cooked fillets. Serve tomato salsa alongside.

Serves: 4

Kim Neall

BROWNED REDFISH OR GROUPER

Any non-oily fish, such as Redfish or Warsaw grouper	Tony Chachere's seasoning
Flour	Butter

Cut fish into serving-size pieces. Coat with flour and shake off excess. Shake a generous, but not too generous as to make it too salty, amount of Chachere's seasoning on fish. In Florida, there isn't a law that says you have to blacken the fish and smoke up the kitchen. Just brown fish, in butter, over medium or medium-low heat until a fork sticks through fish easily enough to indicate it is done. Set on paper towel briefly before serving.

Bob Hurchalla

GROUPER FROMAGE

1 cup mayonnaise
2 cups shredded Monterey Jack
  cheese
½ cup chopped onion, sautéed
1 teaspoon hot pepper sauce
1 teaspoon cayenne pepper

4 (8-ounce) grouper fillets
  Dash of salt
  Dash of black pepper
  Dash of garlic powder
1 lemon, halved

Preheat oven to 350 degrees.

Combine mayonnaise, cheese, sautéed onion, hot sauce and cayenne pepper; set aside. Add water to a greased 9x13-inch baking dish to a depth of ¼ inch. Sprinkle grouper with salt, pepper and garlic powder. Place fish in baking dish and squeeze lemon juice over the top. Bake 10 to 20 minutes, depending on thickness of fish. When almost done, top each fillet with ½ cup of cheese mixture. Bake 8 to 10 minutes longer.

Serves: 4

Janel Weigt

GROUPER WITH TOMATO AND BASIL

2 tablespoons extra virgin olive oil,
  divided
1 (1-pound) fillet grouper or red
  snapper, skinned and halved
  crosswise
¼ teaspoon salt, plus extra to taste

⅛ teaspoon black pepper, plus extra
  to taste
½ cup coarsely chopped plum
  tomatoes
1 small clove garlic, minced
2 tablespoons thinly sliced fresh basil

Place 1 tablespoon oil in a nonstick 10-inch skillet with a tight-fitting lid. Add fish and turn to coat. Arrange fish in skillet, skin-side down, and season with salt and pepper.

In a bowl, combine tomatoes, garlic and basil with remaining 1 tablespoon olive oil. Season with salt and pepper. Mound tomato mixture on top of fish. Cover skillet with lid. Cook over medium-high heat for 8 minutes or until cooked through.

Serves: 2

Colleen Hynes

GARLIC GROUPER

Grouper fingers (these can be cut
   from fillets if you can't find
   their actual fingers)
Garlic powder

Salt and freshly ground black
   pepper
Butter, melted

Preheat oven to 375 degrees.

Arrange grouper in a pie pan, fitting fingers tight against one another. Season with a generous amount of garlic powder, salt to taste and a fair amount of black pepper (it helps "civilize" the garlic). Pour melted butter over grouper fingers. Bake 6 minutes or until a fork will easily stick through the grouper.

Never bake Red or Warsaw grouper fillets, as whole fillets will bake up rubbery; instead, cut into "fingers". These 2 grouper varieties, along with the always tender Snowy grouper variety, have a heartier flavor than other groupers that will not disappear in the face of garlic.

Jim Hurchalla

GROUPER MACADAMIA

2   eggs
1   tablespoon water
1   (3-ounce) jar macadamia nuts,
     crushed
1   sleeve Ritz crackers, crushed

4   (6-ounce) grouper fillets
    Salt and pepper to taste
2   cups flour
1   cup olive oil

Preheat oven to 375 degrees.

Beat eggs with water and place in a shallow dish. Combine crushed nuts and crackers in a separate shallow dish. Season grouper with salt and pepper and dust with flour. Dip fillets in egg wash, then roll in cracker mixture, patting mixture firmly onto grouper. Sauté fillets in oil over high heat until browned. Transfer to oven and bake 5 minutes or until done.

Serves: 4

Jill LeSerra

CURRIED GROUPER

⅓ cup cooking oil	1 teaspoon curry powder
⅓ cup apple cider or juice	1 teaspoon salt
2 tablespoons chopped fresh parsley	1½ pounds grouper fillets, or other firm fish

Combine all ingredients except grouper and mix thoroughly. Pour mixture over grouper and marinate 30 minutes, stirring occasionally. Grill fish on both sides until done.

Barbara Graunke

BAKED GROUPER PARMIGIANO

2 (8-ounce) grouper fillets, or any firm white fish	1 tablespoon fresh lemon juice
½ cup mayonnaise	1 tablespoon minced fresh dill
¼ cup freshly grated Parmesan cheese	Black pepper to taste
	½ teaspoon paprika

Preheat oven to 350 degrees.

Place grouper fillets in a greased baking dish. In a small bowl, whisk together mayonnaise, cheese, lemon juice, dill and black pepper. Spread mixture over fillets. Sprinkle with paprika. Bake 10 minutes or until just cooked through.

Serves: 2

Janel Weigt

EASY DIJON MACKEREL

Olive oil   Spanish mackerel fillets
Dijon mustard

Preheat oven to 350 degrees.

Beat oil into mustard, using as much oil as can be blended in without separating. (Mixture should taste like a sauce rather than "hot doggy".) Cover fillets with mustard sauce. Bake 8 minutes or until done, checking the thickest part of the fillets with a fork periodically for doneness.

Baking mackerel this way makes it very succulent.

James Hurchalla

MAHI MAHI WITH
CARAMELIZED ONION CRUST, HORSERADISH
CRÈME FRAÎCHE AND STEAMED SPINACH

4	ounces olive oil, divided	1	pound mahi mahi fillets
2	large red onions, sliced		Salt and pepper to taste
3	ounces balsamic vinegar	1	cup water
2	ounces sugar	½	cup Japanese bread crumbs
1	stick unsalted butter, softened	8	ounces fresh spinach, cleaned

Preheat oven to 350 degrees.

Heat 2 ounces olive oil in a large saucepan over high heat until smoking. Add onions and sauté while continuously stirring for 15 to 20 minutes or until well browned and translucent. Add balsamic vinegar, sugar and butter. Reduce heat to low and simmer about 5 to 6 minutes. Place onion mixture on a tray and cool completely. Refrigerate overnight.

Season fillets with salt and pepper. Sauté fish over medium-high heat in remaining 2 ounces olive oil for 2 minutes on each side. Place fish in a baking dish with 1 cup water. Divide onion mixture evenly over top of fillets. Sprinkle with bread crumbs. Bake 8 to 10 minutes.

To serve, steam spinach until wilted. Place spinach on the bottom of a serving plate. Arrange fish on spinach. Top with onions and add a dollop with Horseradish Crème Fraîche.

Horseradish Crème Fraîche

6	ounces crème fraîche or sour cream	3	ounces prepared horseradish

Combine crème fraîche and horseradish and mix well. Refrigerate overnight.

Caramelized onions and horseradish crème fraîche should be prepared a day ahead.

Chef Michael D'Aquila
The Black Marlin, Stuart, Florida

MAHI MAHI WITH
MOJO AND BLACK BEAN PURÉE

Grapefruit Mojo

Zest and juice of 4 Florida grapefruit
Zest and juice of 2 limes
1 small white onion, finely julienned

1 teaspoon chopped garlic
2 tablespoons cider vinegar
6 tablespoons olive oil
¼ teaspoon cracked black pepper to taste

Mahi Mahi
4 (8-ounce) mahi mahi fillets
2 tablespoons salad oil

Grapefruit sections for garnish

Combine all mojo ingredients. Ladle enough mojo over fish to cover, reserving any remaining mojo. Marinate fish in mojo for 2 hours.

Heat salad oil in a skillet until very hot. Add fish and cook about 2 minutes on each side. To serve, ladle black bean purée onto a serving plate. Set fillets on purée. Ladle a little of reserved mojo on fish. Garnish with grapefruit sections. Serve with mashed potatoes, if desired.

Serves: 4

Black Bean Purée (optional)
1 clove garlic, chopped
1 small onion, chopped
1 habanero or jalapeño chile, chopped

1 cup cooked or canned black beans
1 cup chicken broth
Salt and pepper to taste

Sauté garlic, onions and chiles until soft. Add beans and broth and cook 15 minutes. Transfer mixture to a blender and process until smooth. Season with salt and pepper.

Holly Whitney

The river at night is a magical place. As you bend the oars there are swirls of phosphorescent light - miniature universes of incalculably small creatures that emit light when disturbed. The fisher by night has one Milky Way above him and others at his oar tips or in the propeller's wake.

~ Ernest Lyons

MAHI MAHI MAUI STYLE

2	tablespoons butter, divided	1	teaspoon honey
1	clove garlic, chopped	1	tablespoon sesame seeds
1	tablespoon teriyaki sauce		Mahi mahi fillets
2	tablespoons lemon juice		Fresh parsley for garnish

Melt 1 tablespoon butter in a skillet set at 250 degrees or over medium heat. Add garlic and sauté until tender; remove from heat. Stir in teriyaki sauce, lemon juice, honey and sesame seeds. Pour mixture over fish and marinate 30 minutes. Heat remaining 1 tablespoon butter in skillet over medium heat. Add fish and sauté 4 to 5 minutes on each side while basting with marinade. Garnish with parsley.

Serves: 4

Bill Fusselbaugh

DIJON GRILLED DOLPHIN

	Olive oil	Herbes de Provence (preferably
	Dijon mustard	with rosemary)
1	teaspoon minced garlic	Mahi mahi fillets, cut into
		rectangles and triangles

In a large bowl, bit by bit, beat as much olive oil into the mustard as it will hold without separating. Add garlic and enough herbes de Provence for the sauce to be visually well populated with it. Add fillet pieces and toss with a fork until well coated. Grill fillets, turning once, until a fork sticks into various pieces easily enough to indicate they are done.

Blue Runner, Skipjack tuna, Permit and Rainbow Runner are also especially good in this recipe.

Bob Hurchalla

CRISPY MAHI MAHI

¼ cup lemon juice	1½ teaspoons paprika
2 tablespoons Italian salad dressing	½ teaspoon dried thyme
2 cups crushed potato chips	2 pounds skinless mahi mahi fillets,
½ cup Parmesan cheese	cut into serving pieces
¼ cup chopped fresh parsley	2 tablespoons vegetable oil

Preheat oven to 500 degrees.

Combine lemon juice and salad dressing in a shallow bowl. In a separate bowl, combine potato chips, cheese, parsley, paprika and thyme. Dip fillets in liquid mixture, then roll in potato chip mixture. Place fish on a lightly greased baking dish. Drizzle with vegetable oil. Bake 10 to 12 minutes or until fish flakes with a fork.

Serves: 6

Gretchen Hurchalla

MAHI WITH BASIL BUTTER

1 cup olive oil	¼ teaspoon garlic powder
¼ teaspoon white pepper	Juice of 1 lemon
¼ teaspoon salt	Mahi mahi fillets

Combine all ingredients except fish for a marinade. Place fish in a glass dish or bowl. Pour marinade over fish. Marinate at room temperature for 1 hour.

To cook, grill fish 4 to 5 minutes on each side. Serve with Basil Butter.

Basil Butter
2 sticks butter
½ cup chopped fresh basil

Combine butter and basil in a food processor and process to combine. Transfer to a serving dish.

Holly Whitney

MAHI MAHI WITH RUM

¼	cup rum or flavored rum	4	tablespoons butter
½	cup fresh lime juice	1	tablespoon Old Bay seasoning
2	onions, sliced into rings		Black pepper to taste
1	lemon, sliced		Cayenne pepper to taste
2	teaspoons dried oregano	2	pounds mahi mahi fillets

Preheat oven to 350 degrees.

Combine all ingredients except fish for a marinade. Place fillets in a baking dish. Pour marinade over fish. Cover dish and refrigerate overnight. Bake, covered, for 20 to 30 minutes or until fish flakes with a fork.

Serves: 6

Doug Funsch

POACHED POMPANO
WITH CLAM SAUCE

12 littleneck clams, in the shell, washed	1½ pounds Florida pompano fillets, cut into serving-size pieces
½ pound shrimp, peeled and deveined	½ cup heavy whipping cream
1 cup dry white wine	½ teaspoon white pepper
1 cup water	½ teaspoon dried marjoram
1 cup sliced onions	½ teaspoon dried savory
	½ teaspoon dried thyme
	2 tablespoons chopped onions

Combine clams, shrimp, wine, water and sliced onions in a large saucepan. Cover and steam 5 minutes or until clams open. Remove clams and shrimp; set aside. After clams have cooled, remove meat from shells; set clam meat aside. Strain cooking liquid into a large skillet. Add fillets. Cover and simmer over medium heat for 8 to 10 minutes or until fish flakes easily with a fork. Remove fillets from skillet and transfer to an ovenproof platter; keep warm in a warm oven. Simmer cooking liquid until reduced to about ¾ cup. Stir in cream, pepper, marjoram, savory and thyme. Simmer until sauce thickens slightly. Add clam meat, shrimp and chopped onions and heat. Serve sauce over fillets.

Serves: 6

Nan Funsch

ROSEMARY BAKED SALMON

1 tablespoon dried rosemary, crumbled, or 2 tablespoons fresh minced	⅔ cup bread crumbs
2 cloves minced garlic	1½ pounds salmon steaks
Salt and pepper to taste	1 tablespoon plus 1 teaspoon olive oil

Preheat oven to 425 degrees.

Combine rosemary, garlic and salt and pepper in a mortar or bowl and mash to a paste. Using a fork or food processor, mix paste with bread crumbs. Season both sides of salmon steaks with salt. Arrange salmon steaks in a lightly greased baking dish. Press equal amounts of bread crumb mixture onto top of each steak. Drizzle with olive oil. Bake 10 to 12 minutes or until fish is cooked throughout.

Jill Myers

POACHED SALMON
WITH CILANTRO AND GINGER

1½ pounds skinned salmon fillets	1 tablespoon chopped fresh cilantro
Black pepper to taste	1½ teaspoons finely chopped fresh ginger
3 tablespoons lime zest	
2 tablespoons fresh lime juice	
3 tablespoons chopped Vidalia onions	Salt to taste

Preheat oven to 450 degrees.

Wash and pat dry salmon and arrange in a baking dish. Season with pepper. In a bowl, combine lime zest and juice, onions, cilantro and ginger. Pour mixture over salmon and marinate 15 minutes.

Spread foil on a baking sheet and place salmon in center of foil. Top salmon with marinade and season with salt. Fold edges of foil around salmon and crumple to seal. Bake 20 minutes or until opaque throughout.

Serves: 4

Olga Maness

DILLED SALMON ON PARCHMENT PAPER

4	skinless salmon fillets	2	tablespoons chopped fresh dill
4	tablespoons butter, melted	1	shallot, finely chopped
¼	cup fresh lemon juice		

Preheat oven to 400 degrees.

Cut 4 pieces of parchment paper into 12-inch squares. Place a fillet on half of each square. Combine butter and lemon juice and drizzle over fish. Sprinkle with dill and shallots. Fold parchment paper over fillets and fold edges on the side and ends. Bake 12 to 15 minutes or until parchment puffs and fish flakes easily. Cut paper above each fillet to display fish.

Serves: 4

Julie Clark

SALMON CAKES

1	(16-ounce) can red or pink salmon, deboned and drained	1	egg
1	small onion, chopped	1	tablespoon flour, or enough to bind
			Black pepper to taste

Combine all ingredients and mix well, using enough flour to bind mixture together. Form mixture into patties about the size of your hand. Fry in oil or sauté in a sprayed nonstick skillet until golden brown. Serve with cheesy noodles and a green salad.

Recipe doubles nicely. If making ahead, you may chill combined ingredients in refrigerator. This also helps the ingredients to stick together better.

Donna Dolan

> **M**y Florida is cruising off-shore in a small boat just as the sun comes up, grabbing a bending rod and boating a king mackerel, watching sea turtles and manta rays, coming back through a boisterous inlet " on a wing and a prayer."
>
> ~ Ernest Lyons

SKILLET SALMON

1	tablespoon olive oil	½	cup cream cheese spread
4	salmon fillets	½	cup chopped cucumbers
1	cup skim milk	2	tablespoons chopped fresh dill

Heat oil in a large skillet over medium-high heat. Add salmon and cook 5 minutes on each side or until fish flakes easily. Remove from skillet and cover with foil; set aside. Mix milk and cream cheese spread in the skillet until well blended. Stir in cucumbers and dill. Return salmon to skillet and cook 2 minutes longer or until heated through.

Serves: 4

Kathy Walker Peterson

ROASTED SALMON
WITH CUCUMBER SOUR CREAM

⅓	cup dry white wine	6	(6-ounce) salmon fillets with skin
⅓	cup fresh orange juice		Salt and pepper to taste
⅓	cup soy sauce, regular or low-salt		

Preheat oven to 400 degrees.

Mix wine, orange juice and soy sauce in a 9x13-inch glass baking dish. Place salmon, skin-side up, in dish. Cover with plastic wrap and refrigerate 2 hours, turning a couple times.

Shake off excess marinade and place salmon, skin-side down, on a foil-lined baking sheet. Bake 14 minutes or until fish is opaque in the center. Sprinkle with salt and pepper and transfer to individual serving plates. Serve with chilled cream sauce.

Cucumber Sour Cream

1	cup packed fresh baby spinach leaves	3	tablespoons whole grain Dijon mustard
1	cup packed arugula leaves	½	cup seeded, peeled and finely chopped cucumbers
½	shallot		Salt and pepper to taste
¾	cup sour cream		

Place spinach, arugula and shallot in a food processor and process until finely chopped. Add sour cream and mustard and blend. Transfer to a medium bowl and stir in cucumbers. Season with salt and pepper. Cover and refrigerate about 1 hour before serving.

Serves: 6

Mary Hutchinson

GRILLED RED SNAPPER AND MANGO WITH CILANTRO-LIME VINAIGRETTE

6 tablespoons olive oil	4 (5- to 6-ounce) red snapper fillets
5 tablespoons chopped fresh cilantro, divided	1 large mango, peeled and cut into thick wedges
3 tablespoons fresh lime juice	¾ teaspoon cumin seeds
1½ teaspoons lime zest	8 large red-leaf lettuce leaves
Salt and pepper to taste	

Whisk together olive oil, 4 tablespoons cilantro, lime juice and zest in a small bowl. Season with salt and pepper. Brush mixture over all sides of fish and mango; reserve remaining mixture. Sprinkle fish and mango with salt, pepper and cumin seeds. Grill mango and fish, without turning, for 6 minutes or until fish is just opaque in center and mango is soft and beginning to brown. Overlap 2 lettuce leaves on each of 4 plates. Top with fish and mango. Drizzle remaining vinaigrette on top and sprinkle with remaining 1 tablespoon cilantro.

Lauren Palmero

BAKED SNAPPER À LA AL'S

1 skinned large snapper fillet	2 tomatoes, sliced
Salt to taste	Black pepper to taste
1 onion, sliced	Dash of garlic powder
1 green bell pepper, sliced	1 stick butter, melted
3 stalks celery, chopped	

Preheat oven to 350 degrees.

Place fillet on a foil-lined broiler pan. Season with salt. Cover fish with onions, bell peppers, celery and tomatoes. Sprinkle with black pepper and garlic powder. Pour butter over the top. Bake 20 minutes or until fish flakes when tested with a fork.

Go light on the garlic powder, as snapper's delicate flavor cannot overcome as much garlic as grouper's heartier flavor. If substituting, avoid using just any grouper for the snapper, because Red or Warsaw grouper are rubbery if cooked as fillets instead of fingers.

Bob Hurchalla

Adapted from a Barb Hendry recipe for whole snapper in the original Florida Flavors cookbook.

SNAPPER WITH TAPENADE AND RADISH AND GREEN ONION SALAD

½ cup olive oil
2 tablespoons balsamic vinegar
1 tablespoon fresh lemon or
  grapefruit juice
½ tablespoon honey
¾ tablespoon Worcestershire sauce
2 tablespoons butter

3 (10-ounce) packages fresh
  spinach
  Salt and pepper to taste
4 (7-ounce) red snapper fillets, or
  other mild white fish, such as
  flounder
½ cup olive tapenade

Combine olive oil, balsamic vinegar, juice, honey and Worcestershire sauce and stir until honey dissolves; set aside. Melt butter in a large saucepan over medium-high heat. Add spinach and sauté until wilted. Season with salt and pepper. Sauté fish over medium-high heat for 3 minutes on each side or until opaque, or bake at 500 degrees for 9 minutes. Divide spinach among 4 plates. Spoon olive oil vinaigrette over spinach. Place a fish fillet atop spinach on each plate. Spread tapenade over fish. Top with Radish and Green Onion Salad.

Serves: 4

Radish and Green Onion Salad
½ cup finely shredded radishes
½ cup finely chopped green onions

⅓ cup Oriental sesame oil
  Salt and pepper to taste

Toss all ingredients together in a small bowl.

Sarah Heard

GRILLED RED SNAPPER WITH TOMATO SALSA

1¼ cups plum tomatoes, seeded and chopped
⅓ cup chopped onions
¼ cup kalamata olives, sliced
1 large clove garlic, minced
2 tablespoons minced fresh chives
2 tablespoons chopped fresh basil

1 tablespoon chopped fresh rosemary
3 tablespoons olive oil, divided
1 tablespoon capers, drained
2 teaspoons lemon juice
1 teaspoon anchovy paste
Salt and pepper to taste
8 (6- to 7-ounce) red snapper fillets

Combine tomatoes, onions, olives, garlic, chives, basil, rosemary, 1 tablespoon olive oil, capers, lemon juice and anchovy paste in a medium bowl. Cover with plastic wrap and let stand at room temperature 30 minutes. Season with salt and pepper.

Brush fillets with remaining 2 tablespoons olive oil. Season with salt and pepper. Grill fillets 3 to 4 minutes per side. Top with tomato salsa and serve.

Priscilla Peterson

BAKED SNAPPER WITH WHITE WINE

3 russet potatoes (about 2¼ pounds), peeled and cut into ¼-inch thick rounds
½ cup olive oil, divided
3 cloves garlic, minced
1½ tablespoons chopped fresh oregano
1 teaspoon salt

¼ teaspoon crushed red pepper flakes
¾ cup dry white wine
¼ cup water
4 (5- to 6-ounce, ¾-inch thick) red snapper fillets
Salt and pepper to taste
¼ cup chopped fresh parsley, divided

Preheat oven to 450 degrees.

Arrange potato slices in a 9x13-inch metal baking pan, overlapping if needed. In a small bowl, mix ¼ cup olive oil, garlic, oregano, 1 teaspoon salt and pepper flakes. Pour mixture over potatoes. Pour wine and water over potatoes and cover pan. Bake 20 minutes. Uncover and bake 35 minutes longer or until potatoes are tender. Place fish on potatoes and drizzle with remaining ¼ cup olive oil. Season to taste with salt and pepper and sprinkle with 2 tablespoons parsley. Bake, uncovered, for 18 minutes or until fish is opaque in the center. Sprinkle with remaining 2 tablespoons parsley and serve.

Serves: 4

Virginia Lueders

SNAPPER BOCA CHICA

1½ pounds snapper fillets	½ cup lime juice
½ cup honey	2 teaspoons paprika
1½ cups orange juice	1 teaspoon salt

Score the top of snapper fillets in a large checkerboard fashion with 6 shallow cuts. Combine honey, orange juice and lime juice in a flat bottom dish and mix well. Place fish in juice mixture and marinate 1 hour in the refrigerator.

Combine paprika and salt. Transfer fish to a boiler pan and season top of fillets liberally with paprika mixture. Broil 10 minutes per inch thickness of the fillets or until fish flakes easily when tested with a fork. Meanwhile, bring marinade to a boil in a saucepan. Reduce heat and simmer 5 minutes. Baste fish with hot marinade once before removing from oven.

Serves: 4

Jane Roberts

GRAND MARNIER YELLOWTAIL

Sauce

½ cup white wine	7 ounces hollandaise sauce
2 tablespoons Grand Marnier liqueur	1 ounce frozen orange juice concentrate, or to taste
1 tablespoon grated fresh ginger	

Fish

7 (6-ounce) whole yellowtail fillets	¼ teaspoon dried thyme
½ tablespoon orange juice	Salt and pepper to taste
½ teaspoon butter, melted	

Combine wine, Grand Marnier and ginger in a saucepan. Cook until reduced by half. Strain through a small strainer and discard ginger. Return reduction to saucepan and add hollandaise sauce. Stir in orange juice concentrate. Mix over low heat until warm; do not boil.

For the fish, arrange fillets in a baking dish. Drizzle with orange juice and butter. Season with thyme and salt and pepper. Broil until fish is done. To serve, ladle sauce onto individual plates. Place a fillet over sauce on each plate and serve.

Serves: 6

Bob Smith

MEXICAN RED SNAPPER

1	(28-ounce) can diced tomatoes, well drained, juice reserved	2	tablespoons chopped fresh parsley
¼	cup extra virgin olive oil	1	teaspoon dried Mexican oregano
¼	cup finely chopped white onions	¼	cup chopped green olives
4	large cloves garlic, chopped	2	tablespoons raisins
3	small bay leaves	2	tablespoons drained capers
			Salt and pepper to taste
		6	(4- to 5-ounce) red snapper fillets

Preheat oven to 425 degrees.

Place drained tomatoes in a bowl and crush with a masher to a coarse purée. Drain tomatoes again, reserving juice. Heat oil in a large skillet over medium-high heat. Add onions and garlic and stir. Add tomato purée and cook 1 minute. Add bay leaves, parsley, oregano and ¼ cup reserved tomato juice. Simmer 3 minutes or until sauce thickens. Add olives, raisins, capers and all remaining tomato juice. Simmer 8 minutes or until sauce thickens again. Season with salt and pepper. Remove bay leaves.

Spread 3 tablespoons sauce on bottom of a 15x10-inch baking dish. Arrange fillets over sauce. Sprinkle fillets with salt and pepper. Spoon remaining sauce over fish. Bake, uncovered, for 18 minutes or until fish is opaque in center.

Serves: 6

Ev Roarke

 **SNOOK FINGERS**

Snook
Italian bread crumbs
Garlic powder to taste
Salt and pepper to taste

Butter
Olive oil
⅓ cup Key lime juice

Cut snook into 1x3-inch "fingers". Combine bread crumbs, garlic powder and salt and pepper in a mixing bowl. Heat butter and oil in a skillet at 350 degrees or medium heat. Dip fish in bread crumb mixture, then add to skillet. Cook 5 to 7 minutes on one side. Turn and cook on other side 5 to 7 minutes longer. When done, turn off heat or remove from heat. Pour lime juice over fish and cover 3 to 4 minutes. Remove from skillet and serve.

Bill Reamer

SAM'S SNOOK FINGERS

1   cup all-purpose flour
1   teaspoon salt
1   teaspoon baking powder
½   teaspoon dried dill or Cajun
     powder
¾   cup beer
½   cup milk

2   eggs, lightly beaten
2   pounds skinned and deboned
     snook fillets, or other firm white
     fish, cut into "fingers"
2   quarts vegetable oil for frying
     Salt and pepper to taste
     Cinnamon or Cajun seasoning
     (optional)

Combine flour, salt, baking powder and dill in a large bowl. In a separate bowl, combine beer, milk and eggs. Dip fish fingers in egg wash, then roll in dry ingredients until well coated. Place on paper towel. Repeat dry ingredient coating after 3 minutes.

Heat vegetable oil to 375 degrees in a deep fryer. Fry fingers in hot oil until golden brown and fish flakes easily with a fork. Cook in batches of 4 to 6 fingers at a time to maintain temperature. Remove fingers from oil and drain on paper towel. Season lightly with salt and pepper. For added zest, dust lightly with cinnamon or Cajun seasoning. Serve piping hot.

For extra crispy and crunchy fish fingers, add corn flake crumbs to the dry coating mixture.

Serves: 4 to 6

Sam Yates

TIPSY TILAPIA

4	tablespoons butter	¼	cup chopped fresh parsley
1-1½	cups cooking sherry	½	(16-ounce) can hearts of palm,
1	pound tilapia fillets		sliced
8	cloves garlic, minced		Juice of ½ lemon
1	onion, minced		

Preheat oven to 350 degrees.

Melt butter in a baking dish in oven. Add sherry to melted butter. Arrange fillets in dish. Top fish with garlic, onions, parsley and hearts of palm. Squeeze lemon juice over all. Fish should be completely covered with liquid; if not, add more sherry to cover. Bake 30 to 35 minutes. Serve with brown and wild rice.

Jane VanWieren

SESAME CRUSTED TUNA LOIN
WITH GINGER VINAIGRETTE

8	ounces tuna loin	2	ounces mixed greens
	Salt and pepper to taste	2	ounces Ginger Vinaigrette
3	ounces white sesame seeds		(recipe below)
½	ounce sesame oil		

Season tuna with salt and pepper and coat with sesame seeds. Heat oil in a skillet over high heat. Sear tuna on each side for 30 seconds. Remove tuna and slice diagonally. Toss mixed greens with Ginger Vinaigrette. Divide greens among individual serving plates. Arrange tuna slices over greens.

Ginger Vinaigrette

4	ounces white balsamic vinegar	1	ounce puréed ginger
2	ounces water	1	ounce corn or canola oil
½	ounce sugar		Salt and pepper to taste

Combine vinegar, water, sugar and ginger in a bowl. Slowly whisk in oil. Season with salt and pepper.

Kristan Altimus

HERB TUNA WITH AÏOLI

¼	cup sesame oil	1	tablespoon sesame seeds
⅓	cup soy sauce	3	tablespoons fresh orange juice
2	tablespoons chopped fresh basil	2	large cloves garlic, finely chopped
2	teaspoons chopped fresh thyme	½	cup mayonnaise
2	teaspoons dried tarragon	2	pounds tuna steaks

Whisk together sesame oil, soy sauce, basil, thyme, tarragon, sesame seeds, orange juice and garlic in a bowl for a marinade. Place mayonnaise in a separate bowl. Add 3 tablespoons of marinade to mayonnaise and mix to make the aïoli. Refrigerate until ready to serve. Pour remaining marinade into a plastic zip-top bag or shallow dish. Place tuna in bag or dish and coat with marinade. Marinate at least 1 hour. Cook tuna over a hot grill for 2 minutes per side for medium-rare doneness. The tuna can be served right off the grill or chilled. Serve tuna with aïoli.

Serves: 4 as a main course, 6 to 8 as an appetizer

Mary Hutchinson

GRILLED TUNA
WITH PINEAPPLE-NECTARINE SALSA

1	teaspoon lime zest	1	teaspoon vegetable oil
2	tabaylespoons fresh lime juice	¼	teaspoon salt
2	tablespoons fresh orange juice	⅛	teaspoon white pepper
1	tablespoon chopped fresh cilantro	1	pound tuna, cut into 4 pieces

Combine all ingredients except tuna in a plastic zip-top bag. Add tuna and turn bag to coat fish. Seal and refrigerate 1 hour, turning occasionally. Grill fish over medium-high heat for 5 to 7 minutes on each side or to desired degree of doneness. Serve tuna with Pineapple-Nectarine Salsa.

Serves: 4

Pineapple-Nectarine Salsa

1	medium nectarine, diced	2	tablespoons diced red onions
1	(8-ounce) can pineapple tidbits in it own juice	1	tablespoon chopped fresh cilantro
1	kiwifruit, peeled and diced	1	teaspoon fresh lemon juice

Combine all salsa ingredients in a bowl. Cover and refrigerate.

Colleen Hyne

GLAZED YELLOWFIN TUNA

1½	pounds (1-inch thick) tuna steaks	½	teaspoon ground cumin
1	tablespoon Dijon mustard	½	teaspoon ground thyme
2	teaspoons honey	2	tablespoons chopped fresh parsley

Place tuna in a microwave-safe dish. Mix together mustard, honey, cumin and thyme. Drizzle mixture evenly over tuna. Microwave on high for 3 to 4 minutes. Sprinkle with parsley. Let stand 2 minutes before serving.

Serves: 6

Gretchen Hurchalla

SEARED TUNA WITH WASABI-BUTTER SAUCE

2   tablespoons white wine vinegar
1¼ cups white wine
¼   cup minced shallots
1   tablespoon wasabi paste
1   tablespoon soy sauce
2   sticks unsalted butter, cubed

1   cup chopped fresh cilantro
6   (6-ounce, about 1-inch thick)
    fresh tuna steaks
1   tablespoon olive oil
    Salt and pepper to taste

Combine vinegar, wine and shallots in a small saucepan over medium heat. Simmer until liquid is reduced to 2 tablespoons. Strain and return liquid to saucepan, discarding shallots. Stir in wasabi paste and soy sauce. Gradually whisk in butter, one cube at a time, over low heat, allowing mixture to emulsify between additions. Do not bring to a boil. When all butter in incorporated, stir in cilantro and remove from heat. Pour mixture into a small bowl; set aside.

Heat a large skillet over medium-high heat. Brush tuna with olive oil and season with salt and pepper. Sear tuna in hot skillet for 3 to 5 minutes on each side, being careful to not overcook. Serve with wasabi sauce.

Serves: 6

Alexa Muir

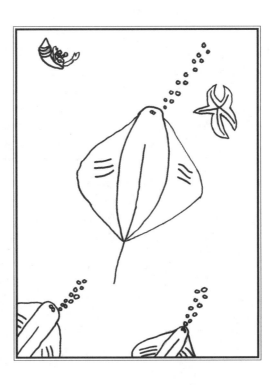

STEAMED CLAMS
WITH CILANTRO AND RED PEPPER

5 tablespoons unsalted butter, divided
1½ cups thinly sliced scallions
1¼ cups chopped fresh cilantro, divided
2 cups sake or dry vermouth

5 cloves garlic, pressed
½ teaspoon crushed red pepper flakes
1 teaspoon Worcestershire sauce
4 dozen clams, scrubbed
Salt and pepper to taste

Melt 4 tablespoons butter in a large pot over medium heat. Add scallions and cook 3 minutes. Add 1 cup cilantro, sake, garlic, pepper flakes and Worcestershire sauce. Increase heat to high and bring to a boil. Add clams and cover pot. Cook 7 minutes or until clams open, shaking pot often. Using a slotted spoon, transfer to one large bowl or smaller soup bowls. Discard any unopened clams. Boil remaining cooking liquid over high heat for 1 minute or until slightly thickened. Whisk in remaining 1 tablespoon butter. Season with salt and pepper. Pour sauce over clams and sprinkle with remaining ½ cup cilantro.

Peter Lueders

CLAMS WITH JALAPEÑO, LEMON AND BASIL

4 tablespoons butter
4 cloves garlic, minced
1 tablespoon minced jalapeño
1 cup canned tomato sauce
½ cup white wine

2 tablespoons fresh lemon juice
6 pounds clams, scrubbed
½ cup finely chopped fresh basil
1½ tablespoons lemon zest
Black pepper to taste

Melt butter in a very large pot over medium-high heat. Add garlic and jalapeño and stir until garlic is golden. Add tomato sauce, wine and lemon juice and bring to a boil. Add clams. Cover pot and boil 9 minutes or until clams open. Discard any unopened clams. Add basil and lemon zest. Season with black pepper. Transfer all to a large bowl and serve.

Serves: 8

Peter Lueders

CRAB CAKES WITH LEMON DILL SAUCE

3 tablespoons butter, divided	1 cup bread crumbs, divided
1 scallion, finely chopped	1 egg
2 tablespoons finely chopped red bell pepper	½ teaspoon minced fresh parsley
1 clove garlic, minced	1 pound white or claw crabmeat, picked over to remove shell
3 tablespoons whipping cream	¼ cup Parmesan cheese
1 tablespoon Dijon mustard	2 tablespoons vegetable oil
Cayenne pepper	

Melt 1 tablespoon butter in a heavy skillet over medium heat. Add scallions, bell peppers and garlic and sauté 3 minutes or until bell peppers are limp. Add cream, mustard and cayenne and mix well. Add ½ cup bread crumbs, egg and parsley and mix well. Gently fold in crabmeat. Form mixture into 8 patties, about ½-inch thick. Combine remaining ½ cup bread crumbs and Parmesan cheese in a bowl. Pat crumb mixture onto both sides of patties. Refrigerate 2 hours or until firm. Heat oil and remaining 2 tablespoons butter in a skillet. Add crab cake patties and cook 3 minutes on each side or until golden brown. Or, place crab cake patties on a baking sheet, drizzle with oil-butter mixture and bake at 400 degrees for 7 to 10 minutes, turning once. Serve with Lemon Dill Sauce.

Lemon Dill Sauce

1 cup mayonnaise	1 tablespoon lemon zest
¼ cup buttermilk	2 teaspoons fresh lemon juice
2 tablespoons chopped fresh dill	1 small clove garlic, minced
1 tablespoon minced fresh parsley	

Combine all ingredients in a bowl and stir well. Refrigerate until chilled; sauce thickens as it chills.

Janel Weigt

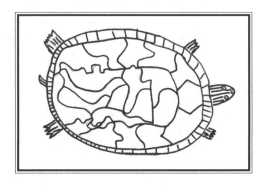

BALTIMORE CRAB CAKE

1 pound crabmeat	4 saltine crackers, crushed, plus
1 tablespoon mayonnaise	more for coating
1 tablespoon prepared mustard	Salt and pepper to taste
	Dash of cayenne pepper

Combine crabmeat, mayonnaise, mustard and 4 crushed crackers. Season with salt and both peppers. Form mixture into patties and dredge in extra crushed crackers. Deep fry in 350 to 375 degree oil until brown.

Theresa Barrett

 CRABMEAT ROYALE

4 tablespoons butter	⅛ teaspoon black pepper
8 ounces mushrooms, sliced	¼ cup dry vermouth
2 cups fresh crabmeat	¼ cup whipping cream
¼ cup chopped fresh parsley	4 ounces Swiss cheese, cut into strips

Preheat oven to 350 degrees.

Melt butter in a skillet. Add mushrooms and sauté 3 minutes or until tender. Add crabmeat and cook and flake. Stir in parsley, black pepper, vermouth and cream. Blend together and pour into a shallow casserole dish or 4 individual casserole dishes. Top with cheese strips. Bake 15 to 20 minutes or until bubbly.

Julia Porter Moritz

 CRAWFISH SALAD NASSAU STYLE

2-3 crawfish tails, cooked and diced
1-2 tablespoons diced onions
1 tablespoon diced green bell
    peppers
3 hard-boiled eggs, diced
1 ripe tomato, diced

3 tablespoons lemon juice
3 tablespoons mayonnaise
2 tablespoons olive oil
    Salt and pepper to taste
1 teaspoon hot pepper sauce

Combine all ingredients and mix well. Chill at least 4 hours.

Sue F. Hipson

LOBSTER (OR SHRIMP) FRA DIAVOLO

2 tablespoons olive oil
2 onions, chopped
4 cloves garlic, chopped
1 (28-ounce) can Italian plum
    tomatoes, chopped
1 yellow bell pepper, chopped
⅓ cup white wine or broth
½ teaspoon dried red pepper flakes
¼ teaspoon salt

¼ teaspoon coarsely ground black
    pepper
8 ounces dry fusilli pasta
3½ pounds lobster tails, meat
    removed and cut into ½-inch
    pieces, or 1½ pounds peeled
    and deveined shrimp
¼ cup chopped fresh basil

Heat oil in a large nonstick skillet over medium-high heat. Add onions and garlic and cook 7 to 10 minutes, stirring occasionally, or until golden. Add tomatoes, bell peppers, wine, pepper flakes, salt and pepper. Bring to a boil. Reduce heat and simmer, uncovered, for 20 minutes or until flavors blend and sauce is slightly thickened. Meanwhile, cook fusilli according to package directions; drain and keep warm in a large bowl. Add lobster to tomato sauce and simmer, uncovered, for 5 minutes or until lobster is just opaque. Toss lobster sauce with fusilli. Sprinkle with basil.

Serves: 6

Laura Bianco

 **LOBSTER THERMIDOR**

3 lobsters	Freshly ground black pepper
2 cups whipping cream	½ cup milk
1½ sticks butter, divided	¼ cup prepared mustard
3 tablespoons flour	½ cup Parmesan cheese
1½ teaspoons salt	

Preheat oven to 400 degrees.

Boil lobsters and remove shells; cut meat into bite-size pieces. Simmer cream in a saucepan for 30 minutes, stirring occasionally; do not boil. Melt 4 tablespoons butter in a skillet. Stir in flour, salt, pepper and milk, stirring occasionally until thickened. Mix in warmed cream. Mix in lobster. Rub mustard in a baking dish. Pour lobster mixture into dish. Sprinkle with cheese and dot with remaining stick of butter. Bake, uncovered, for 10 minutes. This is a very rich dish.

Mixture may be placed in clean lobster shells, or served over pastry shells or rice. Chicken may be substituted for the seafood.

Marcia Hendry

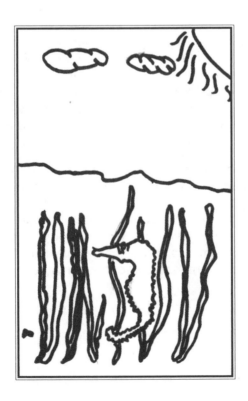

MUSSELS AND TOMATOES

¼	cup olive oil	¼	cup chopped fresh parsley
1	small onion, chopped	¼	cup chopped fresh basil
4	cloves garlic, minced		Dash of salt and pepper
2	(14½-ounce) cans plum tomatoes		Dried hot pepper flakes to taste
½	teaspoon dried oregano	20-30	fresh mussels, scrubbed

Heat olive oil in a large pot. Add onions and garlic and sauté until onions are tender. Add tomatoes, oregano, parsley, basil, salt and pepper and pepper flakes. Cook over medium heat for about 20 minutes. Add mussels, cover and simmer until mussels open. Remove any unopened mussels. Pour mixture into a large dish. Serve with plenty of bread.

Jill Myers

CHILLED MUSSELS WITH WHITE WINE

2	cups dry white wine	4	ounces anchovy fillets
8	dozen mussels, scrubbed	½	teaspoon dried hot pepper flakes
¼	cup olive oil	2	tablespoons vinegar
4	cloves garlic, crushed	2	tablespoons chopped fresh parsley

In a large pot, bring wine to a simmer. Add mussels and cook until all mussels open. Remove mussels and set aside to cool. Increase heat and cook wine until reduced to ⅔ cup. Remove mussels from shells, discarding shells. In a large skillet, heat olive oil. Add garlic and sauté until lightly browned. Stir in anchovies and pepper flakes. Add mussels, reduced wine and vinegar. Simmer 1 to 2 minutes. Remove from heat and allow to cool. Place mixture in a large bowl and cover tightly with plastic wrap. Refrigerate several hours or overnight. Add parsley and toss well.

Holly Whitney

STUFFED MUSSELS

4	dozen mussels, scrubbed	3	cloves garlic, minced
½	cup dry white wine	1	tablespoon minced fresh parsley
2	tablespoons olive oil	4	tablespoons butter, melted
1½	cups bread crumbs		Salt and pepper to taste

Preheat oven to 375 degrees.

Steam mussels in wine and olive oil in a saucepan. When mussels open, remove mussels from shells, reserving cooking liquid and shells. Chop mussels. Mix mussels with bread crumbs, garlic, parsley and butter. Season with salt and pepper. Moisten mixture with cooking liquid. Fill mixture into half-shells. Bake 12 to 15 minutes.

Kim Neall

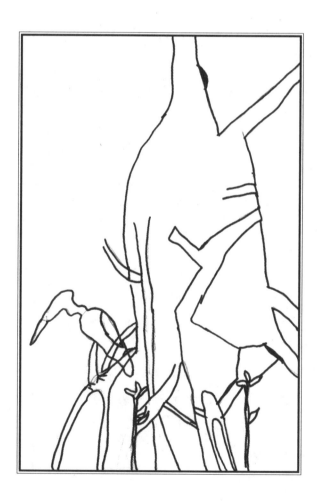

PAN-SEARED SCALLOPS
WITH ASPARAGUS AND BACON

24 medium asparagus spears	24 sea scallops
2 teaspoons olive oil	¾ cup freshly squeezed orange juice
1½ teaspoons salt, divided	2 tablespoons dry vermouth
1 teaspoon black pepper, divided	1 tablespoon butter
⅔ cup diced raw center-cut bacon (about 3½ ounces)	2 tablespoons chopped chives
Olive oil	2 tablespoons shaved Parmesan cheese

Preheat oven to 475 degrees.

Cut off 2½ inches from each asparagus tip. (Reserve remainder of stalks for another use.) Toss asparagus tips with 2 teaspoons olive oil, ½ teaspoon salt and ½ teaspoon pepper in an 8-inch square baking pan. Bake 6 minutes. Remove from pan; set aside. Cook bacon in a large skillet until crisp. Remove from skillet and drain on paper towel. Pour bacon drippings into a measuring cup. Add olive oil to equal ¼ cup.

Sprinkle both sides of scallops with remaining 1 teaspoon salt and remaining ½ teaspoon pepper. Heat bacon drippings and oil mixture in a skillet over medium-high heat until hot. Add scallops and cook 5 minutes, turning once, or until browned on both sides. If needed, cook in batches if scallops do not fit in skillet without touching; set aside and keep warm. Heat skillet over medium-high heat until hot. Add orange juice and vermouth and cook, stirring constantly, until sauce is reduced to ½ cup. Remove from heat and whisk in butter.

To serve, divide scallops among serving plates. Arrange asparagus, tip end up, against the scallops. Drizzle with sauce and sprinkle with bacon, chives and cheese. Serve with rice.

Dorothy Dicks

> We live in a world filled with miracles. There is such an abundance of the amazing and the inconceivable that men stop believing and become bored. Some live their lives without a tinge of understanding about the wonders around them.
>
> ~ Ernest Lyons

THREE IN THE BAG

1½ cups chopped fresh tomatoes	6 tablespoons olive oil, plus extra for brushing, divided
¾ cup chopped leeks, white and light green parts only	12 sea scallops, halved
¾ cup chopped fresh cilantro	2 dozen small clams, littlenecks or cherrystones
¾ cup julienned celery root	
1 tablespoon grated ginger	2 dozen medium shrimp, deveined with tails intact
Pinch of sea salt, or to taste	
Pinch of white pepper, or to taste	6 tablespoons white wine

Preheat oven to 400 degrees.

Cut parchment paper into six 12x14-inch rectangles. Halve paper by folding short bottom edge to top. Fold left edge to right to halve again. Snip off top right and left corners at 45 degree angles.

Blend tomatoes, leeks, cilantro, celery root, ginger, salt and pepper in a bowl. Place a single square of folded parchment paper on a cutting board. Brush with olive oil. Add about ½ cup of tomato mixture to center of square. Top with 4 scallop halves, 4 clams and 4 shrimp. Drizzle with 1 tablespoon wine and 1 tablespoon olive oil. Fold up points of paper to form a sack and secure with a paper clip or staple. Repeat with remaining ingredients.

Place sacks on a baking sheet. Bake 12 to 15 minutes or only until clams open. Serve to guests in paper sacks on a plate, allowing them to open sacks at the table. Serve with lemon wedges and baguettes or crusty Italian bread.

Serves: 6

Bill Wolters

 SCALLOP CASSEROLE

1	small package Spanish yellow rice	12	ounces scallops
1	tablespoon butter		Garlic salt to taste
2	tablespoons flour	1	(14½-ounce) can tomatoes or
1	cup milk		stewed tomatoes
¼	cup Parmesan cheese		Bread crumbs or croutons
8	ounces fresh mushrooms, sliced		

Preheat oven to 300 to 325 degrees.

Prepare rice according to package directions. Prepare a white sauce by melting butter in a saucepan. Blend in flour. Add milk and cook and stir until thickened. Add cheese and mushrooms to sauce. In a shallow pan, stir-fry scallops for 2 minutes, seasoning with garlic salt as desired. Spread cooked rice in the bottom of a casserole dish. Add tomatoes. Layer scallops on top. Cover with sauce and sprinkle with bread crumbs. Bake 30 minutes.

Serves: 5 to 6

V. James Navitsky

COQUILLES ST. JACQUES

1	small onion, chopped	2	slices white bread, torn into small
2	cloves garlic, minced		pieces, reserving a few bits for
1	tablespoon butter		crumbs
2	tablespoons chopped fresh parsley	¾	cup Sauternes or other white wine
1	pound fresh bay scallops	1	cup sliced mushrooms (optional)

Preheat oven to 350 degrees.

Sauté onion and garlic in butter over low heat until onions are clear. Stir in parsley. Add scallops. Cook slowly for 5 minutes. Add bread pieces and wine. If too dry, add a little more butter. Scoop mixture into shells or small ramekin dishes to about two-thirds full. Sprinkle with reserved crumbs. Bake a few minutes or until heated. Serve hot.

For a variation, chopped mushrooms can be added with the scallops.

Serves: 4

Roger and Marjorie Sayers

SEARED PEPPERED SCALLOPS WITH TANGERINE-SOY GLAZE

4 tablespoons peanut oil, divided	½ cup fresh tangerine or orange juice
1½ pounds scallops	1 tablespoon soy sauce
2 teaspoons ground peppercorn and salt blend	½ teaspoon packed tangerine or orange zest
1 tablespoon minced fresh garlic	Salt

Heat 3 tablespoons peanut oil in a large skillet over high heat. Sprinkle scallops with seasoning blend. Working in batches, sauté scallops in hot oil until brown on outside and opaque in the center. Transfer to a serving plate and set aside, reserving skillet drippings. Return skillet to heat and add remaining 1 tablespoon peanut oil to drippings. Add garlic and sauté 30 seconds. Stir in juice, soy sauce and zest. Boil, stirring frequently, for 2 minutes or until sauce thickens to a syrup. Pour sauce over scallops and serve.

Serves: 4

Mary Hutchinson

FAST AND EASY SCALLOPED SCALLOPS

½-¾ cup homemade mayonnaise made with lemon juice (or store-bought with lemon juice added)	Salt to taste
	2 pounds small bay scallops, or halved sea scallops
3-4 grinds black pepper	Cracker meal or plain bread crumbs
¼ teaspoon shallot powder, or ½ teaspoon minced shallots	Butter

Mix mayonnaise, pepper, shallot powder, salt and scallops, using just enough mayonnaise to moisten scallops well. Spoon scallop mixture into greased scallop shells or small au gratin dishes. Top with cracker meal and dot with butter. Broil 5 to 8 minutes under a hot broiler until browned.

Serves: 6 appetizers, 4 entrées

Lucy Wampler

GINGERED SHRIMP

1½ pounds freshly cooked, peeled
    and deveined with tails intact
    large shrimp
¼ cup soy sauce
2   teaspoons chopped ginger

¼ cup distilled vinegar
2   tablespoons sugar
2   tablespoons sake
1½ teaspoons salt
3   tablespoons thinly sliced scallions

Place shrimp in a glass or plastic container. Bring soy sauce to a boil over high heat in a 1-quart saucepan. Stir in ginger and reduce heat to medium. Simmer, uncovered, for 5 minutes or until liquid is reduced by half. Stir in vinegar, sugar, sake and salt. Pour mixture over shrimp. Cover and refrigerate several hours.

To serve, remove shrimp from marinade with a slotted spoon and arrange on a serving plate; discard marinade. Sprinkle with scallions.

Katie Preston

COCONUT LIME SHRIMP
WITH PEANUT SAUCE

1   cup chopped fresh basil
½ cup canned unsweetened
    coconut milk
2   tablespoons chopped garlic
1½ tablespoons fresh lime juice
1   tablespoon minced ginger

2   teaspoons soy sauce
2   teaspoons fish sauce
2   teaspoons light brown sugar
20 raw large shrimp, peeled and
    deveined

Combine all ingredients except shrimp in a food processor. Blend until almost smooth. Transfer mixture to a glass 9x13-inch baking dish or a large zip-top bag. Add shrimp and toss to coat. Cover or seal and marinate in refrigerator for 2 hours.

Soak bamboo skewers in water for at least 30 minutes before grilling. Thread shrimp onto skewers. Grill over high heat for 2 minutes on each side or until done. Baste with marinade while grilling. Serve with Peanut Sauce for dipping.

Peanut Sauce

⅓ cup creamy peanut butter
¼ cup canned low-salt chicken broth
2   tablespoons canned unsweetened
    coconut milk

1   teaspoon fresh lime juice
1   teaspoon soy sauce
1   teaspoon fish sauce
1   teaspoon hot pepper sauce

Combine all sauce ingredients in a food processor and blend until smooth. Cover and refrigerate, but bring to room temperature before serving.

Virginia Lueders

SHRIMP AND SCALLOP SAUTÉ
WITH GINGER CREAM SAUCE

12	ounces shrimp, peeled and deveined	4	ounces white wine, such as dry vermouth
12	ounces scallops	3	cups whipping cream
	Flour for dusting	1	teaspoon sugar
	Butter and oil for sautéing		Salt and white pepper to taste
2	tablespoons finely chopped ginger	2	tablespoons chopped fresh parsley (rinse after chopping, then squeeze dry in a cheesecloth)
½	teaspoon chopped garlic		

Dust shrimp and scallops in flour. Sauté seafood over medium heat in a mixture of butter and oil. (Oil will prevent butter from burning, or use clarified butter.) Continue cooking until very lightly browned. Add ginger and garlic and sauté until garlic starts to brown. Deglaze pan with wine and cook to reduce liquid. Add cream and cook to reduce again. Add sugar and salt and pepper. Toss with parsley. Serve over rice or angel hair pasta or pasta of your choice.

A bunch of chopped fresh chives can be substituted for the ginger.

Serves: 4

Fred Martin
Owner/Chef
Uncle Freddie's Hometown Grille

HERBED SHRIMP IN BEER

2	pounds peeled raw shrimp	2	tablespoons chopped fresh cilantro
1½	cups beer		
2	cloves garlic, minced	1½	teaspoons seasoned salt
½	cup chopped scallions	½	teaspoon black pepper

Combine all ingredients in a bowl. Cover and refrigerate 8 hours or overnight, stirring occasionally. Drain, reserving marinade. Thread shrimp onto skewers. Grill 2 minutes per side or until cooked, basting occasionally with reserved marinade. Or, broil about 4 inches from heat source until done. Marinade can be boiled and served on the side for a dipping sauce.

Serves: 4 to 6

Colleen Hynes

CAJUN LEMON SHRIMP

1 large sweet onion, sliced into thin rings	6 cloves garlic, minced
1 cup chopped red bell peppers	1-3 teaspoons Cajun seasoning
3 tablespoons olive oil	½ teaspoon salt
⅔ cup water	2 pounds raw medium shrimp, peeled and deveined
2 teaspoons lemon zest	2 tablespoons cornstarch
¼ cup fresh lemon juice	¼ cup cold water

Sauté onions and bell peppers in a large skillet over medium heat until just tender. Stir in ⅔ cup water, lemon zest and juice, garlic, Cajun seasoning and salt. Add shrimp and cook and stir until shrimp turn pink. Combine cornstarch with ¼ cup cold water in a small jar and shake until smooth. Add cornstarch mixture to skillet and cook 1 minute or until thickened. Serve over hot white rice, if desired.

Serves: 8

Kevin Henderson

CAJUN SEAFOOD PASTA

1 pound dry fettuccine pasta	1 cup chopped scallions
2 cups heavy whipping cream	1 cup chopped fresh parsley
1 tablespoon chopped fresh basil	½ pound raw shrimp, peeled and deveined
1 tablespoon chopped fresh thyme	
2 teaspoons salt	½ pound scallops
2 teaspoons black pepper	½ cup shredded Swiss cheese
1 teaspoon white pepper	½ cup Parmesan cheese
1½ teaspoons dried red pepper flakes	

Cook pasta in a large pot of boiling salted water until al dente; drain.

Meanwhile, pour cream into a large skillet. Cook over medium heat, stirring constantly, until just boiling. Reduce heat and add basil, thyme, salt, both peppers, pepper flakes, scallions and parsley. Simmer 7 to 8 minutes or until thickened. Stir in shrimp and scallops and cook until shrimp is no longer transparent. Stir in cheeses and blend well. Serve sauce over drained pasta.

Serves: 6

Janie Rust

FLORIBBEAN SHRIMP

¼	cup coconut flakes	1½	cups unsweetened coconut milk
¼	cup cashews	3	tablespoons orange marmalade
16-20	raw large shrimp, peeled and deveined		Salt and pepper to taste
1	tablespoon olive oil	1	cup peeled and diced fresh orange
2	tablespoons unsalted butter	1	cup peeled and diced fresh
2	cloves garlic, finely chopped		maetngo
4	teaspoons finely chopped ginger	1	cup peeled and diced fresh pineapple
¼	cup chopped shallots		
¼	teaspoon cayenne pepper	¼	cup fresh cilantro

Toast coconut and cashews in a dry skillet over low heat, browning slowly and stirring often; set aside to cool.

Wash shrimp and pat dry. Heat olive oil in a skillet. Add shrimp and cook 1 minute on each side or until browned on both sides; drain and set aside. In a separate skillet, heat butter until melted. Add garlic, ginger and shallots and sauté 2 minutes or until transparent. Add cayenne pepper, coconut milk and marmalade. Season with salt and pepper. Stir in orange, mango, pineapple and shrimp and cook 5 to 7 minutes. Transfer to a serving platter and garnish with coconut and cashews. Sprinkle cilantro on top. Serve with rice.

Serves: 4

Kristan Altimus

RED CURRY SHRIMP

1	tablespoon red curry paste	1¼	pounds raw large shrimp, peeled and deveined
1	(13½-ounce) can unsweetened coconut milk	⅓	cup chopped fresh cilantro
1	(8-ounce) bottle clam juice		Salt and pepper to taste

Stir red curry paste in a large skillet over medium heat for about 1 minute. Add coconut milk and clam juice and bring to a boil, whisking until paste dissolves. Boil 7 minutes or until sauce is thick enough to coat a spoon, stirring occasionally. Add shrimp and cook 4 minutes longer or until shrimp turn pink and opaque in the center. Stir in cilantro and season with salt and pepper. Serve with rice, if desired.

Serves: 4

Colleen Hynes

SHRIMP SCAMPI

1½ pounds shrimp, peeled and deveined	1 clove garlic, finely chopped
1 stick butter	½ teaspoon soy sauce
	½ teaspoon Worcestershire sauce

Cook shrimp about 3 minutes. Melt butter in a skillet. Add garlic and sauté until tender. Stir in soy sauce and Worcestershire sauce. Add shrimp and cook 5 minutes or until heated through. Serve with rice.

May Boland

SHRIMP AND LINGUINE

1 tablespoon olive oil	2 tablespoons whipping cream
½ pound raw jumbo shrimp, peeled and deveined	2 slices bacon, cooked and crumbled
¾ cup marinara sauce	4 ounces dry linguine pasta, cooked and drained
½ cup frozen peas	

Heat olive oil in a large skillet over medium-high heat. Add shrimp and cook until shrimp turn pink. Stir in marinara sauce and peas. Reduce heat to low and add cream and bacon. Cook, stirring frequently, until heated through. Add hot pasta and toss to coat.

Serves: 2

Cecilia Wright

 # SHRIMP CURRY

1 large onion, chopped	1 teaspoon salt
½ cup finely chopped apple	¼ teaspoon black pepper
½ cup finely chopped celery	2½-3 pounds shrimp, cooked and peeled
4 tablespoons butter	
1½ cups water	1 pint whole milk or cream
2 level tablespoons curry powder	

Sauté onion, apple and celery in butter until browned. Add water and simmer a few minutes. Stir in curry powder, salt and pepper. Add shrimp and milk and cook gently until sauce thickens. Serve on a bed of rice.

Frances M. Austin

SUMMERTIME SHRIMP AND PENNE PASTA

1	pound raw medium shrimp, peeled and deveined	⅔	cup red wine vinegar
6	ounces fresh snow peas	¼	cup chopped fresh parsley
1	pound penne pasta, or pasta of choice, cooked and drained	1	teaspoon dried oregano
		1½	teaspoons dried basil
1	pint cherry tomatoes, halved	½	teaspoon garlic salt
6	scallions with tops, chopped	½	teaspoon freshly ground black pepper
⅔	cup olive oil		

Cook shrimp in boiling water for 3 to 5 minutes or until shrimp turn pink; drain, rinse with cold water to stop cooking and drain again. Meanwhile, fill a small saucepan with water and bring to a boil. Stir in snow peas and cook 1 minute. Drain and rinse with cold water to cool; pat dry. Combine shrimp, snow peas, pasta, tomatoes and scallions in a large bowl. In a separate bowl or a jar, combine olive oil, vinegar, parsley, oregano, basil, garlic, salt and pepper. Mix well and pour over shrimp mixture. Toss until mixed. Refrigerate until ready to serve.

Patty Henderson

THAI SHRIMP

1	medium onion, chopped	¼	cup chunky peanut butter
1	(8-ounce) package fresh portobella mushrooms, sliced	1	tablespoon ground ginger
		3	tablespoons cornstarch
	Olive oil	3	tablespoons cold water
1	(16-ounce) jar salsa	2	pounds cooked shrimp, peeled, deveined and tails removed
¼	cup honey		
¼	cup soy sauce	4	cups cooked rice
¼	cup Dijon mustard		

Sauté onions and mushrooms in a skillet in olive oil until tender; set aside. In a saucepan, bring salsa, honey, soy sauce, mustard, peanut butter and ginger to a slow boil, stirring occasionally. Reduce heat. Dissolve cornstarch in cold water and stir into sauce. Cook until thickened. Gently stir in sautéed vegetables and shrimp. Simmer 2 minutes. Serve over rice.

Serves: 4 to 6

Mary Hutchinson

BROILED SCAMPI MAISON

3 shallots, minced
4 cloves garlic, minced
4 sticks butter
1 tablespoon Worcestershire sauce
½ cup lemon juice
1 cup sherry

1 cup prepared mustard
Salt and pepper to taste
2 pounds raw large shrimp
½ cup oil
Chopped fresh parsley

Sauté shallots and garlic in butter. Add Worcestershire sauce, lemon juice, sherry and mustard. Boil 5 minutes, stirring occasionally. Season with salt and pepper. Split and devein shrimp, leaving shell with tail intact. Arrange shrimp on a broiler-proof pan and brush with oil. Broil 5 minutes. Arrange shrimp on a serving platter and cover with butter sauce. Sprinkle with parsley.

Chef John W. Donahue
Plaza Café

CREAMED GRITS WITH SAUTÉED SHRIMP

2 tablespoons olive oil, divided
1 sweet onion, sliced, such as
    Vidalia, Maui or Florida Sweet
Salt and pepper to taste
1¼ cups whole milk
½ cup quick-cooking white grits
½ cup whipping cream
4 tablespoons butter, divided

24 raw large shrimp, peeled and
    deveined
¼ cup lager beer
3 tablespoons fresh lemon juice
6 cloves garlic, chopped
4 plum tomatoes, seeded and
    chopped
2 teaspoons chopped fresh thyme

Heat 1 tablespoon olive oil in a medium skillet over medium-high heat. Add onion and sauté until golden. Season with salt and pepper; set aside. Combine milk and grits in a medium saucepan. Bring to a boil, whisking constantly. Reduce heat and simmer 5 minutes or until grits are tender, stirring frequently. Stir in cream and 2 tablespoons butter until melted. Season with salt and pepper.

Meanwhile, heat remaining 1 tablespoon olive oil in a skillet over medium-high heat. Add shrimp and sauté 1 minute. Add beer, lemon juice and garlic. Simmer 2 minutes or until shrimp are opaque in the center and the sauce is reduced. Mix in tomatoes, thyme and remaining 2 tablespoons butter. Season with salt and pepper. To serve, divide grits among 4 serving plates. Top with onions, then shrimp and sauce.

Serves: 4

Brenda Matthews

CHEESE AND SHRIMP STUFFED ROASTED POBLANOS WITH RED BELL PEPPER SAUCE

8	large poblano chiles	¼	cup chopped red bell peppers
½	pound peeled and deveined cooked shrimp, chopped	2	tablespoons chopped shallots
⅔	cup goat cheese, softened	2	tablespoons chopped fresh cilantro
½	cup shredded Panela or Monterey Jack cheese	2	tablespoons chopped fresh basil
			Salt and pepper to taste
			Basil leaves for garnish

Preheat oven to 350 degrees.

Char poblanos over a gas flame or in a broiler until blackened on all sides. Enclose chiles in a paper bag and let stand 10 minutes. Peel chiles. Carefully cut a slit in chiles along 1 side. Remove seeds, leaving stem attached.

Mix shrimp, both cheeses, bell peppers, shallots, cilantro and basil in a medium bowl. Season with salt and pepper. Fill mixture, dividing equally, into chiles. Pull up sides of chiles to enclose filling. Place stuffed chiles on a baking sheet. Bake, uncovered, for 15 minutes or until heated through and cheese is melted.

To serve, spoon 3 tablespoons Red Bell Pepper Sauce onto each plate. Place a chile on each plate and spoon more sauce over the top. Garnish with basil leaves.

Red Bell Pepper Sauce

2	large red bell peppers	1	jalapeño chile pepper, seeded and minced
1	tablespoon olive oil		
¼	cup chopped shallots	1	cup low-salt chicken broth
2	cloves garlic, minced		Salt and pepper

Char and peel bell peppers the same way as poblano chiles. Chop peppers. Heat oil in a medium skillet over medium heat. Add shallots, garlic and jalapeño and sauté 5 minutes or until shallots are tender; cool slightly. Transfer mixture to a blender. Add chopped bell peppers and broth. Purée until smooth. Season to taste with salt and pepper.

Kristen Gray

Our planet is a gambler's heaven. Everyone has won. Never say that you're unlucky. The mathematical odds for any particular person to be born—or for any other living creature to be ushered into the miracle of life, are incalculable. Even for one generation.

~ Ernest Lyons

SPICY SHRIMP WITH SOBA NOODLES

Dressing

¼	cup rice vinegar	1	teaspoon sugar
¼	cup soy sauce	2	tablespoons toasted sesame seeds
2	tablespoons sake	1	jalapeño pepper, seeded and
2	tablespoons fresh lemon juice		minced
2	tablespoons fresh orange juice	1	tablespoon minced fresh ginger
¼	cup oil	½	teaspoon minced garlic
1	tablespoon sesame oil		

Salad

8	ounces dry soba noodles, or your favorite Oriental noodles	¼	cup chopped fresh basil
		1	pound large shrimp or prawns
½	cup bean sprouts	3	tablespoons oil, divided
½	cup julienned carrots	1	tablespoon dried red pepper
¼	cup chopped fresh cilantro	¾	cup snow peas

Whisk together all dressing ingredients and let stand at least 30 minutes. Dressing may be made 1 day ahead and kept covered in the refrigerator. Return to room temperature before adding to salad.

For salad, cook noodles until al dente in boiling salted water; drain in a colander, rinse with cool water and drain well. Transfer noodles to a large bowl and toss with bean sprouts, carrots, cilantro and basil. In a separate bowl, toss shrimp with 2 tablespoons oil and dried pepper. Heat remaining 1 tablespoon oil in a skillet until hot. Cook shrimp and snow peas in oil until just cooked through and shrimp are opaque. Toss noodle mixture well with dressing. Top with shrimp and snow peas.

Sarah Heard

SHRIMP HUNGARIAN

3	pounds shrimp	½	cup chile sauce
1	onion, chopped	1	pint whipping cream
4	tablespoons butter		Salt and pepper to taste

Cook shrimp in boiling water for 10 minutes; drain, peel and devein. Sauté onion slowly in butter. Add chile sauce and cream. Heat thoroughly; do not boil. Mix in shrimp. Season with salt and pepper. Serve over rice, brown rice is best.

Jean Taylor

CREAMY SEAFOOD AND SPINACH PASTA

8	ounces dry pasta, such as rigatoni	¼	cup white wine or chicken broth
1	tablespoon olive oil	1	(16-ounce) jar Alfredo pasta sauce
1	small onion, chopped	¼	cup water
⅓	cup oil-packed sun-dried tomatoes, patted dry, thinly sliced	¼	teaspoon cracked black pepper
		½	pound shrimp
		½	pound scallops
1	large clove garlic, minced	1	(6-ounce) package fresh spinach

Cook pasta according to package directions; drain and return to pot.

Meanwhile, heat olive oil in a large skillet over medium-high heat. Add onions, tomatoes and garlic. Cook and stir 2 to 3 minutes or until just tender. Stir in wine and bring to a boil. Stir in Alfredo sauce, ¼ cup water and pepper. Simmer, stirring occasionally, for 4 minutes or until hot. Add shrimp and scallops and cook, stirring occasionally, until seafood is cooked through, shrimp are pink and scallops are opaque. Stir in spinach. Stir seafood sauce into drained pasta and serve.

Two cups cooked and cubed chicken can be substituted for the seafood.

Serves: 4

Janel Weigt

DON ALLYN'S BAKED STUFFED SHRIMP

2	pounds raw jumbo shrimp, peeled with tails intact	1	tablespoon lemon juice
		½	cup finely shredded cooked crabmeat
1	medium onion, finely chopped		
3	cloves garlic, minced	1½	cups plain bread crumbs
¼	cup finely chopped celery	1	egg, lightly beaten
2	tablespoons butter		

Butterfly shrimp and place on a greased baking sheet; set aside. Sauté onion, garlic and celery in butter for 1 to 2 minutes. Stir in lemon juice and cook 2 minutes longer. Remove pan from heat. Blend in crabmeat, bread crumbs and egg. Spoon equal amounts of stuffing mixture onto each butterflied shrimp. Broil shrimp 5 inches from heat source for 5 to 6 minutes or until browned.

Don Allyn

Vegetables and Side Dishes

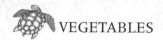

DILLED ASPARAGUS

1	pound fresh asparagus	1	tablespoon chopped fresh parsley
¼	cup red wine vinegar	2	teaspoons fresh dill, or ¾ teaspoon
¼	cup olive oil		dried
1	tablespoon sugar	2	teaspoons minced onion
½	teaspoon salt	1	(2-ounce) jar pimiento, drained
¼	teaspoon black pepper		and chopped

Cook asparagus until just tender. Rinse under cool water; drain on paper towel. Combine vinegar, oil, sugar, salt, pepper, parsley, dill, onion and pimiento and stir well. Lay asparagus in a non-metal container and pour dressing mixture over top. Cover container and chill at least 8 hours, stirring occasionally. Serve at room temperature.

Patty Henderson

CROCKPOT BEANS

1	pound ground beef, browned, crumbled and drained	1	(16-ounce) can black-eyed peas, drained
¾	pound bacon, cooked, drained and crumbled	1	cup brown sugar
2	(28-ounce) cans quality baked beans	1	large onion, chopped
		1	cup ketchup
1	(16-ounce) can kidney beans, drained	3	tablespoons white vinegar
		1	tablespoon liquid smoke
			Dash of black pepper

Combine all ingredients in a crockpot. Simmer on low for 8 hours.

Serves: 4

Demma Bailey

My Florida is surf casting from the beach with no one in sight a mile each way.

~ Ernest Lyons

BAKED BEANS

1	pound bacon	2	tablespoons molasses
3	large onions, chopped	2	(1-pound, 12-ounce) cans baked
¾	cup cider vinegar		beans
1	cup brown sugar	2	(15-ounce) cans butter beans
1½	teaspoons dry mustard	2	(15-ounce) cans kidney beans

Preheat oven to 350 degrees.

Cook bacon in a skillet; remove bacon, reserving all or at least half of bacon grease in pan. Add onions to skillet and cook until clear. Add vinegar, sugar, mustard and molasses to onions. Simmer about 20 minutes. Combine all beans in a large casserole dish. Pour onion mixture over beans and mix thoroughly. Crumble bacon over top and mix in. Bake 1 hour or until heated through.

Serves: 10 to 12

Jean Jacobs

BROCCOLI CASSEROLE

2	(10-ounce) packages frozen chopped broccoli	¼	teaspoon salt Dash of black pepper
2	tablespoons butter	1	cup milk
2	tablespoons all-purpose flour	1	(3-ounce) package cream cheese

Topping
½	cup torn sliced American cheese	1	cup soft bread crumbs
2	tablespoons butter, melted		

Preheat oven to 350 degrees.

Cook broccoli in microwave according to package directions; drain.

In a saucepan, melt 2 tablespoons butter. Blend in flour, salt and pepper. Add milk and cook and stir until bubbly. Reduce heat and blend in cream cheese until smooth. Remove sauce from heat and mix lightly with broccoli. Transfer to a 1½-quart casserole dish.

Top casserole with cheese. Toss melted butter with bread crumbs and sprinkle over cheese. Bake 40 to 45 minutes.

Serves: 6

Patricia Florio

BROCCOLI CORN CASSEROLE

2	(15-ounce) cans quality cream-style corn	1	tablespoon dried onion
2	(10-ounce) packages frozen chopped broccoli, thawed and drained	1	cup fine cracker crumbs, divided
		1	stick butter, melted, divided
		1	teaspoon salt
2	eggs, beaten	¼	teaspoon black pepper

Preheat oven to 350 degrees.

Combine corn, broccoli, eggs, onion, ½ cup cracker crumbs, ¼ cup butter, salt and pepper. Pour mixture into a lightly greased 2-quart casserole dish. Sprinkle remaining ½ cup cracker crumbs on top and drizzle with remaining ¼ cup butter. Bake 45 minutes or until brown and bubbly.

Serves: 6 to 8

Mary Jo Boman

CHEDDAR CABBAGE WEDGES

1	medium head cabbage (about 3 pounds)	½	teaspoon salt
		⅛	teaspoon black pepper
½	cup chopped green bell pepper	2	cups milk
¼	cup chopped onion	¾	cup shredded Cheddar cheese
4	tablespoons butter or margarine	½	cup mayonnaise
¼	cup flour	3	tablespoons bottled chili sauce

Preheat oven to 375 degrees.

Cut cabbage into 8 wedges, leaving a portion of the core on each wedge. Steam wedges in boiling salted water in a large kettle for 10 to 15 minutes; drain. Cut away core and place wedges in a greased 3-quart baking dish.

In a medium saucepan, sauté bell peppers and onions in butter until tender. Stir in flour, salt and pepper and cook until bubbly. Gradually add milk and cook and stir until thickened. Pour sauce over cabbage. Bake, uncovered, for 15 minutes. In a small bowl, combine cheese, mayonnaise and chili sauce. Spoon mixture over cabbage. Bake 5 minutes longer.

Serves: 4 to 6

Marie Carlton

BRAISED RED CABBAGE

3	tablespoons unsalted butter	1	teaspoon salt
1	medium head red cabbage (about 2 pounds), very thinly sliced	2	tablespoons brown sugar
		3	tablespoons red wine vinegar
		¼	teaspoon white pepper
1	small red onion, chopped		

Melt butter in a large sauté pan or Dutch oven over medium-high heat. Add cabbage and cook, stirring or turning with tongs, for 5 minutes or until cabbage wilts. Mix in onions and salt and cook about 5 minutes longer, stirring occasionally. Add brown sugar and vinegar and reduce heat to medium-low. Cover and continue to cook, stirring or turning occasionally, for 15 to 20 minutes or until cabbage is very tender and almost all of the liquid has evaporated. Taste and adjust sugar, salt or vinegar as needed. Stir in pepper and remove from heat.

Serves: 6

This dish may be prepared at least one day in advance and reheated over medium-low heat when ready to serve.

Don Sweat

COPPER PENNY SALAD

2	pounds sliced carrots	½	cup salad oil
2	medium onions, sliced into rings and separated	1	(10¾-ounce) can condensed tomato soup, undiluted
1	large green bell pepper, cut into pieces	1	teaspoon Worcestershire sauce
		1	tablespoon prepared mustard
¾	cup sugar		Salt and pepper to taste
⅔	cup vinegar		

Cook carrots in salted water until tender; drain. Combine carrots, onions and bell peppers in a large bowl.

Prepare a dressing by heating sugar and vinegar in a saucepan until sugar dissolves. Add oil, soup, Worcestershire sauce, mustard and salt and pepper. Let stand until cool. Mix dressing to blend and pour over vegetables. Marinate overnight. Salad will keep 2 weeks.

Lynn Siegel

HORSERADISH CARROTS

8 carrots, sliced lengthwise	1-2 tablespoons horseradish
¾ cup mayonnaise	1 teaspoon chopped fresh parsley
½ cup carrot juice	Buttered bread crumbs
1 tablespoon chopped onions	

Preheat oven to 350 degrees.

Cook carrots until tender. Place carrots in a greased flat casserole dish. Blend mayonnaise, carrot juice, onions, horseradish and parsley. Pour mixture over carrots. Top with buttered bread crumbs. Bake 15 minutes.

Mary Louise Smith

 # LEMON-ORANGE CARROTS

2 cups sliced fresh carrots	4 teaspoons lemon juice
⅓ cup orange marmalade	2 tablespoons butter or margarine

Cook carrots in a small amount of water in a saucepan until tender, boiling off all the liquid. Add marmalade, lemon juice and butter. Stir until carrots are evenly coated. Serve warm.

Serves: 4

Cathy Maddalena

CAULIFLOWER WITH PARSLEY MUSTARD DRESSING

2 cloves garlic, peeled	1 head cauliflower, cut into florets
2 tablespoons red wine vinegar	1 large red bell pepper, cut into
1 teaspoon Dijon mustard	slivers
1 teaspoon extra virgin olive oil	2 tablespoons chopped fresh parsley

Blanch garlic cloves in boiling water in a small saucepan for 2 minutes; drain. When cool, mince garlic and transfer to a mixing bowl. Add vinegar and mustard and mix well. Whisk in oil and mix well. In a covered steamer, steam cauliflower 3 to 5 minutes or until crisp-tender. Add steamed cauliflower, bell pepper and parsley to mixing bowl with garlic mixture. Mix well. Cover and refrigerate until serving.

Paul Davis

GRAMMY'S BAKED CORN

3   eggs, beaten
2   tablespoons flour
2   tablespoons sugar
1   cup milk

2   (15-ounce) cans cream-style corn
     Salt to taste
     Pats of butter

Preheat oven to 350 degrees.

Mix eggs, flour, sugar and milk. Add corn and salt. Pour mixture into a casserole dish. Top with pats of butter. Bake 60 minutes.

If doubling recipe, use 1 ½ cups milk.

Jill Roberts

BAKED CORN PUDDING

1   (15-ounce) can cream-style corn
1   (15-ounce) can whole kernel corn,
     drained
1   (8-ounce) container sour cream
1   stick butter, melted

1   (7-ounce) box corn muffin mix
2   eggs, slightly beaten
¾   cup shredded Cheddar cheese
1   (4-ounce) can chopped green
     chiles, drained

Preheat oven to 350 degrees.

Combine all ingredients in a large bowl. Pour mixture into a greased 9x13-inch pan. Bake 60 minutes.

Serves: 6 to 8

Elaine Clark

CORN OYSTERS

3   ears corn
1   cup finely crushed saltine cracker
     crumbs (30 crackers)
2   eggs

⅓   cup milk
⅓   teaspoon black pepper
2   tablespoons vegetable oil
     Hot pepper sauce

Cut raw kernels from ears of corn to yield 1 ½ cups. Mix corn kernels with cracker crumbs, eggs, milk and pepper in a bowl. Heat oil in a large skillet over medium heat. Drop corn mixture into skillet by heaping tablespoons; do not overcrowd skillet. Cook 2 minutes on each side or until browned. Repeat with remaining mixture. Serve with hot sauce.

Anna Taylor

PASTEL DE ELOTE (MEXICAN CORN PIE)

3	eggs	4	ounces Monterey Jack cheese, cut into ½-inch cubes
1	(8¾-ounce) can cream-style corn (¾ cup)	4	ounces sharp Cheddar cheese, cut into ½-inch cubes
1	(10-ounce) package frozen corn, thawed and drained	1	(4-ounce) can chopped mild green chiles
1	stick butter, melted	½	teaspoon salt
½	cup yellow cornmeal	⅛	teaspoon Worcestershire sauce
1	cup sour cream		

Preheat oven to 350 degrees.

Beat eggs in a large bowl. Add both corns, butter, cornmeal, sour cream, both cheeses, chiles, salt and Worcestershire sauce. Stir until thoroughly mixed. Pour into a well greased 10-inch pie plate. Bake, uncovered, for 60 minutes.

Serves: 8 for a luncheon or as a side dish

Lloyd Wescoat

Pie may be baked and stored in refrigerator for up to 3 days. Reheat at 350 degrees for about 20 minutes. May also be frozen after baking and kept for up to 3 months. Thaw and reheat at 350 degrees for about 20 minutes.

If doubling recipe, use a large rectangular glass dish.

GREEN BEAN AND MOZZARELLA CHEESE SALAD

2	cups fresh green beans, cooked and drained	1	cup shredded non-fat mozzarella cheese
6	plum tomatoes, chopped	¼	cup chopped fresh basil
		⅓	cup Italian dressing

Combine beans, tomatoes, cheese and basil in a large bowl. Pour dressing over top. Marinate at least 1 hour in refrigerator.

Serves: 8

Tippy Greenleaf

JALAPEÑO-CORN CASSEROLE

1 cup dry long-grain rice
1 medium onion, chopped
1 medium-size green bell pepper, chopped
1 cup chopped celery
1 stick butter or margarine
1-2 large jalapeño peppers, seeded and chopped

2 (15-ounce) cans cream-style corn
1½ cups shredded mild Cheddar cheese
1 tablespoon sugar
Green pepper rings, cherry tomatoes and chopped fresh parsley for garnish

Preheat oven to 350 degrees.

Cook rice according to package directions and set aside in a large mixing bowl.

Sauté onion, bell pepper and celery in butter in a large skillet until tender. Add sautéed vegetables to reserved rice. Stir in jalapeño peppers, corn, cheese and sugar and mix well. Spoon corn mixture into a lightly greased 2-quart casserole. Bake 40 to 45 minutes or until thoroughly heated. Garnish, if desired.

Serves: 8

Shannon Bothwell

SESAME GREEN BEANS

1½ pounds fresh green beans
3-4 chicken bouillon cubes
1 tablespoon sesame oil

¼ cup soy sauce
½ teaspoon ground ginger
1 tablespoon toasted sesame seeds

Wash green beans in a large bowl filled with cold water and ice cubes. Trim off ends and snap beans in half. Fill a large pot half full with water. Bring to a boil over high heat. Add bouillon cubes. Add beans, reduce heat to medium-high and cook about 10 minutes, stirring occasionally. When done, turn off heat and drain beans in a colander. Return empty pot to same burner. Add sesame oil, soy sauce and ginger to pot and mix. Add drained beans and mix to thoroughly coat beans. Top with toasted sesame seeds.

Serves: 4 to 6

To toast sesame seeds, place a small saucepan over medium heat. Add sesame seeds. Gently move pan over heat for a few minutes or until seeds are golden brown.

Michelle Wright

FRENCH STRING BEANS

2   (16-ounce) cans French-cut green
     beans, undrained
3   cloves garlic, minced
2   tablespoons bacon drippings
1   (10¾-ounce) can condensed
     cream of mushroom soup
1   stick butter, divided

1   tablespoon flour
1   teaspoon paprika
1   teaspoon chili powder
1   cup shredded sharp Cheddar
     cheese
1   cup cracker crumbs

Preheat oven to 350 degrees.

Combine undrained beans, garlic and bacon drippings in a saucepan. Boil gently for 30 minutes. Drain, reserving juice. Transfer beans to a 2-quart casserole. Pour condensed soup over beans. Melt 4 tablespoons butter in saucepan. Stir flour, paprika and chili powder into melted butter. Add reserved cooking juice and cheese. Pour mixture over beans. Sprinkle crumbs on top and dot with remaining 4 tablespoons butter. Bake 30 minutes or until bubbly.

Lillie Davis

LENTILS WITH GARLIC AND HERBS

2¼ cups chicken broth, divided
2   cups water
1   cup dried lentils, rinsed and
     drained
2   bay leaves
4   teaspoons chopped fresh
     rosemary, or 2 teaspoons dried

4   medium cloves garlic, pressed
½   medium onion, chopped (1 cup)
2   teaspoons cider vinegar
2   teaspoons olive oil
     Salt and pepper to taste

Bring 2 cups broth and water to a boil in a large pot. When boiling rapidly, pour lentils into pot slowly so water continues to boil. Add bay leaves, rosemary and garlic. Reduce heat slightly and simmer 20 minutes.

Meanwhile, heat remaining ¼ cup broth in a small skillet. Add onions and cover. Cook until onions are transparent and golden, but not brown, adding more broth if needed to prevent onions from burning. When lentils are tender, add onions and vinegar to lentils. Cook over high heat, uncovered, for 10 minutes or until liquid evaporates. Stir in oil and season with salt and pepper.

Dagmar Bothwell

OKRA SUPREME

2 cups sliced okra
1 large onion, chopped
½ cup chopped green bell pepper
1 cup sliced celery
1 cup corn kernels (4 to 5 ears)
3 large tomatoes, peeled and chopped
¾ cup water
2 cloves garlic, minced

1 teaspoon seasoned salt
2 tablespoons chopped fresh parsley
1 bay leaf
2 tablespoons Worcestershire sauce
2 tablespoons soy sauce
½ teaspoon black pepper
3 tablespoons bacon drippings
Salt if needed

Combine all ingredients in a large saucepan. Cook over medium heat for 15 to 20 minutes. Adjust seasonings to taste. Remove bay leaf before serving. Serve over rice.

Use fresh vegetables, if possible.

This is a recipe my mother made up to use an abundance of vegetables and has become one of our favorites. It was also printed in a national cookbook, chosen from over 12,000 entries.

Ann T. Combs

CHEESE AND ONION PIE

1 cup crushed saltine crackers
2 sticks butter, melted, divided
3 cups thinly sliced sweet onions
8 ounces imported Swiss cheese, shredded

1 tablespoon flour
1 teaspoon salt
Dash of cayenne pepper
3 eggs, well beaten
1 cup milk, scalded

Preheat oven to 325 degrees.

Combine cracker crumbs and 4 tablespoons melted butter and press into a 9-inch pie pan. Sauté onions in remaining 1½ sticks butter. Place onions on crust. Combine cheese, flour, salt and cayenne pepper in a bowl. Add eggs and milk and mix well. Pour mixture over onions. Bake 40 minutes. Serve hot or at room temperature.

Serves: 6 to 8

Joan Giesler

ONION KUCHEN

2	medium onions, sliced and separated into rings	1	egg, beaten
3	tablespoons butter	1	(8-ounce) container sour cream
2	(4½-ounce) cans refrigerated biscuits	¼	teaspoon salt
		1	teaspoon poppy seeds

Preheat oven to 375 degrees.

Sauté onions in butter for 5 minutes or until tender; set aside. Separate biscuits and arrange in the bottom of a lightly greased 8-inch round pan. Press biscuits together to cover bottom of pan. Bake 5 minutes. Spoon onions over biscuits; set aside. Combine egg, sour cream and salt and stir well. Pour mixture over onions and sprinkle with poppy seeds. Bake 30 minutes or until set. Let dish stand 5 minutes before serving.

Serves: 4 to 6

Sharyon Daigneau

SPINACH PIE

2	(10-ounce) packages frozen chopped spinach	8	ounces mozzarella cheese, shredded
½	medium onion, chopped	½	cup grated Parmesan cheese
4	tablespoons butter	2	frozen pie crusts, thawed, divided
½	cup heavy whipping cream		Egg white or milk
3	eggs, beaten		Sesame seeds (optional)

Preheat oven to 325 to 350 degrees.

Cook spinach according to package directions; drain well. In a saucepan, sauté onions in butter. Mix in spinach and remove from heat. In a separate bowl, combine cream and eggs. Add spinach mixture to bowl. Stir cheeses into cream and spinach mixture. Pour mixture into a pie crust. Top with second pie crust. Brush egg white or milk over top crust for a glaze. Sprinkle with sesame seeds, if desired. Bake 40 minutes.

Serves: 6 to 8

Debra Bolle

TAC'S CREAMED SPINACH

1   (10-ounce) package frozen
    chopped spinach
1   large clove garlic, minced
2-3 tablespoons bacon drippings
2   tablespoons flour

1-2 tablespoons water
1   cup sour cream
    Garlic salt to taste
    Black pepper to taste

Thaw spinach and squeeze out juice, reserving juice. In a skillet, sauté garlic in bacon drippings. Add reserved spinach juice to skillet and bring to a boil. Reduce heat. Mix flour and water into skillet to make a gravy. Cook and stir until thickened. Fold in spinach, sour cream, garlic salt and pepper. Cook until heated through.

Serves: 4

Barbara Blaydon

SPINACH PIE WITH FETA

1   pastry sheet, thawed
3-4 scallions, finely chopped
1   stick butter or margarine, divided
1   (10-ounce) package frozen
    chopped spinach, cooked and
    well drained

8   ounces feta cheese, crumbled
3   eggs, beaten
½   cup cottage cheese
1   teaspoon lemon juice

Preheat oven to 350 degrees.

Cut pastry sheet in half. Roll out each half to fit in a 9x13-inch baking dish. Sauté scallions in 1 tablespoon butter. In a bowl, combine spinach, feta cheese, eggs, cottage cheese and lemon juice.

Line bottom and part way up the sides of a greased 9x13-inch baking dish with one pastry sheet half. Melt remaining butter. Brush pastry in dish with some of butter. Pour spinach mixture on top. Cover tightly with other pastry sheet half, tucking edges into the bottom sheet. Spread remaining melted butter on top and around sides. Bake about 1 hour or until golden brown.

Serves: 6

Margaret Henry

ACORN SQUASH

1 tablespoon butter or margarine
½ medium onion, coarsely chopped
(about 1 cup)
2 cups peeled and cubed acorn
squash (½-inch cubes)
½ cup raisins

1 tablespoon coarsely chopped
walnuts
3 tablespoons water
Salt and freshly ground black
pepper to taste

Melt butter in a medium saucepan. Add onions and sauté 5 minutes or until golden but not browned. Add squash and sauté 2 minutes longer. Add raisins and walnuts and sauté 5 minutes, stirring occasionally. Add water and salt and pepper. Cover and remove from heat. Let stand, covered, for 20 minutes or until ready to serve.

Dagmar Bothwell

SQUASH DELIGHT

2 (10-ounce) packages frozen
cream spinach
2 large butternut squash
2 large sweet potatoes
2 large turnips or parsnips

½ teaspoon nutmeg, or to taste
½ teaspoon ginger, or to taste
Honey
Shredded cheese (Cheddar,
provolone or Monterey Jack)

Place pouches of spinach in a large pot of boiling water. Meanwhile, cut unpeeled squash, potatoes and turnips or parsnips into ¾-inch cubes. Add cubed vegetables to pot of boiling water. Return to a rolling boil and cook 6 minutes.

Lightly rub olive oil over a large rectangular glass dish and prewarm dish. Drain vegetables and transfer to warmed dish. Mix in both pouches of spinach. Sprinkle with nutmeg and ginger and drizzle with honey. Cover with cheese. Broil 4 minutes or until cheese browns.

Patrick Hayes

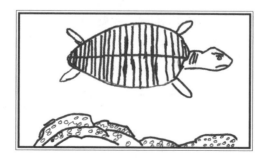

YELLOW SQUASH CASSEROLE

2-3 pounds yellow squash, sliced
Salt and pepper to taste
1 stick butter or margarine, melted
1 cup sour cream
1 (10¾-ounce) can condensed
  cream of chicken soup

2 onions, finely chopped
1 (5-ounce) can sliced water
  chestnuts, drained
1 (2-ounce) jars pimientos, drained
1 (8-ounce) package herb seasoned
  stuffing mix, divided

Preheat oven to 350 degrees.

Cook squash in boiling water until tender; drain, reserving 1½ cups liquid. Season squash with salt and pepper and mash. Combine reserved cooking liquid with butter, sour cream, condensed soup, onions, water chestnuts, pimientos and half the stuffing mix. Stir in squash. Transfer mixture to a 2½-quart casserole dish. Top with remaining stuffing mix. Bake 30 minutes.

Serves: 16

Mary Louise Smith

SQUASH CASSEROLE

8 medium zucchini or yellow
  squash, cut into ¼-inch rounds
3 sausage patties
1 small onion, sliced
1 (8-ounce) package shredded
  cheese

Saltine crackers
1 (10¾-ounce) can condensed
  cream of mushroom soup
1 (5-ounce) can evaporated milk
4 tablespoons butter

Preheat oven to 350 degrees.

Cook squash in salted boiling water for 5 minutes or until crisp-tender; drain well. Meanwhile, brown sausage patties; drain and crumble. Layer squash and onion slices in a greased 3-quart baking dish. Cover with crumbled sausage and cheese. Top with whole saltine crackers. Combine condensed soup and milk and heat in a microwave for 2 minutes. Pour mixture over casserole and dot with butter. Bake 30 minutes.

Julie Clark

BAKED TOMATOES

1 slice bread, torn into pieces	1 teaspoon salt
1 (28-ounce) can tomatoes	1 teaspoon black pepper
1 cup sugar mixed with a heaping tablespoon flour	3 tablespoons butter, melted

Preheat oven to 400 degrees.

Combine all ingredients and place in a casserole dish. Bake 1 hour.

Serves: 4 to 7

Leslie Warren

LISA'S TOMATO BAKE

1 (4½-ounce, 5-count) can refrigerated biscuits (not buttermilk)	Salt and pepper to taste
	¼ cup sliced scallions, green and white parts
3-4 large tomatoes, sliced	1 cup mayonnaise
2 tablespoons chopped fresh basil	1½ cups shredded Colby-Jack cheese

Preheat oven to 425 degrees.

Separate biscuits and press into the bottom (not up the sides) of a lightly greased 9- or 10-inch pie plate. Arrange tomato slices over biscuits. Sprinkle with basil and salt and pepper. In a small bowl, mix scallions, mayonnaise and cheese. Spread mixture over tomatoes, covering slices completely. Bake 20 to 25 minutes. Remove from oven and let stand 15 minutes before cutting into wedges.

Serves: 6

Lisa Massing

FRIED TOMATOES WITH GRAVY

6	slices ripe tomatoes, stems removed		Sugar
	Bread crumbs or flour	3	tablespoons flour
4	tablespoons butter or oil	¾	teaspoon salt
		1½	cups milk

Cover tomato slices with bread crumbs or flour. Cook slices in butter until brown on bottom. Turn and sprinkle with sugar. Cook until brown on other side. Transfer to a platter, leaving 1 or 2 slices in pan. Stir flour and salt into butter and remaining tomato slices. Gradually add milk. Cook and stir until gravy is thickened. Pour gravy over tomato slices on platter.

To make fried green tomatoes, slice green tomatoes and dip in crumbs or flour. Cook in a skillet in butter or oil until brown. Sprinkle with sugar after turning.

Mary Louise Smith

BAKED TOMATO-BASIL PUDDING

3	medium tomatoes, chopped (peeling and seeding optional)	2	tablespoons chopped fresh basil
½	cup herbed croutons, divided	3	tablespoons brown sugar
1½	tablespoons butter, divided		Salt and freshly ground black pepper to taste
⅓	cup minced scallions		

Preheat oven to 350 degrees.

Mix together tomatoes and ¼ cup croutons in a medium bowl; set aside. In a blender or food processor, pulse remaining ¼ cup croutons into crumbs; set aside.

Melt 1 tablespoon butter over medium heat in a 10-inch skillet. Add scallions and basil and sauté 2 minutes or until scallions begin to wilt. Add scallion mixture to tomatoes along with brown sugar and salt and pepper. Stir to mix well. Spoon mixture into a greased 2-quart casserole dish. Wipe out skillet and return to medium heat. Melt remaining ½ tablespoon butter in skillet. Add crouton crumbs and toss to coat. Sprinkle crumbs over tomatoes. Bake 30 minutes. Turn off heat and leave pudding in oven 15 minutes longer. Serve warm.

Serves: 4

We use cherry tomatoes when we have a bumper crop.

Dorothy Dicks

241

TOMATO PIE

1 (8-ounce) can refrigerated crescent rolls	4 tomatoes, diced, or 5-6 plum tomatoes plus 1 regular tomato
1 medium onion, chopped	1 cup mayonnaise
1 green bell pepper, chopped	1 cup shredded mozzarella or Cheddar cheese

Preheat oven to 350 degrees.

Line a greased 9-inch pan with crescent roll dough; set aside. Sauté onions and peppers. Layer onion mixture and tomatoes over dough. Combine mayonnaise and cheese and spread over vegetable layers. Bake 40 to 45 minutes. Let stand 20 to 30 minutes before cutting to allow pie to set.

Serves: 4 to 6

Mary Boland

APRICOT-GLAZED YAMS

1 (29-ounce) can yams, drained	¼ teaspoon salt
1 (16-ounce) can apricot halves, undrained	¼ teaspoon cinnamon
	⅓ cup golden raisins
3 tablespoons brown sugar	3 tablespoons dry sherry
1 tablespoon cornstarch	¼ teaspoon orange zest

Preheat oven to 350 degrees.

Place yams in an 11x7-inch baking dish. Drain apricots, reserving syrup. Arrange apricots over yams. Add water to reserved syrup to equal 1 cup.

Combine brown sugar, cornstarch, salt and cinnamon in a medium saucepan. Add raisins and reserved syrup mixture and stir well. Bring to a boil over medium heat. Stir in sherry and orange zest. Pour syrup mixture over yams and apricots. Bake, uncovered, for 20 minutes, basting occasionally.

Serves: 4

Dagmar Bothwell

FLORIDA Classic FLAVORS YUCCA CON MOJO

3-4 yucca roots, peeled
1 large onion, thinly sliced
2 cloves garlic, crushed

Juice of 1 lemon
¾ cup vegetable oil

Cut yucca roots into serving size, about 6 to 8 pieces per root. Cook yucca in boiling salted water for 40 minutes or until tender; drain.

Meanwhile, prepare mojo. Combine onions, garlic and lemon juice in a heat resistant bowl. Heat oil. When oil starts to boil, pour over onion mixture. Serve mojo over hot, drained yucca.

Aida Fry

TUSCAN GRILLED VEGETABLES

Marinade
¼ cup balsamic vinegar
½ cup extra virgin olive oil
½ teaspoon oregano or herbes de Provence
1 tablespoon finely chopped garlic

¼ teaspoon coarsely crushed rosemary
Salt and coarsely ground black pepper to taste

Vegetables
1 (8- to 10-inch) zucchini, cut lengthwise into ¼-inch thick strips
2 (6-inch) yellow squash, cut lengthwise into ¼-inch thick strips
1 large red bell pepper, cut lengthwise into 2-inch wide strips

1 large green bell pepper, cut lengthwise into 2-inch wide strips
1 (8-inch) eggplant, cut lengthwise into ¼-inch thick strips

Combine all marinade ingredients in a plastic or glass bowl. Add all vegetables except eggplant to marinade and turn once. Add eggplant to mixture and press into marinade. (Eggplant is added last because it absorbs a lot of marinade.) Cover bowl with plastic wrap and let stand 15 minutes. Turn and allow vegetables to marinate 15 minutes longer. Drain vegetables. Cook on a hot barbecue or skillet grill. When vegetables get brown grill lines, reduce heat to medium and turn vegetables. Grill until second side has brown grill lines and vegetables are softened. Vegetables are best served at room temperature or slightly chilled. Arrange in a radiating star pattern on a serving platter.

Serves: 6

Noel Trachtenberg

ZUCCHINI GOAT CHEESE GRATIN

2	pounds zucchini, cut diagonally into ¼-inch slices	8	ounces goat cheese
3	tablespoons unsalted butter	½	cup heavy whipping cream
1	large onion, thinly sliced	¼	cup freshly grated Parmesan cheese
	Salt and freshly ground black pepper	4	cups dry bread crumbs

Preheat oven to 350 degrees.

Cook zucchini in boiling salted water 2 minutes or until crisp-tender; drain and pat dry. Melt butter in a skillet. Add onions and sauté until translucent. Arrange one-third of zucchini in a greased 9x13-inch baking dish. Season with salt and pepper. Spread half of onions over zucchini. Repeat layers, seasoning with salt and pepper and ending with zucchini. Crumble goat cheese into a small saucepan. Stir in cream. Cook over low heat for 3 to 4 minutes or until smooth and thick. If sauce is too thick, thin with extra cream. Pour sauce over zucchini layers. Combine Parmesan cheese and bread crumbs and sprinkle over vegetables. Bake 35 to 40 minutes.

Serves: 6

This dish can be prepared in advance and refrigerated or frozen. Bring to room temperature before baking.

Shannon Bothwell

MY FRIEND JEANNIE'S ZUCCHINI PIE

3	cups unpeeled diced zucchini	1	cup biscuit mix
1	large onion, chopped	4	eggs, beaten
½	cup grated Parmesan or Romano cheese	¼	cup chopped fresh parsley
½	cup salad oil	1	teaspoon salt
		½	teaspoon black pepper

Preheat oven to 350 degrees.

Combine all ingredients in a large bowl and mix well until zucchini is coated with batter. Transfer to a greased 9-inch pie plate or 9-inch baking dish. Bake 35 to 40 minutes or until lightly browned. Serve warm or cold.

Serves: 6

Patricia Florio

JIM SAN'S VEGETABLES
WITH RICE STICKS AND MISO SAUCE

2 packages miso mix, white or red
1⅓ cups hot water
8 ounces tofu, cut into 1-inch squares
2 tablespoons sesame oil, or more if needed
1 (14-ounce) can artichoke hearts, drained and sliced
1 medium eggplant, sliced, sweated and cut into ½-inch squares

1 medium red bell pepper, diced
3-4 scallions, diced, white and green parts
1 medium tomato, sliced or diced, or 3 plum tomatoes
8 ounces mushrooms of choice (shiitake preferred), sliced
4 nests dry rice sticks
4 ounces bean sprouts, or more if desired

Mix the miso with hot water; set aside. In a skillet, fry tofu in sesame oil until a golden crust forms on the tofu; set aside. Add more sesame oil to skillet if needed and sauté artichokes in skillet for 2 minutes. Add eggplant and sauté 1 minute. Add bell pepper, scallions, tomato and mushrooms and cook 1 minute or until vegetables are al dente. Meanwhile, bring water to a boil, then remove from heat. Add rice noodles to water and soak for 3 minutes; drain. Stir miso, tofu and bean sprouts into vegetable mixture. Sauté 1 minute. Serve over rice nests in individual pasta bowls.

Serves: 4

Jim Wilbers

ZUCCHINI CASSEROLE

4 zucchini, sliced
1 small onion, chopped
1 cup sour cream
1 cup shredded carrots
1 (10½-ounce) can condensed cream of chicken soup

1 (7-ounce) package dry stuffing mix
1 stick butter, melted
¼ cup Parmesan cheese

Preheat oven to 375 degrees.

Steam zucchini for 2 to 3 minutes. In a skillet, sauté onions until softened. In a large bowl, combine zucchini, onions, sour cream, carrots and condensed soup. Mix stuffing mix with butter; set aside. Layer half of vegetable mixture in a large, greased baking dish. Spread stuffing mixture over vegetables. Layer remaining vegetables mixture over stuffing. Sprinkle Parmesan cheese on top. Bake 25 minutes or until warm throughout.

Serves: 6 to 8

Kathy Zogran

SWEET POTATO AND BACON SALAD

2	pounds sweet potatoes, peeled and cut into 1-inch chunks	2	tablespoons apple cider vinegar
1	small apple, unpeeled and cut into ½-inch pieces	2	tablespoons Dijon mustard
⅔	cup sliced celery	1¼	teaspoons salt
½	cup white grape juice	¼	teaspoon black pepper
¼	cup olive oil	½	cup chopped walnuts
		9	slices bacon, cooked and crumbled

Cook potatoes until tender; drain and transfer to a large bowl. Add apple and celery to bowl and toss. In a separate bowl, whisk together grape juice, olive oil, vinegar, mustard, salt and pepper until blended. Pour dressing mixture over potato mixture and toss. Let stand about 30 minutes. Add walnuts and bacon just before serving.

Serves: 10 to 12

Mary Hutchinson

POTATO AND CHEESE GALETTE

1	(9- or 10-inch) pie crust	½	cup heavy whipping cream
5	small Yukon gold potatoes		Salt and pepper to taste
1	cup ricotta cheese	1	cup marinara sauce or other favorite tomato sauce
4	eggs, beaten		

Preheat oven to 350 degrees.

Roll out prepared pie crust and put in a pie pan or thaw frozen crust if already in pan. Slice potatoes paper-thin and hold in salted water until ready to use. Combine ricotta cheese, eggs, cream and salt and pepper and blend well. Alternate layers of potatoes and cheese mixture in pie crust, making a couple thin layers of potatoes topped by a thin layer of cheese mixture. Repeat until the pan is layered to the top, ending with a good layer of cheese mixture on top. Bake 45 minutes or until potatoes are tender when tested with a toothpick and the top is evenly browned. Slice and serve with marinara sauce on the top.

Serves: 4 to 6

Pat Ries

CURRIED POTATOES

1 pound new potatoes, unpeeled and halved	2 tablespoons butter or margarine
1 small onion, sliced	1 tablespoon snipped fresh parsley
1 clove garlic, minced	1 teaspoon lemon juice
¼ teaspoon curry powder	¼ teaspoon salt
	Dash of cayenne pepper

Cook potatoes and onions in lightly salted water over medium heat in a covered saucepan for 15 minutes or until potatoes are just tender; drain.

Meanwhile, cook garlic and curry powder in butter in a small saucepan for about 1 minute. Stir in parsley, lemon juice, salt and cayenne pepper. Add butter mixture to vegetables and toss gently to mix.

Serves: 4

Nancy Scott

 # DELICIOUS COMPANY POTATOES

1 (2-pound) bag frozen hash browns (cubes)	½ cup finely chopped onions
1 stick butter, melted	10 ounces Cheddar cheese, shredded
1 (10½-ounce) can condensed cream of chicken soup	1 (16-ounce) container sour cream

Preheat oven to 350 degrees.

Combine all ingredients and spread evenly in a 9x13-inch pan. Bake 35 minutes. This dish works well for barbecue or brunch.

Serves: 12 or more

For a topping, combine 4 tablespoons melted butter and 2 cups crushed corn flakes. Sprinkle over mixture before baking.

Nancy Dillard
Siboney Oleson
Carole Stemle

POTATOES WITH LEMON-BUTTER SAUCE

2 pounds small red potatoes	2 tablespoons chopped fresh chives
2 tablespoons butter or margarine	or scallions
2 tablespoons fresh lemon juice	¼ teaspoon ground nutmeg
	Salt and pepper to taste

Cut potatoes into 1-inch chunks and place in a pot of cold water to cover. Cover pot and bring to a boil. Cook 20 minutes or until tender.

Meanwhile, melt butter in a small pan or in the microwave on high for 30 seconds. Stir in lemon juice, chives, nutmeg and salt and pepper. When potatoes are done, drain and transfer to a serving bowl. Pour lemon-butter sauce over the top.

Serves: 4

Lois Andrews

FRENCH POTATO SALAD WITH BACON AND HONEY MUSTARD SAUCE

Salad

1 pound new potatoes, unpeeled	¼ cup finely diced red onions
2 tablespoons olive oil	1 cup Honey Mustard Sauce
4 ounces bacon	(recipe below)
Salt and pepper to taste	½ cup chopped fresh parsley

Preheat oven to 400 degrees.

Halve potatoes and place, cut-side down, on a baking sheet. Drizzle with olive oil. Cut bacon and drape over potatoes. Season with salt and pepper. Bake until potatoes are crisp on the outside and tender on the inside and the bacon is crisp; cool. Toss potatoes and bacon in a large bowl with onions and Honey Mustard Sauce. Sprinkle with parsley and serve at room temperature.

Honey Mustard Sauce

1 cup Hellmann's mayonnaise	¼ cup prepared honey mustard

Mix all sauce ingredients until well blended. Refrigerate until ready to use.

Karen Cotler

MASHED GARLIC POTATOES

1½ pounds potatoes, unpeeled and
    cut into 1-inch pieces
5   cloves garlic, peeled
⅓   cup sour cream
2   tablespoons milk

2   tablespoons chopped fresh
    parsley
½   teaspoon salt
⅛   teaspoon black pepper

Combine potatoes and garlic in a 2-quart saucepan. Add enough water to cover
and bring to a boil. Reduce heat and cook 8 to 10 minutes or until potatoes are
tender. Drain and transfer potatoes and garlic to a large bowl. Add sour cream,
milk, parsley, salt and pepper. Mash mixture with an electric mixer or hand masher.

Serves: 6

Kathy Walker Peterson

UNCLE BUCKS POTATO CASSEROLE

8-10 potatoes
1   (8-ounce) package cream
    cheese, softened

11 ounces sour cream
1   stick butter
2   tablespoons chopped chives

Preheat oven to 350 degrees.

Place potatoes in a large pot and add enough water to cover. Bring to a boil and
cook until just tender; drain and rinse with cold water. Peel potatoes and mash until
smooth. Mix in cream cheese, sour cream, butter and chives. Transfer to a baking
dish and refrigerate overnight. Bake 35 minutes.

Ted Houk

KENTUCKY BOURBON SWEET POTATOES

3-4 medium sweet potatoes
¾   cup sugar
1   stick margarine or butter
⅓   cup bourbon

½   teaspoon vanilla
½   cup coarsely chopped walnuts or
    pecans

Preheat oven to 350 degrees.

Cook sweet potatoes until tender. Peel potatoes and mash until smooth. Add sugar,
margarine, bourbon and vanilla. Transfer to a 1-quart baking dish. Sprinkle nuts
around outside edge of potatoes. Bake 30 minutes.

June Henderson

SWEET POTATO CASSEROLE

Casserole

4	cups cooked sweet potatoes	2	eggs
6	tablespoons margarine	1	teaspoon vanilla
½	cup sugar	¼	cup milk

Topping

¼	cup flour	1	(8-ounce) can crushed pineapple,
¼	cup sugar		undrained
1	stick margarine, softened		Chopped pecans

Preheat oven to 350 degrees.

Beat together all casserole ingredients. Spread mixture in a 9x13-inch baking dish.

For topping, combine flour, sugar, margarine and pineapple and spread over casserole. Sprinkle pecans on top. Bake 45 minutes.

Kay De Nicola

GARLIC POTATO SALAD

	K-Paul's Vegetable Magic	2	tablespoons chopped fresh
6-8	medium to large potatoes,		parsley, or more to taste
	peeled and cubed	2	tablespoons chopped chives, or
	Olive oil		more to taste
	Wine vinegar	½	cup chopped celery
¼	cup chopped onions		Lemon juice to taste
¼	cup chopped scallions		Lemon pepper to taste
4-6	garlic cloves, pressed		Prepared mustard to taste

Season a pot of gently boiling water with Vegetable Magic. Add potatoes and simmer 15 to 20 minutes or until fork tender but not falling apart; drain. Toss potatoes with olive oil and vinegar to coat. Stir in onions and scallions. Add garlic, parsley and chives. Mix well and refrigerate overnight. Before serving, add celery, lemon juice and lemon pepper. Add mustard and additional parsley, chives and Vegetable Magic to taste.

Chopped hard cooked eggs and mayonnaise may be added, but are definitely not necessary for this delicious salad.

Dan Krauer

POTATO AMANDA

2 baking potatoes, peeled and diced into large cubes
2 large onions, diced into large cubes
2-3 green bell peppers, chopped
¾ (6-ounce) can black olives, sliced
1 teaspoon dried oregano
¼ cup chopped fresh parsley
¼ cup olive oil
Salt and pepper to taste
1 cup freshly grated Asiago or Parmesan cheese

Preheat oven to 350 degrees.

Sauté potatoes, onions, bell peppers, olives, oregano and parsley in olive oil in a large skillet over medium heat until vegetables are tender. Layer half the vegetable mixture in a 1-quart casserole dish. Sprinkle half of cheese on top. Repeat layers. Bake, covered, for 30 minutes.

Eileen Geiger

SWEET POTATO CASSEROLE

Casserole
2 tablespoons cornstarch
1 cup milk, divided
1 large can yams (sweet potatoes), mashed
6 tablespoons margarine or butter
2 eggs, well beaten
1 cup sugar
Dash of cinnamon

Topping
1 cup crushed corn flakes
½ cup brown sugar
1 cup shredded coconut
1-1½ sticks margarine
½ cup chopped pecans

Preheat oven to 400 degrees.

In a large bowl, dissolve cornstarch in a small amount of the milk. Stir in remaining milk. Add mashed yams, margarine, eggs, sugar and cinnamon. Mix well and transfer to a 2-quart baking dish. Bake 15 to 20 minutes.

Remove from oven and prepare topping. Combine all topping ingredients in a saucepan. Cook over low heat until margarine melts. Spread over hot casserole. Return to oven and bake 15 to 20 minutes longer.

Pat Navaretta

COLCANNON
Classic Irish recipe.

1½ pounds potatoes, peeled	1 leek, chopped, white part only
Coarse salt	1 cup milk
1 head savoy cabbage, finely	4 tablespoons butter, divided
shredded (4 cups)	Freshly grated nutmeg to taste

Cook potatoes until tender. Mash and season with salt. Cook cabbage and leek in milk until tender. Add 2 tablespoons butter and nutmeg to taste. Fold together potatoes and cabbage mixture. Spread mixture in a square baking dish, leaving a small well in the center. Brown top under a broiler. Place remaining 2 tablespoons butter in the well. When melted, spoon some of butter over each serving.

Serves: 4

Virginia Slack

HOT OLIVE POTATO SALAD

4 cups potatoes, diced and cooked	¼ cup sliced green olives
½ cup chopped celery	½ cup mayonnaise
½ cup chopped onion	1 teaspoon garlic salt
4 ounces Swiss cheese, shredded	Salt and pepper to taste

Preheat oven to 350 degrees.

Combine all ingredients and transfer to a baking dish. Bake 45 minutes. Serve hot.

Jeanne Houk

POTATO BAKE

1 cup milk	½ green bell pepper
4 eggs	4 tablespoons margarine, softened
1 cup cubed Cheddar cheese	3-4 cups cubed potatoes
1 medium onion	Salt and pepper to taste

Preheat oven to 350 degrees.

Process milk, eggs, cheese, onion, bell pepper and margarine in a blender. Add potatoes and blend until potatoes are chopped. Season with salt and pepper. Transfer mixture to a baking dish. Bake 1 hour.

Heather Arnold

EASY BLACK BEANS AND RICE

1 medium onion, chopped
1 tablespoon oil
1 (14½-ounce) can stewed
   tomatoes, undrained

1 (15-ounce) can black beans,
   undrained
½ teaspoon dried oregano
½ teaspoon minced garlic
1½ cups dry instant brown rice

Sauté onions in oil until tender but not brown. Add tomatoes, beans, oregano and garlic. Bring to a boil. Stir in rice and return to a boil. Reduce heat to a simmer. Cover and cook 5 minutes or until rice is cooked. Remove from heat and let stand 5 minutes before serving.

Serves: 4 to 6

Judy Wakeman

KEY WEST BLACK BEANS AND RICE

2 cups canned black beans, rinsed
   and drained
2 cups cooked rice
½ cup chopped red onions
1½ cups chopped fresh cilantro

⅔ cup olive oil
⅓ cup Key lime juice
3 cloves garlic, minced
   Salt and pepper to taste

Combine beans, rice, onions and cilantro in a bowl. In a small jar, mix olive oil, lime juice and garlic. Pour oil mixture over bean mixture. Mix well and season with salt and pepper. Flavor improves if prepared a day ahead.

Serves: 4 to 6

Anna Taylor

COCONUT RICE

¾ cup canned coconut milk
1½ cups water
1 clove garlic, minced
½ teaspoon salt

1 cup dry basmati rice
2 tablespoons chopped fresh basil
3 tablespoons toasted coconut

Combine coconut milk, water, garlic and salt in a medium saucepan. Bring to a boil. Stir in rice. Reduce heat and simmer, covered, until all liquid is absorbed. Sprinkle with basil and coconut just before serving.

Serves: 4 to 6

Dagmar Bothwell

PLANTAINS AND RICE

1 cup long-grain white rice	⅓ cup orange juice
1 tablespoon canola oil	1½ tablespoons brown sugar
1 pound ripe plantains or firm	½ teaspoon ground allspice
bananas	Salt and freshly ground black
3 tablespoons hot jalapeño pepper	pepper to taste
jelly	

Rinse rice with cold water and place in a large pot. Add 3 to 4 quarts water and bring to a boil. Cook 10 minutes or until rice is cooked through but still firm. Drain rice and rinse with warm water. Transfer rice to a serving bowl and toss with oil.

Meanwhile, peel plantains and cut into small cubes. Melt jelly in a large nonstick skillet. Stir in orange juice. Add plantains and cook 5 minutes. Stir in brown sugar and allspice. Toss plantain mixture with rice. Season with salt and pepper.

Jan Anderson

 ## PEAS 'N RICE
A Bahamian Big Deal

2 ounces salt pork or bacon, diced	1 pinch black pepper
¼ cup cooking oil	1 teaspoon salt
1 small onion, diced	1 cup cooked black-eyed peas
½ teaspoon dried thyme	3 cups water
1 tablespoon tomato paste	1½ cups dry rice

Cook salt pork or bacon in oil in a ½-gallon pot. When almost brown, add onions and cook until golden brown. Add thyme, tomato paste, pepper and salt. Cook until most of liquid evaporates. Add peas and simmer about 15 minutes, stirring occasionally. Add water and bring to a boil over medium heat. Stir in rice. Simmer, uncovered, until water disappears from top of rice. Cover and cook over low heat for 45 minutes.

Serves: 4

Ronda Owens

SOUTHERN SAUSAGE AND WILD RICE

1 (6-ounce) package long-grain and
    wild rice mix
1 pound bulk pork sausage
1 (10¾-ounce) can condensed
    cream of mushroom soup
1 cup chopped fresh mushrooms
½ cup chopped onions

½ cup chopped green bell peppers
¼ cup chopped celery
1 cup shredded sharp Cheddar
    cheese
½ cup chicken broth
1 teaspoon dried parsley
½ teaspoon black pepper

Preheat oven to 350 degrees.

Cook rice according to package directions. Meanwhile, brown and crumble sausage in a skillet. Drain excess fat from sausage. Combine rice, sausage, condensed soup, mushrooms, onions, bell peppers, celery, cheese, broth, parsley and pepper in a greased 2-quart casserole. Bake 1 hour.

Serves: 6 to 8

Patrick Murray

WINTER MINT WILD RICE

2 cups dry wild rice, rinsed and
    drained
1 cup cooked long-grain rice
2 tablespoons canola oil
1 cup diced celery
1 cup diced onions
1 cup dried cherries

1 tablespoon finely grated orange
    zest
1 teaspoon dried thyme
1 cup pecan halves
    Salt and pepper to taste
½ cup chopped fresh mint leaves

Bring 4 cups boiling salted water to a boil. Add wild rice and reduce heat to medium. Continue to boil, uncovered, for 40 minutes or until rice is tender but not mushy, adding more water if needed. Drain rice and transfer to a large bowl. Add long-grain rice and toss to mix. Heat oil in a skillet. Add celery, onions, cherries, orange zest, thyme and pecans. Cook and stir 10 to 15 minutes or until vegetables are softened. Add mixture to rice and toss. Season with salt and pepper. Stir in mint leaves.

Serves: 8

Mary Ann Hasenfus

JIM EMERT'S WILD RICE
WITH CRANBERRIES AND PEARS

1½ cups dry wild rice, rinsed
½ cup dried cranberries
¼ cup Merlot or Pinot Noir wine
⅓ cup olive oil
3 tablespoons red wine vinegar
1 teaspoon Dijon mustard

Dash of salt
6 scallions, chopped
2 large firm-ripe pears, peeled and diced
½ cup chopped pecans, toasted

Add wild rice to 3 cups boiling salted water. Reduce heat and simmer 25 to 30 minutes or until rice is tender but firm to the bite; drain and set aside.

Meanwhile, soak cranberries in wine. In a small bowl, whisk together oil, vinegar, mustard and salt. Mix oil dressing with cranberries. Toss rice, dressing and pears together. Top with pecans and serve warm or at room temperature.

Judy Simmons

GOLDEN COUSCOUS

1 large yellow bell pepper, diced
1 medium onion, finely chopped
3 tablespoons extra virgin olive oil, divided
2¼ cups fresh or canned whole kernel corn

½ teaspoon salt
¼ teaspoon black pepper
1½ cups canned chicken broth
1 cup couscous
2 teaspoons turmeric
1 teaspoon cumin

In a large skillet, sauté bell peppers and onions in 1 tablespoon olive oil until tender. Add corn and sauté 4 minutes. Stir in salt and pepper; remove from heat and set aside.

Bring broth to a boil in a large saucepan over medium heat. Stir in remaining 2 tablespoons olive oil, couscous, turmeric and cumin. Remove from heat. Cover and let stand 5 minutes or until liquid is absorbed. Gently stir in reserved vegetable mixture. Serve warm or at room temperature.

Serves: 6

Dagmar Bothwell

MEXICAN RICE SALAD

1 cup dry long-grain white rice
1¾ cups chicken broth, or water plus
    1 chicken bouillon cube
1 teaspoon turmeric
1 teaspoon cumin
1 (16-ounce) can yellow or white
    corn kernels, drained
1 (16-ounce) can black beans,
    drained and rinsed
1 green bell pepper, chopped
1 red bell pepper, chopped
1 medium onion, chopped
½ cup sliced stuffed green olives

1 small bunch cilantro, stems
    discarded and chopped
⅓ cup lime juice (bottled Key West
    juice is acceptable)
1 tablespoon Dijon mustard
½ cup olive oil
    Salt and pepper to taste
    Red pepper flakes to taste
1 avocado, cut into small chunks
    (optional)
    Sliced scallions or cherry
    tomatoes for garnish (optional)

Combine rice and broth in a medium pan. Add turmeric and cumin. Bring to a boil. Reduce to very low heat and cook, covered, until all liquid is absorbed.

Meanwhile, combine corn, beans, all bell peppers, onions, olives and cilantro in a large bowl. In a small bowl, whisk together lime juice and mustard. Whisk in olive oil. Pour dressing mixture over vegetable mixture and toss to coat. Season with salt and pepper and pepper flakes. Fluff rice with a fork or spoon and add to vegetable mixture. Add avocado just before serving. Season as needed with more lime juice or salt and garnish.

Serves: 4 to 6

Shannon Bothwell

ORANGE-CINNAMON RICE PILAF

2 tablespoons butter
¾ cup finely chopped onions
1½ cups dry white rice
6 tablespoons fresh orange juice
1 tablespoon orange zest

¾ teaspoon cinnamon
¾ teaspoon cumin
½ teaspoon salt
2½ cups low-salt chicken broth
    Black pepper

Melt butter in a saucepan over medium-high heat. Add onions and cook until just tender. Stir in rice, orange juice, orange zest, cinnamon, cumin, salt and broth. Bring to a simmer. Reduce heat to low. Cook, covered, for 20 minutes or until broth is absorbed and rice is done. Season with pepper and serve.

Serves: 6

Mary Hutchinson

MUSHROOM-BARLEY CASSEROLE

⅔ cup quick-cooking barley
¼ cup chopped onions
2 tablespoons butter or margarine
1 (4-ounce) can mushroom stems
   and pieces
2 tablespoons chopped pimiento

2 tablespoons snipped fresh parsley
2 teaspoons instant chicken
   bouillon
¼ teaspoon crushed dried rosemary
1¾ cups water

Preheat oven to 350 degrees.

In a small skillet, sauté barley and onions in butter until barley is lightly browned and onions are tender. Drain mushrooms, reserving 3 tablespoons liquid. Stir mushrooms and reserved liquid, pimiento, parsley, chicken bouillon, rosemary and water into skillet. Transfer to a 1-quart casserole. Bake, covered, for 1 hour or until barley is tender. Uncover and bake 10 minutes longer or until liquid is absorbed.

Serves: 4 to 5

Nancy Scott

GALLO PINTO NICARAGUAN RICE AND BEANS

2 teaspoons oil
1 small onion, diced
2 cups dry long-grain rice
1 teaspoon salt, or to taste
½ teaspoon cumin

1 cup cooked red beans, drained
   with 1¾ cups liquid reserved
2 cloves garlic, minced
1 teaspoon Worcestershire sauce
1¾ cups water

Heat oil in a large pan over medium heat. Add onions and sauté until golden. Add rice and sauté over medium-high heat for about 5 minutes, stirring constantly. Add salt, cumin, beans and garlic. Cook and stir about 1 minute. Add Worcestershire sauce and reserved bean liquid, then water. Stir once and bring to a boil. Cook, uncovered, for about 2 minutes. Reduce heat to low and cover; do not stir. Cook, covered, for 13 minutes. Remove from heat, keep covered and let stand 10 minutes. Fluff rice before serving.

Marybeth Pena

COUSCOUS WITH TOMATOES AND CILANTRO

¾ cup tomato juice
¾ cup chicken broth
1 cup quick-cooking couscous
1 cup diced tomato
½ cup chopped fresh cilantro
2 teaspoons olive oil
Salt and freshly ground black
pepper to taste

Combine tomato juice and broth in a saucepan and bring to a boil. Place couscous in a serving bowl. Pour boiling liquid over couscous and stir with a fork. Let stand 5 minutes. Add tomato, cilantro and oil and fluff with a fork to separate grains. Season with salt and pepper.

This is a great accompaniment for seafood dishes.

Serves: 4

Jan Anderson

LINGUINI WITH FRESH TOMATO AND BASIL

3 ripe medium tomatoes, chopped
⅓ cup thinly sliced fresh basil
1 tablespoon olive oil
1 clove garlic, minced
½ teaspoon salt
¼ teaspoon black pepper
8 ounces dry linguini, cooked and
drained
¾ cup shredded Parmesan cheese

Combine tomatoes, basil, olive oil, garlic, salt and pepper in a large bowl. Add linguini and cheese and toss.

Serves: 6

Kathy Walker-Peterson

HOT NOODLES WITH WALNUTS

4 quarts water
1 tablespoon salt
8 ounces medium egg noodles
5 tablespoons butter or margarine
¾ cup ground or finely chopped
walnuts
Parmesan cheese
Finely chopped fresh parsley

Bring water to a boil in a large saucepan. Stir in salt and noodles and cook 8 to 10 minutes or until tender; drain well. In a large skillet, melt butter over low heat. Add noodles and walnuts. Cook, stirring constantly, until heated through. Sprinkle with cheese and parsley. Serve warm.

Serves: 6

Ella Fay and Leroy Jackson

THREE-CHEESE SPIRALS

1 (16-ounce) package spiral pasta	1½ cups small curd cottage cheese
1 egg	1 pound American cheese, cubed
1½ cups sour cream	2 cups shredded Cheddar cheese

Preheat oven to 350 degrees.

Cook pasta according to package directions; drain. Meanwhile, process egg, sour cream and cottage cheese in a blender until smooth. Transfer to a large bowl. Add American and Cheddar cheeses. Stir in drained pasta until evenly coated. Transfer to a greased shallow 3-quart baking dish. Bake, uncovered, for 15 minutes. Stir and bake 15 to 20 minutes longer or until bubbly and edges begin to brown.

Serves: 8 to 10

Janel Weigt

LINDA'S NOODLE PUDDING

6 ounces farmer cheese	1 teaspoon salt
6 ounces cottage cheese	1 teaspoon vanilla
2 (3-ounce) packages cream cheese	1 cup milk
4 eggs	8 ounces wide noodles, cooked and
1 cup sour cream	well drained
1 stick unsalted butter	Cinnamon sugar to taste for
¾ cup sugar	topping

Preheat oven to 400 degrees.

Cream together all cheeses. Add eggs, one at a time. Mix in sour cream, butter, sugar, salt, vanilla and milk. Fold mixture into drained noodles and transfer to a greased baking pan or dish. Sprinkle cinnamon sugar on top. Bake 15 minutes. Reduce temperature to 350 degrees and bake 1 hour longer.

Nancy Marin

> If you have eyes to see, travel out through the back country and take a walk in the woods. The wild flowers are in bloom everywhere. They may be more shy and less conspicuous than their northern cousins but we have them in legions.
>
> ~ Ernest Lyons

Desserts

NEW ORLEANS
GARDEN DISTRICT BREAD PUDDING

1	loaf Italian bread, sliced, crusts removed	3	eggs, beaten
½	teaspoon nutmeg	1	teaspoon vanilla
1	teaspoon cinnamon	1½	cups sugar
1	stick butter, melted	1	cup raisins (optional)
		3	cups milk

Preheat oven to 350 degrees.

Tear bread into pieces into a bowl. Mix in nutmeg, cinnamon, butter, eggs, vanilla, sugar, raisins and milk. Transfer to a greased 3-quart casserole or baking pan. Bake 45 minutes or until pudding is soft but not firm. Serve with rum sauce.

Serves: 6

Rum Sauce

3	tablespoons flour	1	(16-ounce) package brown sugar
1	cup water	1	teaspoon vanilla
1	stick butter, melted	½	cup rum
½	cup granulated sugar		

To make rum sauce, mix flour and water together in a blender. Mix in melted butter. Pour mixture into a saucepan. Add both sugars and bring to a boil. Cook and stir until thickened. Remove from heat and cool. When cool, stir in vanilla and rum. Serve warm over warm pudding.

Patty Henderson

NO'CHO MAMA'S BANANA PUDDING

	Pepperidge Farms Chessman cookies	1	(8-ounce) package cream cheese, softened
6	bananas	1	(14-ounce) can sweetened condensed milk
1	(3-ounce) package instant vanilla pudding mix	½	(8-ounce) container frozen whipped topping, thawed
1	teaspoon vanilla		

Arrange a single layer of cookies in the bottom of a 9x13-inch pan. Slice bananas on top. In a bowl, prepare pudding according to package directions, substituting vanilla for 1 teaspoon of milk; set aside. In a separate bowl, blend cream cheese with sweetened condensed milk. Stir pudding into cream cheese mixture. Fold in whipped topping. Spread mixture over bananas. Top with more cookies. Freeze 2 hours, then transfer to refrigerator. Incredibly good!

Pat Cook

PEACH AND BERRY BREAD PUDDING

3 cups heavy cream	2 eggs
1½ cups sugar	10 medium peaches, peeled and
1 tablespoon vanilla	thinly sliced
½ teaspoon salt	1 cup blackberries or strawberries
10 croissants, cut into 1-inch cubes	Vanilla ice cream
6 egg yolks	

Preheat oven to 300 degrees.

Combine cream, sugar, vanilla and salt in a heavy 4-quart pan. Warm over medium-low heat just until steam comes off surface; do not boil. Remove from heat and pour over cubed croissants. Let stand 30 minutes.

In a large bowl, whisk together egg yolks and eggs. Gently stir in croissant mixture. Fold in peaches and berries. Pour mixture into a greased 9x13-inch baking dish. Bake 1½ hours or until a knife inserted in the center comes out clean. Cool slightly. To serve, cut into squares and serve with ice cream.

Serves: 12

Bonnie Brashear

CINNAMON BREAD CUSTARD

16 slices cinnamon or cinnamon	¾ cup granulated sugar
raisin bread	3 cups milk
1 stick unsalted butter, melted	1 cup heavy cream
4 eggs	1 tablespoon vanilla
2 egg yolks	Powdered sugar

Preheat oven to 350 degrees.

Brush both sides of each bread slice with melted butter. Arrange bread in rows in 2 layers in a greased 9x13-inch pan. In a large bowl, beat together eggs and egg yolks. Whisk in granulated sugar, milk, cream and vanilla. Pour egg mixture over the bread slices, making sure each slice is evenly moistened. Place pan in a larger roasting or baking pan. Add enough warm water in outer pan to reach halfway up sides of inner dish. Bake in upper third of oven for 25 minutes or until top is lightly and evenly browned and the custard is set. Transfer to a rack and cool about 15 minutes. Cut into squares and sprinkle lightly with powdered sugar. May serve with berries on top.

Paula White

 BROWNIES

BROWNIES

1   (20-ounce) package brownie mix
     with walnuts
2   cups powdered sugar
1   stick butter, softened, or 4 ounces
     cream cheese

¾   teaspoon almond extract
1   (12-ounce) package semi-sweet
     chocolate chips
1   tablespoon butter

Prepare brownie mix according to package directions in a 9x13-inch pan; cool. Mix powdered sugar, softened butter and almond extract. Ice cooled brownies with sugar mixture. Melt chocolate chips and 1 tablespoon butter and pour over cooled brownies. Cut into squares immediately and refrigerate.

Debbie Thomas

SWEDISH WHITE BROWNIES

2   eggs
1½   cups sugar, divided
     Pinch of salt
1   stick butter, melted

1   cup flour
1   teaspoon almond extract
½   cup chopped pecans

Preheat oven to 325 degrees.

Beat together eggs, 1 cup sugar, salt, butter, flour and almond extract. Spread batter in an 8-inch square greased pan. Sprinkle remaining ½ cup sugar and pecans on top. Bake 30 minutes. Cut into squares when cool.

Serves: 6

Nancy Farrow

The spirit of the mangrove swamp, well-established, centuries old, is one of complacent victory. It has seized the land from the shallows and held it through the hurricanes of the centuries.

~ Ernest Lyons

BETTER THAN LIFE BROWNIES

1 (18-ounce) package German
   chocolate cake mix
⅔ cup evaporated milk, divided
1½ sticks margarine, softened

1 cup chopped pecans
1 (14-ounce) package caramels,
   unwrapped
1 cup semi-sweet chocolate chips

Preheat oven to 350 degrees.

Mix together cake mix, ⅓ cup evaporated milk, margarine and pecans. Spread half of batter in a greased 9x13-inch baking pan. Bake 15 minutes.

Meanwhile, melt together caramels and remaining ⅓ cup evaporated milk in a saucepan, stirring often. Pour caramel mixture over baked layer. Sprinkle with chocolate chips. Add remaining batter. Bake 20 minutes longer or until done.

Serves: 10 to 12

Danielle Rader

HEPBURN'S BROWNIES

2 (1-ounce) squares unsweetened
   chocolate
1 stick unsalted butter (not
   margarine), plus extra for pan
1 cup sugar

2 eggs, lightly beaten
½ teaspoon vanilla
¼ cup all-purpose flour
½ teaspoon salt
1 cup coarsely chopped walnuts

Preheat oven to 325 degrees.

Melt chocolate and butter in a heavy saucepan. Remove from heat and stir in sugar. Add eggs and vanilla and beat vigorously. Stir in flour, salt and walnuts. Mix well. Use butter to grease an 8-inch square pan. Quickly pour batter into pan. Bake 40 minutes. Cool before cutting into 1½-inch squares.

Especially good with a scoop of ice cream (any flavor)!

Susan Murphy

JILL'S FAMOUS FUDGE BROWNIES

1½ sticks butter, melted
1½ cups sugar
1½ teaspoons real vanilla
3   eggs
¾   cup all-purpose flour

½   cup cocoa powder
½   teaspoon baking powder
½   teaspoon salt
1   cup mini chocolate chips

Preheat oven to 350 degrees.

Combine all ingredients except chocolate chips in a large mixing bowl. Beat with an electric mixer until well blended. Stir in chocolate chips. Spread batter in a greased 8-inch square or rectangular jellyroll pan. Bake 40 to 45 minutes in square pan, 30 to 35 minutes in jelly roll pan or until brownies pull away from sides of pan. Cool completely. Cut into desired serving size.

Serves: 12 to 18

Jill Levy

FRESH COCONUT CAKE

2	sticks butter, softened	1	teaspoon salt
2	cups sugar	1	cup milk
5	egg whites, room temperature	1	tablespoon coconut extract
3	cups sifted cake flour	2	cups freshly grated coconut
1	tablespoon baking powder		

Preheat oven to 350 degrees.

Cream butter and sugar in a mixing bowl until smooth. Add egg whites and beat 5 minutes or until light and fluffy. Sift together flour, baking powder and salt. Add dry ingredients alternately with milk and coconut extract to creamed mixture. Blend until smooth. Stir in coconut. Divide batter evenly between two greased and floured 9-inch pans. Bake 35 to 45 minutes. Serve with whipped cream and fresh strawberries tossed with sugar.

To remove coconut meat, crack open a fresh coconut, pry meat off the sides, peel off the brown skin and grate the white coconut meat.

Charles Rosselli
Executive Pastry Chef, Sailfish Point Country Club

HARVEY WALLBANGER CAKE

1	(18¼-ounce) package yellow cake mix	4	eggs
		¼	cup vodka
1	(3-ounce) package vanilla instant pudding mix	¼	cup Galliano liqueur
		¾	cup orange juice
½	cup vegetable oil		

Preheat oven to 350 degrees.

Combine all ingredients in a bowl and beat for 5 minutes. Pour batter into a greased and floured tube or Bundt pan. Bake 45 to 50 minutes. Cool 5 minutes before removing from pan. Cool completely on a wire rack.

Serves: 8 to 10

Kelly Pelletier

TROPICAL CAKE

1⅓ cups water
3   egg whites
1   (18¼-ounce) package yellow cake mix
2   cups milk
1   (3.4-ounce) package instant banana cream pudding mix

1   (15-ounce) can unsweetened crushed pineapple, drained
2   cups frozen whipped topping, thawed
¼   cup shredded coconut, toasted

Preheat oven to 350 degrees.

Combine water, egg whites and cake mix in a large bowl. Beat with an electric mixer on low speed for 30 seconds. Increase to medium speed and beat 2 minutes. Pour batter into a greased 9x13-inch baking pan. Bake 35 minutes or until cake springs back when touched lightly in the center. Cool on a wire rack.

In a medium bowl, combine milk and pudding mix. Beat at low speed for 2 minutes or until thickened. Cover and chill 5 minutes. Stir in pineapple. Using the handle of a wooden spoon, poke about 40 holes in the top of the cake. Spread pineapple mixture over cake. Top with whipped topping and sprinkle with coconut. Store in refrigerator.

Serves: 14 to 16

Kirk Baker

 FRENCH COCONUT CAKE

1   stick butter, melted
1⅓ cups sugar
3   eggs, beaten
1   tablespoon vinegar

1   teaspoon vanilla
1   can flaked coconut
1   pie crust, unbaked

Preheat oven to 350 degrees.

Combine all ingredients except pie crust. Pour into unbaked pie crust. Bake 45 minutes.

Claudia Barton

FRIEDA'S ORANGE CAKE

1   stick butter, softened
1   cup granulated sugar
1   cup chopped dates
1   orange, peeled, seeded and
        chopped

2   eggs, at room temperature
¼   cup cream
¾   cup buttermilk
2   level cups cake flour
1   teaspoon baking soda

Preheat oven to 350 degrees.

Cream butter and sugar together in a bowl. Mix in dates and orange. Carefully stir in eggs. In a separate bowl, mix cream and buttermilk. In another bowl, sift flour and baking soda together. Add milk mixture and dry ingredients, alternately, to batter. Pour batter into 2 greased and floured 8-inch cake pans. Bake 25 minutes. Cool completely before spreading icing over cake.

Frieda's Orange Icing
1   stick butter, softened
3   cups powdered sugar
2   tablespoons frozen orange juice
        concentrate

2   tablespoons water
1   teaspoon vanilla

Mix all icing ingredients to a smooth spreading consistency.

Jean Harper Lee

SWEET POTATO CAKE

A moist, delicious cake.

2   cups sugar
1   stick margarine
¾   cup egg substitute
2   (14½-ounce) cans unsweetened
        mashed sweet potatoes
3   cups cake flour
1½ teaspoons cinnamon

1   teaspoon baking powder
1   teaspoon baking soda
½   teaspoon nutmeg
½   teaspoon salt
2   teaspoons vanilla
¼   cup sweetened flaked coconut
¼   cup finely chopped pecans

Preheat oven to 350 degrees.

Beat sugar and margarine. Gradually mix in egg substitute and beat well. Add 2½ cups sweet potatoes (about 1½ cans) and beat well. Mix in flour, cinnamon, baking powder, baking soda, nutmeg, salt, vanilla, coconut and pecans. Stir well. Pour batter into a greased 10-inch tube pan. Bake 1 hour, 25 minutes or until a wooden toothpick inserted in the center comes out clean. Cool before removing from pan.

Margaret Gray

BANANA UPSIDE DOWN CAKE

1	cup brown sugar	½	teaspoon salt
2	tablespoons water	1	stick butter, melted
4	tablespoons butter	1	cup granulated sugar
3	ripe bananas	2	eggs
1½	cups flour	½	cup milk
2	teaspoons baking powder	1	teaspoon vanilla

Preheat oven to 325 degrees.

In a saucepan over medium-high heat, cook brown sugar and water until mixture bubbles and caramelizes, stirring often. Add 4 tablespoons butter and stir until well mixed. Pour mixture in an 8-inch square baking pan. Cut bananas lengthwise into three slices each, then cut slices in half crosswise. Arrange slices over caramelized sugar in the pan.

In a bowl, combine flour, baking powder and salt; set aside. In a separate bowl, combine 1 stick melted butter and granulated sugar using an electric mixer. Beat in eggs on low speed. Add milk and vanilla and mix until well blended. Blend in dry ingredients, adding one-third at a time. Pour batter into pan over bananas. Bake 50 minutes or until cake starts to pull away from the sides of the pan and springs back when touched in the center. Cool in pan on a rack for 5 minutes. Invert onto a serving plate and remove pan.

Serves: 6

John Wakeman

MAHONEY'S POPPY SEED CAKE

1	(18¼-ounce) package yellow cake mix	4	eggs
		¾	cup sherry
1	(3-ounce) vanilla pudding mix	⅓	cup poppy seeds
1	(8-ounce) container sour cream	1	stick margarine, softened

Preheat oven to 350 degrees.

Combine all ingredients in a large bowl. Beat with an electric mixer for 2 minutes or until smooth. Pour batter into a greased and floured Bundt pan. Bake 45 minutes or until a wooden toothpick inserted in the center of cakes comes out clean.

Serves: 8 to 10

Elaine Clark

BLUE RIBBON CARROT CAKE

Cake

2 cups flour	2 cups sugar
2 teaspoons baking soda	1 teaspoon vanilla
2 teaspoons cinnamon	1 (8-ounce) can crushed pineapple,
½ teaspoon salt	drained
3 eggs	2 cups grated carrots
¾ cup vegetable oil	3½ ounces shredded coconut
¾ cup buttermilk	1 cup chopped walnuts

Buttered Glaze

1 cup sugar	1 stick butter
½ teaspoon baking soda	1 tablespoon corn syrup
½ cup buttermilk	1 teaspoon vanilla

Cream Cheese Frosting

1 stick butter, softened	2 cups powdered sugar
1 (8-ounce) package cream cheese,	1 teaspoon orange juice
softened	1 teaspoon orange zest
1 teaspoon vanilla	

Preheat oven to 350 degrees.

Sift together flour, baking soda, cinnamon and salt; set aside. In a large bowl, beat eggs. Add oil, buttermilk, sugar and vanilla and mix well. Gradually add dry ingredients and continue to mix well. Stir pineapple, carrots, coconut and walnuts into batter. Pour batter into a well greased 9x13-inch baking pan. Bake 55 minutes or until a wooden toothpick inserted in the center of cake comes out clean.

While cake bakes, prepare glaze and frosting. For glaze, combine sugar, baking soda, buttermilk, butter and corn syrup in a saucepan and bring to a boil. Cook 5 minutes, stirring frequently; be careful to not burn sauce. Remove from heat and stir in vanilla. When cake is done baking, use a wooden toothpick to poke holes in cake. Pour glaze slowly over hot cake until absorbed. Allow cake to cool completely.

To make frosting, cream butter and cream cheese together until fluffy. Add vanilla, powdered sugar, orange juice and orange zest and beat until smooth. Spread over cooled cake.

Serves: 10 to 12

Barbara Blaydon

TEXAS SHEET CAKE

Cake

2	sticks butter		1	teaspoon salt
1	cup water		1	teaspoon baking soda
¼	cup cocoa powder		2	eggs, beaten
2	cups flour		½	cup sour cream
2	cups sugar			

Preheat oven to 325 degrees.

Combine butter, water and cocoa powder in a saucepan. Bring to a boil over medium heat, stirring often. Meanwhile, sift together flour, sugar, salt and baking soda. Add dry ingredients to boiling mixture in saucepan. Remove from heat. Add eggs and sour cream and stir well. Pour batter into a greased and floured jelly roll pan. Bake 25 minutes. Cool completely. Spread icing over cooled cake and sprinkle with nuts. Cut into squares.

Serves: 10 to 12

Icing

1	stick butter		4	cups sifted powdered sugar
5½-6	tablespoons milk		1½	teaspoons vanilla
¼	cup cocoa powder		¾	cup chopped nuts for topping

For icing, combine butter, milk and cocoa in a saucepan. Bring to a boil, stirring often. Remove from heat and mix in powdered sugar and vanilla.

Sharyon Daigneau

RAISIN FROSTING

1	cup sugar		1	tablespoon flour
1	cup plus 1 tablespoon water, divided		1	teaspoon vanilla
			1½	cups ground raisins

Combine sugar and 1 cup water in a saucepan. Bring to a boil. Make a paste with flour and remaining 1 tablespoon water and stir into boiling syrup. Add vanilla and raisins and bring to a boil. Refrigerate until cooled. Use on yellow or white cake.

This was a favorite of my father, Dale Clark. His mother made this for him on his birthday and when she died, I took on the tradition.

Susan Zarnowiec

OATMEAL CAKE

Cake

1 stick butter or margarine	1½ cups flour
1 cup quick-cooking oatmeal	1 teaspoon baking soda
1½ cups boiling water	1 teaspoon cinnamon
2 eggs	½ teaspoon ground ginger
1 cup brown sugar	½ teaspoon ground cloves
1 cup granulated sugar	½ teaspoon salt

Topping

1 stick butter, melted	1 cup shredded coconut
1 cup brown sugar	1 cup chopped nuts
1 egg	1 tablespoon cream or milk

Preheat oven to 350 degrees.

Combine butter and oatmeal in a bowl. Pour boiling water over mixture and let stand 20 minutes. Add eggs, both sugars, flour, baking soda, cinnamon, ginger, cloves and salt and mix by hand. Pour batter into a greased 9x13-inch pan. Bake 30 to 35 minutes.

Meanwhile, combine all topping ingredients. Pour topping over hot or warm cake. Broil until golden brown.

Serves: 12 to 24

Charmaine Truitt

ROCKY ROAD CAKE

1 (18¼-ounce) package devil's food cake mix	4 eggs, well beaten
	1 cup chopped walnuts
1 cup water	1 cup mini marshmallows
1 cup mayonnaise	1 cup semi-sweet chocolate chips

Preheat oven to 350 degrees.

Combine cake mix, water, mayonnaise and eggs in a bowl. Beat at least 3 minutes or until mixed well, scraping sides of bowl often. Stir in walnuts, marshmallows and chocolate chips. Pour batter into a greased and floured tube pan. Bake 50 to 55 minutes or until a toothpick inserted in the center comes out clean. Cool. Eat as is or topped with ice cream.

Marjorie Sayers

SOUR CREAM POUND CAKE

2 sticks butter, softened	¼ teaspoon baking soda
3 cups sugar	1 cup sour cream
6 eggs, separated	1 teaspoon vanilla
3 cups flour	

Preheat oven to 325 degrees.

Cream butter and sugar in a bowl. Mix in egg yolks. In a separate bowl, beat egg whites until stiff, but not dry. Add beaten egg whites alternately with flour to creamed mixture. Mix baking soda with sour cream and add to batter. Beat well. Mix in vanilla. Pour batter into a greased tube pan. Bake 1 hour, 10 minutes to 1 hour, 30 minutes or until a wooden toothpick inserted in the center of cake comes out clean, but cake is still moist.

Serves: 8 to 10

Jean Jacobs

POUND CAKE

1½ sticks margarine or butter, softened	1 teaspoon baking powder
2 cups sugar	5 tablespoons milk, room temperature
5 eggs, room temperature	1 teaspoon vanilla
2 cups sifted flour	1 teaspoon lemon juice

Preheat oven to 325 degrees.

Beat butter with an electric mixer on medium speed until creamy. Gradually add sugar and continue beating until light and fluffy. Add eggs, one at a time, beating batter until yellow yolk disappears. Combine flour and baking powder in a separate bowl. Mix milk with vanilla and lemon juice in another container. Add dry ingredients alternately with liquid mixture to batter, beginning and ending with dry ingredients. Mix after each addition until blended. Pour batter into a tube pan greased with shortening and dusted with flour. Place cake in center of oven and keep door closed until minimum baking time has elapsed. Bake 1 hour or until a toothpick inserted in the center comes out clean. Cool in pan on a wire rack for 10 minutes. Remove from pan and cool completely on rack.

Kris Kerr

PUMPKIN SWIRL CHEESECAKE

Crust

2 cups gingersnap cookie crumbs	6 tablespoons butter, melted
½ cup finely chopped pecans	

Filling

3 (8-ounce) packages cream cheese, softened	1 cup canned pumpkin
1 cup sugar, divided	1 teaspoon cinnamon
1 teaspoon vanilla	¼ teaspoon nutmeg
3 eggs	Dash of ground cloves

Preheat oven to 325 degrees if using a silver pan, 300 degrees for a dark nonstick pan.

Combine all crust ingredients and press into the bottom and 2 inches up the sides of a 9-inch springform pan.

For filling, beat cream cheese, ¾ cup sugar and vanilla with an electric mixer on medium speed just until blended. Reserve 1½ cups batter. Mix remaining batter with pumpkin, cinnamon, nutmeg, cloves and remaining ¼ cup sugar. Spoon half of pumpkin batter over crust. Add half of plain batter in spoonfuls. Repeat layers. Drag a knife through the batter in several directions for a marbled effect.

Bake 55 minutes or until center is almost set. Run a knife around the rim of pan to loosen cake; cool before removing rim of pan. Refrigerate 4 hours or overnight.

Amanda Tilton Martin

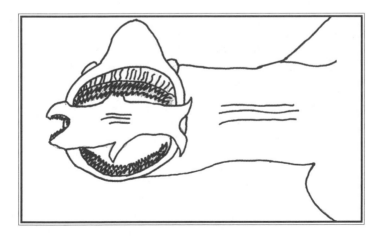

COCONUT CHEESECAKE

Crust

6 tablespoons unsalted butter, melted, divided

¾ cup graham cracker crumbs

½ cup shredded coconut, toasted, cooled

2 tablespoons sugar

Filling

3 (8-ounce) packages cream cheese, softened

1 cup sugar

4 _lespoons unsalted butter, softened

3 tablespoons cornstarch

4 eggs

1¼ cups canned sweetened cream of coconut

¼ cup coconut rum

Preheat oven to 350 degrees.

To prepare crust, brush a 9-inch cake pan with 2-inch sides with 1 tablespoon melted butter. Line pan with parchment paper and lightly brush with some of remaining melted butter. In a medium bowl, mix crumbs, coconut, sugar and remaining melted butter. Press mixture into the bottom of prepared pan. Bake 10 minutes or until lightly browned on the edges. Cool. Reduce oven temperature to 300 degrees.

For filling, beat cream cheese, sugar, butter and cornstarch with an electric mixer until blended. Beat in eggs one at a time. Beat in cream of coconut and rum. Pour batter over cooled crust. Place pan in a large roasting pan and add enough water to roasting pan to come 1 inch up sides of cake pan. Cover roasting pan with foil. Bake at 300 degrees for 1 hour. Remove foil and bake 40 minutes longer or until cake is pale brown, puffed and just set in the center. Cool in water bath for 2 hours. Remove from water and run a knife around edges to loosen cake. Chill in pan 3 hours.

To remove cake from pan, bake at 350 degrees for 2 minutes. Remove from oven. Cover a plate with foil and place over cake. Invert cake, gently shaking cake onto plate. Remove pan and parchment paper. Place another plate on cake and invert again so cake is right-side up. Serve with strawberries or other fruit.

Serves: 10 to 12

Mary Hutchinson

CHEESECAKE SQUARES

Crust

18	graham cracker squares, crushed to make 1½ cups crumbs	1	tablespoon sugar
1	stick butter or margarine, melted	½	teaspoon cinnamon

Filling

2	(8-ounce) packages cream cheese	1	teaspoon vanilla
3	eggs		

Cream Topping

1	cup sour cream	1	teaspoon vanilla
3	tablespoons sugar		

Preheat oven to 350 degrees.

Mix all crust ingredients and press into the bottom of a 9x13-inch glass baking pan.

Combine all filling ingredients and beat together until smooth. Pour filling over crust. Bake 20 minutes. Cool 10 minutes.

Combine all topping ingredients and pour over top of partially cooled cake. Bake 10 minutes longer. Cut into 2-inch squares. Serve plain or top with pie filling.

Amount of sour cream in topping can be doubled, but increase second baking time to 15 minutes.

Jean Hagen

JESSIE'S CHEESECAKE

Crust
1	box Zwieback cookies	½	cup sugar
1	stick butter, melted		

Filling
4	(8-ounce) packages cream cheese, softened	4	eggs, separated, room temperature
1	cup sugar	1	tablespoon lemon juice
¼	cup milk, room temperature	2	teaspoons vanilla

Preheat oven to 350 degrees.

Crush all but 5 or 6 of cookies; set whole cookies aside. Mix cookie crumbs with butter and sugar. Press mixture into the bottom of a 9-inch springform pan.

For filling, cream together cream cheese and sugar. Beat in milk, well beaten egg yolks, lemon juice and vanilla until well blended. In a separate bowl, beat egg whites until soft peaks form. Fold beaten egg whites into batter. Pour batter over crust. Bake 40 to 50 minutes, checking after 40 minutes.

Serves: 10

Bryna Potsdam

UNBELIEVABLE CHEESECAKE

2	(8-ounce) tubes refrigerated crescent rolls	1½	cups sugar, divided
		1	teaspoon vanilla
2	(8-ounce) packages cream cheese, softened	1	stick butter, melted
		1	teaspoon cinnamon

Preheat oven to 400 degrees.

Unroll 1 tube of crescent rolls and spread over the bottom of a 9x13-inch pan. Blend cream cheese, 1 cup sugar and vanilla until smooth and spread over bottom layer of crust. Unroll second tube of crescent rolls and place over cream cheese layer. Pour melted butter over top. Mix remaining ½ cup sugar and cinnamon and sprinkle over butter. Bake 20 to 30 minutes; do not overbake. Cool and slice into finger food-size pieces.

Ruth Dudziak

PUMPKIN CHEESECAKE

Crust

15 gingersnap cookies, crushed   4   tablespoons butter, melted

Filling

3   (8-ounce) packages cream cheese,   ⅔   cup evaporated milk
      softened   2   tablespoons cornstarch
1   cup granulated sugar   1½ teaspoons cinnamon
¼   cup brown sugar   ½   teaspoon nutmeg
2   eggs   1   teaspoon vanilla
1   (15-ounce) can pumpkin

Topping

1   (16-ounce) container sour cream   1   teaspoon vanilla
⅓   cup sugar

Preheat oven to 350 degrees.

Combine crust ingredients and press into the bottom of a springform pan. Bake 5 minutes; cool.

For filling, beat cream cheese and both sugars until fluffy. Beat in eggs, pumpkin and evaporated milk. Add cornstarch, cinnamon, nutmeg and vanilla. Beat well and pour over cooled crust. Bake at 350 degrees for 1 hour or until edge is set but center still moves slightly.

Mix all topping ingredients and spread over warm cheesecake. Bake 5 minutes longer. Cool in refrigerator overnight before removing sides of pan. Garnish as desired.

Dagmar Bothwell

KATHY'S CREAMY CHEESECAKE

Crust

1½ cups graham cracker crumbs
½ teaspoon nutmeg
¼ cup powdered sugar

¼ cup chopped pecans
5 tablespoons butter, melted

Filling

2 (¼-ounce) envelopes unflavored gelatin
½ cup cold water
½ cup hot water
2 egg whites
1½ (8-ounce) packages cream cheese, softened

¼ cup lemon juice
½ teaspoon vanilla
¼ teaspoon salt
¾ cup sugar
1 tablespoon lemon zest
1 (16-ounce) container sour cream

Preheat oven to 400 degrees.

Mix together crust ingredients with a fork and press into a pie pan. Bake 10 minutes; cool.

For filling, soften gelatin in cold water. Add hot water to dissolve; set aside. Beat egg whites until stiff; set aside. Combine cream cheese, lemon juice, vanilla, salt and sugar in a large bowl with an electric mixer until fluffy. Stir in zest and dissolved gelatin. Fold in sour cream and beaten egg whites. Pour filling over cooled crust and chill.

Top with strawberry glaze, cherry topping, blueberries or fruit topping of your choice. Flavored pancake syrup mixed with fresh fruit makes a quick and easy topping.

Kathy Wiggins

OREO CHEESECAKE

18-20	chocolate sandwich cookies	2	teaspoons vanilla
4	(8-ounce) packages cream cheese, softened	2	teaspoons cornstarch
		4	eggs
1⅓	cups sugar	½	cup heavy cream

Preheat oven to 350 degrees.

Trim bottom one-third off of cookies so that there is a flat edge; reserve trimmings. Stand 12 cookies, rounded-side up, around the inside edge of a greased 8x3-inch springform pan. Break remaining cookies into small pieces and combine with reserved cookie trimmings; set aside.

In a large bowl, beat cream cheese until smooth. Gradually beat in sugar, vanilla and cornstarch, scraping sides of bowl as needed. Add eggs, one at a time, beating after each addition. Stir in cream. Spread one-fourth of mixture into prepared pan. Sprinkle with a third of cookie crumbs. Alternate layers of cheese mixture and cookie crumbs, ending with cheese mixture. Wrap bottom and sides of pan with double layers of foil to prevent leaking. Bake 1 hour. Turn off oven and leave cake in oven for 1 hour longer with oven door closed. Refrigerate several hours or overnight. Garnish with whipped cream or extra cookie pieces.

Serves: 10

Pam Fogt

TRIPLE CITRUS CHEESECAKE

Crust

20	chocolate sandwich cookies, crushed	4	tablespoons butter, melted

Filling

4	(8-ounce) packages cream cheese, softened	1	tablespoon lemon juice
1	cup sugar	1	tablespoon Key lime juice
2	tablespoons flour	1	tablespoon orange juice
1	teaspoon vanilla	1	teaspoon lemon zest
4	eggs	1	teaspoon lime zest
		1	teaspoon orange zest

Preheat oven to 300 degrees if using a dark, nonstick pan, 325 degrees for a silver pan.

Mix cookie crumbs and melted butter in a bowl. Press mixture firmly into the bottom of a 9-inch springform pan. Bake 10 minutes.

For filling, beat cream cheese, sugar, flour and vanilla with an electric mixer on medium speed until well blended. Add eggs, one at a time, mixing on low speed after each addition. Mix just until blended; overbeating may cause cheesecake to crack while baking. Stir in fruit juices and zest. Pour filling over crust. Bake 1 hour, 15 minutes or until center is almost set. Run a knife around sides to loosen cake. Cool before removing rim of pan. Refrigerate 4 hours or overnight. Store leftovers in refrigerator.

Serves: 10

Sharyon Daigneau

MR. CORBIN'S FAMOUS PEACH COBBLER

4 (29-ounce) cans sliced peaches in heavy syrup
1 (15-ounce) can sliced peaches
1-2 cups sugar to taste
3 sticks butter or margarine, cut into pieces

2 teaspoons nutmeg
2 teaspoons vanilla
5 unbaked pie crusts (refrigerated or frozen, thawed)

Preheat oven to 400 degrees.

Drain and discard juice from 2 of the large cans and from the small can of peaches. Place peaches in a large bowl along with remaining 2 large cans peaches including syrup. Stir in sugar, butter, nutmeg and vanilla. Mix well. Place one-fourth of peach mixture in a round Dutch oven. Top with a pie crust. Bake until crust starts to brown. Repeat layers and baking 3 more times, using 2 crusts for top layer. Cut top layer crusts into strips and lay across top. Bake until golden. Total cooking time will be a little over 1 hour.

Serves: A large group

Ronald Corbin
Director of OPUS, MCHS

 MANGO COBBLER

2 small mangoes, or 1 large
1 cup sugar, plus extra for sweetening fruit

4 tablespoons butter, softened
1 cup biscuit mix
½ cup milk

Preheat oven to 350 degrees.

Peel and slice mangoes and add sugar to taste. Cream butter and 1 cup sugar. Mix in biscuit mix and milk. Pour mixture into a casserole dish. Top with mango slices. Bake 50 minutes.

Joan Jefferson

> The swamp is eternally being born, living, dying, and its smell is a combination of the smells of plants, birds, animals, reptiles, fish, insects and the untold legions of microscopic things that ultimately devour us all.
>
> ~ Ernest Lyons

NO-DOUGH BLUEBERRY-PEACH COBBLER

1	stick butter or margarine	½	cup milk
1	cup flour	2	cups fresh or frozen sliced
1¼	cups sugar, divided		peaches
2	teaspoons baking powder	2	cups fresh or frozen blueberries

Preheat oven to 350 degrees.

Melt butter in a 2-quart baking dish; set aside. In a bowl, combine flour, ¾ cup sugar and baking powder. Add milk and stir until blended. Spoon batter over butter in dish; do not stir. Combine peaches, blueberries and remaining ½ cup sugar in a separate bowl. Spoon mixture over batter; do not stir. Bake 45 to 55 minutes.

Serves: 6

Susan Fogarty

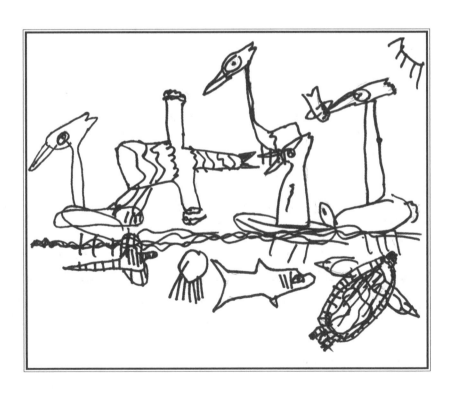

TRIPLE CHOCOLATE CINNAMON COOKIES

¼ cup flour	7 tablespoons sugar
¼ cup cocoa powder	2 eggs
1¾ teaspoons cinnamon	8 ounces semi-sweet chocolate
¼ teaspoon baking powder	chips, melted and cooled
Pinch of salt	8 ounces milk chocolate chips
6 tablespoons unsalted butter,	1 cup chopped walnuts, toasted
softened	Walnut halves

Preheat oven to 350 degrees.

Combine flour, cocoa powder, cinnamon, baking powder and salt; set aside. Beat together butter, sugar and eggs until smooth. Mix in melted chocolate. Stir chocolate mixture into dry ingredients. Add chocolate chips and walnuts. Drop by tablespoonfuls 1 inch apart onto a greased baking sheet. Top each with a walnut half. Bake 11 minutes or until dry and cracked on top but soft when lightly touched. Let stand 5 minutes before removing from baking sheet.

Denise Blanton

ORANGE COOKIES

1 cup plain or butter-flavored	1 cup sour milk, or 1 cup milk mixed
shortening	with 1 tablespoon vinegar
2 cups granulated sugar	4 cups flour
1 teaspoon salt	½ teaspoon baking powder
2 eggs	1 teaspoon vanilla
Juice and zest of 1 orange	1 cup powdered sugar, or as
1 teaspoon baking soda	needed

Preheat oven to 375 degrees.

Cream shortening, granulated sugar and salt. Add eggs and orange zest and mix well. Dissolve baking soda in milk. Mix flour and baking powder. Add milk and flour mixtures alternately to creamed mixture. Mix in vanilla. Drop by teaspoonfuls onto a lightly greased baking sheet. Bake 8 to 9 minutes. Cool.

Combine orange juice with enough powdered sugar to make a smooth, spreadable frosting. Spread frosting over cooled cookies.

Karen Parker

CREAM CHEESE SUGAR COOKIES

1   cup sugar
2   sticks butter, softened
1   (3-ounce) package cream cheese,
      softened
½   teaspoon salt

½   teaspoon almond extract
½   teaspoon vanilla extract
1   egg yolk
2   cups flour

Preheat oven to 375 degrees.

Combine all ingredients except flour and blend well. Stir in flour until well blended. Dough can be used immediately with a cookie press; or refrigerate at least 2 to 3 hours, roll out dough on a floured surface and cut with cookie cutters. Decorate, if desired. Place cookies 1 inch apart on ungreased baking sheets. Bake 7 to 10 minutes or until light golden brown; do not overcook. Cool completely and store in an airtight container.

Lemon or Key lime zest (from about ½ of either fruit) can be added to dough to give it a tropical flare.

Yield: 5 to 6 dozen cookies

Jill Levy

CHOCOLATE BUTTER COOKIES

½   cup sugar
1½ sticks butter, softened
1   egg yolk

1   teaspoon almond extract
1½ cups flour
¼   cup cocoa powder

Preheat oven to 375 degrees.

Combine sugar, butter, egg yolk and almond extract in a large bowl. Beat with an electric mixer on medium speed for 2 to 3 minutes or until light and fluffy. Gradually add flour and cocoa and beat until well mixed. Shape into 1-inch balls or use a cookie press. Place cookies 1 inch apart on baking sheets. Bake 7 to 9 minutes or until set. Cool.

You may want to decorate with melted chocolate chips, melted almond bark, nuts, colored sugar or whatever you like.

Yield: 3 dozen cookies

Eleanor Drazovich

POTATO CHIP COOKIES

2   sticks butter, softened
2   sticks margarine, softened
1   cup sugar

2   teaspoons vanilla
3½ cups flour
5   ounces potato chips, crushed

Preheat oven to 350 degrees.

Beat together butter, margarine, sugar and vanilla in a large bowl. Gradually add flour and mix well. Stir in crushed potato chips. Drop by teaspoonfuls onto a baking sheet. Bake 12 to 15 minutes.

Yield: 6 dozen small cookies

Noni Crossett

MERINGUE COOKIES

2   egg whites, room temperature
½   teaspoon vanilla
⅓   cup sugar

½   cup chocolate chips
½   cup chopped walnuts or shredded
    coconut

Preheat oven to 325 degrees.

Beat egg whites and vanilla in a small bowl with an electric mixer for 2 minutes or until soft peaks form. Gradually add sugar and beat 4 minutes or until stiff peaks form. Fold in chocolate chips and walnuts. Drop by teaspoonfuls onto baking sheets greased with butter. Bake 10 minutes. Turn off oven, leaving cookies in oven until cool, about 4 hours or overnight.

Yield: 24 to 30 cookies

Derna De Pamphilis

OATMEAL COOKIES

1 cup shortening	1½ cups rolled oats (not quick oats)
¾ teaspoon salt	½ cup chopped nuts
1 teaspoon cinnamon	2 cups flour
½ teaspoon ground cloves	¾ teaspoon baking soda
1½ cups brown sugar	¼ cup buttermilk
2 eggs, beaten	

Preheat oven to 350 degrees.

Cream shortening, salt, cinnamon and cloves in a large bowl. Add brown sugar and mix well. Add beaten eggs and mix well. Mix in oats and nuts. In a separate bowl, sift together flour and baking soda. Add dry ingredients alternately with buttermilk into creamed mixture. Drop by teaspoonfuls onto a greased baking sheet. Bake 10 to 15 minutes.

Yield: 6 dozen cookies

Bertha Goshey

BANANA OATMEAL
CHOCOLATE CHIP COOKIES

2 sticks margarine, softened	1 teaspoon ground cloves
1 cup sugar	1 teaspoon cinnamon
2 eggs	3 ripe bananas, mashed
1 teaspoon vanilla	2 cups rolled oats
2 cups all-purpose flour	1 cup semi-sweet chocolate chips
1 teaspoon baking soda	

Preheat oven to 375 degrees.

Cream margarine and sugar together in a medium bowl until smooth. Stir in eggs and vanilla. Sift together flour, baking soda, cloves and cinnamon. Mix dry ingredients into creamed mixture. Add bananas, oats and chocolate chips and mix until well blended. Drop by rounded spoonfuls onto ungreased baking sheets. Bake 10 to 12 minutes. Remove from baking sheets and cool on wire racks.

Yield: 2 dozen cookies

Janie Rust

CRUNCHY PECAN COOKIES

6	ounces pecans (1½ cups), divided	¼	teaspoon salt
1	cup sugar		Scant ¼ teaspoon cinnamon
¼	cup potato starch	3	egg whites, beaten to stiff peaks

Preheat oven to 375 degrees.

Coarsely chop 1 cup pecans; set aside. Pulse remaining ½ cup pecans in a food processor with sugar, potato starch, salt and cinnamon until finely ground; do not pulse to a paste. Stir mixture into beaten egg whites. Stir in reserved chopped pecans. Drop by half-tablespoonfuls 2 inches apart onto a parchment paper-lined baking sheet. Bake 15 to 17 minutes or until lightly browned and slightly puffed. Slide parchment onto a rack and cool cookies completely before removing from paper. Cookies will crisp as they cool.

Cookies can be made 1 week ahead and kept in an airtight container at room temperature.

Marie Servinsky

FAMILY SUGAR COOKIES

3½	cups flour	2	eggs, beaten
2	teaspoons baking powder	1	teaspoon vanilla
1	teaspoon salt	1	teaspoon lemon flavoring
2	sticks butter	2	tablespoons milk or cream
2	cups sugar	1	egg white, beaten

Preheat oven to 350 degrees.

Sift together flour, baking powder and salt in a bowl. In a separate large bowl, cream butter and sugar. Add beaten eggs and beat until smooth and fluffy. Mix in vanilla, lemon flavoring and milk. Add dry ingredients and blend well. Chill dough. When thoroughly chilled, roll out dough until thin and cut into shapes. Place cookies on a greased baking sheet. Brush lightly with egg white. If desired, sprinkle with sugar, candies or chopped nuts. Bake 10 to 12 minutes or until delicately browned.

Kelly Pelletier

SOFT CHOCOLATE CHIP COOKIES

4½ cups all-purpose flour
2   teaspoons baking soda
4   sticks butter, softened
1½ cups brown sugar
½   cup granulated sugar

2   (3.4-ounce) packages instant
      vanilla pudding mix
4   eggs
2   teaspoons vanilla
4   cups semi-sweet chocolate chips
2   cups chopped walnuts (optional)

Preheat oven to 350 degrees.

Sift together flour and baking soda; set aside. In a large bowl, cream butter and both sugars. Beat in pudding mix until blended. Mix in eggs and vanilla. Blend in dry ingredients. Stir in chocolate chips and walnuts. Drop by rounded spoonfuls onto ungreased baking sheets. Bake 10 to 12 minutes or until edges are golden brown.

Yield: 6 dozen cookies

Janie Rust

PIGNOLI COOKIES

12 ounces almond paste
½   cup granulated sugar
1   cup powdered sugar

4   egg whites, divided
1½ cups pine nuts

Preheat oven to 325 degrees.

Mix almond paste and granulated sugar in a food processor until smooth. Add powdered sugar and 2 egg whites and process until smooth. Whisk remaining 2 egg whites in a small bowl. Place pine nuts on a shallow plate. With lightly floured hands, roll dough into 1-inch balls. Coat balls in beaten egg whites, shaking off excess, then roll in pine nuts, pressing lightly to stick. Arrange balls on 2 lightly greased foil-lined baking sheets. Flatten slightly to form a 1½-inch round. Bake 15 to 18 minutes or until lightly browned. Leave on baking sheet for 1 minute before transferring to a wire rack to cool.

Yield: 3 dozen cookies

Janie Rust

ALMOND BUTTER COOKIES

2   sticks butter, softened
1   cup sugar, plus extra for tops
2   cups flour

1   teaspoon almond extract
1   (2-ounce) package sliced
    almonds, roasted

Preheat oven to 350 degrees.

Cream butter and 1 cup sugar until smooth. Slowly mix in flour and almond extract. Roll dough into balls and place 1 inch apart on a baking sheet. Spray the bottom of a glass with nonstick spray and dip in extra sugar, then press onto dough balls to flatten. Bake 10 to 15 minutes. Sprinkle baked cookies with roasted almonds and drizzle with frosting.

To roast almonds, bake in oven at 350 degrees for about 5 minutes.

Yield: 2 dozen cookies

Frosting
1   cup powdered sugar
1   teaspoon almond extract

2   tablespoons warm water

Mix all frosting ingredients until thick and smooth.

Melissa Neilson

SWEDISH GINGERSNAPS

2   sticks margarine, softened
1   cup sugar
½   cup molasses
2¾ cups flour

1   tablespoon ground ginger
1   teaspoon cinnamon
2   teaspoons ground cloves
1   teaspoon baking soda

Preheat oven to 325 degrees.

Cream margarine, sugar and molasses. In a separate bowl, mix flour, ginger, cinnamon, cloves and baking soda. Slowly add dry ingredients to creamed mixture and blend well. Shape dough into 2 loaves, wrap in plastic wrap and freeze. When needed, remove from freezer and cut into ¼-inch thick (or thinner) slices. Place cookies on a greased baking sheet. Bake 8 to 10 minutes or until dark golden in color.

These cookies can also be rolled and cut with a cookie cutter to make gingerbread men or other designs. Great to have in freezer and bake on a moment's notice.

Doris Bedell

SOUR CREAM COOKIES

1 stick butter, softened	1 teaspoon baking soda
1½ cups brown sugar	1 cup sour cream
2 eggs, well beaten	1 teaspoon vanilla
2½ cups sifted flour	1 teaspoon nutmeg
¼ teaspoon salt	¾ cup raisins
½ teaspoon baking powder	⅔ cup chopped nuts

Preheat oven to 325 degrees.

Cream butter and brown sugar until fluffy. Add beaten eggs. In a separate bowl, mix flour, salt, baking powder and baking soda. Add dry ingredients alternately with sour cream to creamed mixture. Blend in vanilla and nutmeg. Fold in raisins and nuts. Bake 7 to 9 minutes or until light golden brown. If dough is chilled, bake 12 to 15 minutes. Cool before icing.

Icing

6 tablespoons butter	1 teaspoon vanilla
¼ cup half-and-half	1½ cups powdered sugar

Melt butter over medium heat and cook until golden brown. Using a hand mixer for best results, mix in half-and-half, vanilla and powdered sugar.

Kate Harper

OLD FASHIONED GINGERSNAPS

2½ cups flour	5 tablespoons butter, softened
2 teaspoons baking soda	¾ cup sugar, plus extra for rolling
2 teaspoons ginger	1 egg
¼ teaspoon ground cloves	2 cups molasses
¼ teaspoon salt	

Preheat oven to 350 degrees.

Sift together flour, baking soda, ginger, cloves and salt in a medium bowl. In a large bowl, beat butter, ¾ cup sugar, egg and molasses together until light and fluffy. Mix in dry ingredients. Cover and chill at least 1 hour. Working with a small section of dough at a time, roll dough into 1-inch balls. Roll balls in extra sugar to coat. Place balls on a greased baking sheet and press each ball down carefully with a spatula. Bake 12 to 15 minutes. Cool 1 minute before removing from baking sheet.

Yield: About 3½ dozen cookies

Kelly Pelletier

TOASTY MACAROONS

4 (3½-ounce) packages flaked
   coconut, toasted
1⅓ cups sweetened condensed milk

2 teaspoons rum extract
½ teaspoon ground ginger

Preheat oven to 325 degrees.

Combine all ingredients and stir until well blended. Drop by teaspoonfuls onto a foil-lined baking sheet. Bake 15 minutes or until firm. Remove from baking sheet to wire racks to cool completely before storing.

Yield: About 3 dozen

Janie Rust

LEMON SNOWFLAKES

Cookies

2 sticks butter, softened
½ cup powdered sugar

¾ cup cornstarch
1¼ cups sifted flour

Preheat oven to 350 degrees.

Beat butter in a medium bowl until creamy. Gradually blend in sugar. Add cornstarch and flour and blend well. Chill dough overnight. Roll chilled dough into 1-inch balls and place on a greased baking sheet. Flatten balls with the palm of your hand. Bake 15 minutes. When cooled, swirl topping on baked cookies.

Topping

1 cup powdered sugar
2 tablespoons butter, softened

1 tablespoon lemon juice
¼ teaspoon almond extract

Mix all topping ingredients together until smooth.

Norma Titherington

KEY LIME TRIFLE

1	(18¼-ounce) package butter recipe yellow cake mix	3	cups heavy cream
1	stick butter	1	(14-ounce) can sweetened condensed milk
	Zest of 2 limes, divided	½	cup Key lime juice

Prepare cake according to directions on package, using the butter and adding zest of 1 lime to the batter before baking. Bake in a 9x13-inch pan. Cool, then cut into 1-inch squares. While cake is baking, whip cream in a chilled bowl with chilled beaters until soft peaks form. Fold in sweetened condensed milk and lime juice, mixing until just blended. Layer half the cake in a trifle bowl or a large glass bowl. Top with half the cream mixture. Repeat layers. Top with remaining lime zest for garnish. Refrigerate until serving.

Cristina delaVega

TIRAMISU ANACAPRI

1	cup cold water	1	cup hot water
1	(14-ounce) can fat-free sweetened condensed milk	½	cup Kahlúa liqueur
1	(1.4-ounce) package sugar-free vanilla instant pudding mix	1	tablespoon instant espresso, or 2 tablespoons instant coffee granules
1	(8-ounce) package reduced-fat cream cheese, softened	2	(3-ounce) packages cake-like ladyfingers (24 cookies)
1	(8-ounce) container frozen reduced-calorie whipped topping, thawed	3	tablespoons cocoa powder, divided

Whisk together cold water, condensed milk and pudding mix in a large bowl. Cover surface of mixture with plastic wrap and chill 30 minutes or until firm. Remove plastic wrap and beat in cream cheese with an electric mixer on medium speed until well blended. Gently fold in whipped topping.

In a separate bowl, combine hot water, Kahlúa and espresso. Split ladyfingers in half lengthwise. Dip cut side of each ladyfinger half in Kahlúa mixture and place, flat-side down, in a trifle bowl or large glass bowl. Spread one-fourth of pudding mixture evenly over ladyfingers. Sprinkle with 1 tablespoon cocoa powder. Repeat layers, ending with cocoa. Cover and chill at least 8 hours.

Serves: 12

Diane Clapp

LEMON TART

Almond Pastry Shell

1	cup sliced almonds	1	egg yolk
3	tablespoons sugar	2	teaspoons almond extract
1¼	cups cake flour	½	teaspoon salt
1	stick butter		

Lemon Cream

3	eggs	1	cup lemon juice
1	cup sugar	10	tablespoons butter, chilled

Preheat oven to 350 degrees.

Place almonds and sugar in a food processor and grind to a fine powder. Add flour, butter, egg yolk, almond extract and salt and pulse to combine. Mixture will be crumbly. Sprinkle mixture on a greased and floured 9-inch tart ring or pan and press down evenly. Bake 15 minutes or until golden brown. Cool.

For lemon cream, beat eggs with a whisk. Whisk in sugar. Mix in lemon juice. Transfer mixture to a saucepan. Cook over low heat, stirring with a rubber spatula, until mixture reaches 168 degrees. Remove from heat and whisk in butter. Pour into cooled tart shell. Chill until set.

Charles Rosselli
Executive Pastry Chef, Sailfish Point Country Club

TIRAMISU

36	ladyfingers	6	tablespoons sugar
1	cup strong coffee	8	ounces mascarpone cheese
¼	cup Kahlúa liqueur	2	cups whipped cream
6	egg yolks		Cocoa powder for dusting

Layer the bottom of a serving dish with ladyfingers. Combine coffee and Kahlúa and pour over ladyfingers. Set aside to let mixture soak into ladyfingers. In a double boiler, whisk egg yolks with sugar until triple in volume or until very thick. Remove from heat and whip until cool. Fold in cheese and mix well. Fold in whipped cream. Layer half of cream filling over soaked ladyfingers. Dust with cocoa powder. Repeat layers. Refrigerate until set.

Serves: 8 to 10

Lorraine Nehls

FRUIT PIZZA

1   (20-ounce) package refrigerated
    cookie dough
1   (8-ounce) package cream cheese,
    softened
⅓   cup sugar
½   teaspoon vanilla or other
    flavoring (almond, orange or
    lemon)

Fruit of choice (see note below),
    well drained
½   cup orange, peach or apricot
    preserves
1   tablespoon water

Preheat oven to 375 degrees.

Line an ungreased 14-inch pizza pan with cookie dough cut into ⅑-inch slices, overlapping slightly. Bake 12 minutes or until light brown. Remove from oven and cool on a wire rack. In a medium bowl, combine cream cheese, sugar and vanilla. Spread over cookie crust. Arrange fruit over cream cheese layer in a design of your choice. Melt preserves in water in a small saucepan over very low heat, stirring often. Brush preserves as a glaze over fruit, making sure all fruit is covered completely. Refrigerate until ready to serve.

Use fresh blueberries, banana slices, Mandarin orange sections, seedless grapes, strawberry halves or kiwi slices, or choose your own.

Serves: 6 to 8

Lonnie Balaban

MOCK ALMOND ROCCA

    Saltine crackers
2   sticks butter
¾   cup brown sugar

1   (24-ounce) package chocolate
    chips
1   cup chopped walnuts

Preheat oven to 400 degrees.

Line a well greased 9x13-inch baking pan with saltine crackers, salt-side up. Combine butter and brown sugar in a saucepan and bring to a boil. Boil 3 minutes. Pour boiling mixture over crackers. Bake 7 minutes or until bubbly all over. Remove from oven and cover with chocolate chips. Allow chocolate to melt, then spread evenly. Sprinkle with walnuts, pressing gently into chocolate. Chill in refrigerator. Cut into squares before serving.

Serves: 10 to 12

Debbie Thomas

ENGLISH TRIFLE

1 stick butter, softened	1 (3.4-ounce) package instant vanilla pudding mix
1 cup sugar, divided	2 cups cold milk
2 eggs	1 (12-ounce) jar seedless raspberry jam
1¾ cups flour	
½ teaspoon baking powder	½ cup cooking sherry (optional)
½ teaspoon salt	1 pint blueberries
1 pint heavy cream	1 pint strawberries
1 teaspoon vanilla	4 large bananas, sliced

Preheat oven to 375 degrees.

Cream together butter and ½ cup sugar. Beat in eggs one at a time. In a separate bowl, combine flour, baking powder and salt. Fold dry ingredients into creamed mixture. Pour batter into a greased and floured 8-inch square pan. Bake 25 minutes. Cool completely before cutting into squares.

While baking, beat cream until soft peaks form. Add remaining ½ cup sugar and vanilla and beat until stiff peaks form; set aside. In a separate bowl, combine pudding mix and cold milk and beat with an electric mixer for 2 minutes or until thickened.

To assemble, spread half of the cake squares in a deep dish. Spread half of raspberry jam over cake. Layer blueberries, strawberries and bananas on top. Spread half of pudding over fruit and add a layer using half of the cream. Repeat layers. Chill 30 minutes before serving.

Serves: 8 to 10

Kathy Walker

PEANUT BUTTER FUDGE

½ cup milk	1 cup peanut butter
2 cups sugar	2 tablespoons butter

Combine milk and sugar in a saucepan and bring to a boil. Boil 5 minutes. Remove from heat and stir in peanut butter until smooth. Add butter and stir until mixed. Pour into an 8-inch square pan. Fudge will set up quickly. Let cool before cutting.

Karen Parker

STRAWBERRY TARTLETS

12	wonton wrappers	2	teaspoons orange juice
3	tablespoons butter, melted	3	cups sliced fresh strawberries
⅓	cup brown sugar		Whipped cream and fresh mint
¾	cup mascarpone cheese		for garnish (optional)
2	tablespoons honey		

Preheat oven to 325 degrees.

Brush one side of each wonton wrapper with butter. Place brown sugar in a shallow bowl. Press buttered side of wontons into sugar to coat. Press wontons, sugared-side up, into greased muffin cups. Bake 7 to 9 minutes or until edges are lightly browned. Remove wonton cups to a wire rack to cool.

Combine cheese, honey and orange juice in a bowl. Spoon about 1 tablespoon of mixture into each wonton cup. Top with strawberries. Garnish with whipped cream and mint.

Yield: 1 dozen

Janel Weigt

SEVEN LAYER BARS

1	stick butter	1	(6-ounce) package butterscotch
1	cup crushed vanilla wafers		chips
1	cup shredded coconut	1	(14-ounce) can sweetened
1	(6-ounce) package semi-sweet		condensed milk
	chocolate chips	1	cup chopped pecans

Preheat oven to 350 degrees.

Melt butter in a 9x13-inch pan while oven is preheating. When melted, press crushed wafers into butter. Layer coconut, chocolate chips, butterscotch chips, condensed milk and pecans in order listed over wafer crust. Bake 30 minutes. Cool before cutting into bars.

Yield: 48 cookies

Eleanor Drazovich

FRUIT SQUARES

2   sticks butter, softened
1   cup sugar
1   teaspoon vanilla
2   cups flour

1   cup chopped pecans
1   (21-ounce) can fruit pie filling of
    choice

Preheat oven to 350 degrees.

Cream together butter, sugar and vanilla. Stir in flour and pecans and mix well. Spread dough in an 8x11x1-inch nonstick baking sheet. Spread pie filling over dough. Bake 40 to 60 minutes. Cool slightly before cutting into squares. Tastes best warm. Refrigerate leftovers.

Serves: 8 to 10

Melissa Neilson

CREAMY BARS

Base
1   (18¼-ounce) yellow cake mix
2   eggs
½   cup butter-flavored shortening,
    melted

1   tablespoon milk
¾   cup chopped pecans

Topping
1   (8-ounce) package cream cheese,
    softened
2   eggs

3½ cups powdered sugar
1   teaspoon vanilla

Preheat oven to 350 degrees.

Combine all base ingredients in a large bowl. Mix with a fork or an electric mixer on low speed until just moistened. Spread evenly into a greased 9x13-inch pan.

For topping, beat cream cheese in a large bowl with an electric mixer on medium speed until smooth. Beat in eggs, powdered sugar and vanilla until smooth. Spread topping evenly over base. Bake 35 minutes or until edges and top are light golden brown and have a slightly shiny appearance. Cool completely before cutting into 1½-inch squares.

Serves: 3 to 4 dozen

Shelley Evans

CHOCOLATE PEANUT SQUARES

2   sticks margarine, divided
6   (1-ounce) squares semi-sweet
      chocolate, divided
1   cup sweetened shredded coconut
1½ cups graham cracker crumbs

½   cup chopped unsalted peanuts
2   (8-ounce) packages cream cheese,
      softened
1   cup sugar
1   teaspoon vanilla

Melt 1½ sticks margarine and 2 squares chocolate in a microwave on high for 1 to 2 minutes or until melted, stirring every 30 seconds. Stir in coconut, cracker crumbs and peanuts. Press mixture into the bottom of a 9x13-inch baking pan. Chill 30 minutes. In a bowl, mix cream cheese, sugar and vanilla until well blended. Spread mixture over crust and chill 30 minutes longer. Microwave remaining 4 tablespoons butter and 4 squares chocolate on high for 1 to 2 minutes or until melted, stirring every 30 seconds. Spread over cream cheese layer. Chill another 30 minutes. Cut into squares, being sure to cut all the way through crust.

Yield: 4 dozen

Jennifer Strauss

CHOCOLATE RASPBERRY LAYER BARS

1⅔ cups graham cracker crumbs
1   stick butter or margarine, melted
1   (12-ounce) package semi-sweet
      chocolate chips
1   (7-ounce) package flaked coconut
      (2⅔ cups)

1   (14-ounce) can sweetened
      condensed milk
⅓   cup white chocolate chips
1   cup seedless red raspberry jam
⅓   cup finely chopped walnuts
      (optional)

Preheat oven to 350 degrees.

Combine cracker crumbs and butter in a medium bowl. Press mixture firmly into the bottom of an ungreased 9x13-inch baking pan. Sprinkle with semi-sweet chocolate chips, then coconut. Pour condensed milk evenly over the top. Sprinkle with white chocolate chips. Bake 20 to 25 minutes or until lightly browned. Cool completely in pan on a wire rack. Spread jam over top and sprinkle with walnuts. Cut into bars.

Yield: 2 dozen

Kirk Baker

PRALINE GRAHAMS

⅓ (16-ounce) box graham crackers, any style
1½ sticks butter

½ cup sugar
1 cup chopped pecans

Preheat oven to 300 degrees.

Separate each graham cracker into 4 sections and arrange side by side in a jelly roll pan. Melt butter in a saucepan. Stir in sugar and pecans. Bring to a boil. Cook 3 minutes, stirring frequently. Spread mixture over graham crackers. Bake 12 minutes. Remove from pan and cool on wax paper or a wire rack. Store in an airtight container.

These are about the easiest cookies you will ever make. They are tasty, crunchy, crispy and sweet.

Yield: 3½ dozen

Pat Cook

MOM'S BANANA SPLIT DESSERT

2 sticks butter, divided
3 cups graham cracker crumbs, divided
3 medium to large bananas, sliced
½ gallon Neapolitan ice cream
1 cup chopped walnuts

1 cup chocolate chips
2 cups powdered sugar
1 (12-ounce) can evaporated milk
1 teaspoon vanilla
1 (8-ounce) container frozen whipped topping, thawed

Melt 1 stick butter and mix with 2 cups cracker crumbs. Press mixture into a 9x13-inch pan. Layer sliced bananas over crust. Cut ice cream into ½-inch thick slices and place over bananas. Sprinkle walnuts on top. Cover pan with plastic wrap and freeze until firm.

Melt remaining 1 stick butter with chocolate chips in a saucepan over medium heat, stirring constantly. Mix in powdered sugar and evaporated milk. Continue to cook and stir until smooth. Remove from heat and stir in vanilla; set aside to cool. When cooled, spread chocolate mixture over ice cream in pan. Spread whipped topping over chocolate and sprinkle with remaining 1 cup cracker crumbs. Freeze until ready to serve. Remove from freezer 10 minutes before serving.

Chocolate sauce can be made in advance for easy preparation.

This dessert may be stored, covered, in the freezer for several weeks.

Susie Fogarty

CHOCOLATE PEAR PASTRY

1	(17.3-ounce) package frozen puff pastry sheets, thawed	5	ripe pears, such as Comice or Bosc
1	cup chopped hazelnuts (4 ounces)	1	egg, beaten
½	(9-ounce) box chocolate wafer cookies	2	tablespoons sugar
		½	cup semi-sweet chocolate chips

Preheat oven to 400 degrees.

Roll out 1 pastry sheet on a lightly floured surface to an 18x10-inch rectangle. Transfer to a greased baking sheet. Fold over 1½ inches on each of the long sides to make a rim. Use a fork to pierce the center in 1-inch intervals. Repeat with remaining pastry on a second greased baking sheet. Bake both pastries for 10 minutes. Cool on wire racks. Reduce oven temperature to 375 degrees.

Combine hazelnuts and chocolate wafers in a food processor or blender and pulse until mixture resembles sand. Peel pears and cut each in half lengthwise, discarding cores and stems. Distribute crumb mixture along the center of each partially baked pastry. Arrange pears, cut-side down, on crumbs, alternating stem and round ends. Brush the rim of each pastry with egg and sprinkle with sugar. Bake at 375 degrees for 20 to 25 minutes or until pears are tender when poked with a fork. Cool on wire racks. Melt chocolate chips in a small cup in the microwave for 1 to 1½ minutes, stirring until smooth. Drizzle melted chocolate over pastries.

This recipe can be made up to 1 day ahead.

Frozen puff pastry is easier than homemade; 5 hours easier, to be exact.

Marie Servinsky

CRUNCHY MELON PARFAIT

1	(8-ounce) container low-fat vanilla yogurt	½	small honeydew or other melon, cut into 1-inch cubes
1	tablespoon brown sugar	1	cup low-fat granola
		4	strawberries for garnish

Combine yogurt and brown sugar. Spoon half the yogurt mixture into 4 dessert glasses. Top with half the melon cubes. Add half the granola. Repeat layers, ending with granola. Garnish with strawberries.

Serves: 4

Cecilia Wright

SCALLOPED PINEAPPLE

1   stick butter, softened
1   cup sugar
2   eggs, well beaten, room
    temperature
1   (20-ounce) can crushed pineapple,
    undrained

3   cups firmly packed French bread
    cubes, crust included
    (about ½ of a large loaf)
1   cup mini marshmallows

Preheat oven to 350 degrees.

Cream together butter and sugar. Mix in eggs. Add undrained pineapple, bread cubes and marshmallows. Transfer to a greased 1½-quart casserole dish. Bake, uncovered, for 45 minutes.

I have served this for years at cookouts, church buffets, Thanksgiving and Christmas. Super easy and good.

Sally McMeekan

DOUBLE CHOCOLATE KAHLÚA TRUFFLES

2½   cups finely crushed chocolate
     wafers
1   cup finely chopped walnuts
1   cup sifted 10X powdered sugar
⅓   cup Kahlúa or other liqueur
1½-2 tablespoons water

⅔   cup dark or semi-sweet
     chocolate chips
1   tablespoon shortening, plain or
     butter-flavored
1   cup white chocolate chips

Combine wafer crumbs, walnuts, powdered sugar and liqueur in a large bowl. Add enough water so crumbs hold together. Use hands or a teaspoon-size cookie scoop to shape mixture into 1-inch balls. Place balls on a wax paper- or parchment-lined baking sheet.

Melt dark chocolate and shortening together in the microwave in 15 to 20 second increments or on the stove top over low heat. In a separate container or saucepan, melt white chocolate. Using a fork, dip half the balls in dark chocolate and half in white chocolate. Return dipped balls to baking sheet. With a spoon or fork, drizzle white chocolate over dark chocolate balls in a random pattern, and drizzle dark chocolate over white chocolate balls. Refrigerate 30 minutes or until chocolate is set. Store in an airtight container in the refrigerator.

These are no-bake handmade truffles. The better the quality of chocolate, the better the truffles.

Jill Levy

303

ULTIMATE HOT FUDGE SAUCE

1	cup cocoa powder	1	(12-ounce) can evaporated milk
2	cups sugar	1	teaspoon vanilla
1	stick butter		

Combine cocoa and sugar in a bowl. Meanwhile, melt butter in a medium saucepan over medium heat. Stir in cocoa mixture. Gradually add evaporated milk, stirring constantly until mixture reaches a gentle boil. Boil 1 minute. Remove from heat and stir in vanilla. Cool. Store in a covered container in the refrigerator for up to several weeks.

Lillie King Davis

PEANUT BUTTER BALLS

1	(18-ounce) jar crunchy peanut butter	2	(16-ounce) packages powdered sugar
4	sticks margarine	1	(12-ounce) package chocolate chips
1	teaspoon vanilla	1	(4-ounce) bar paraffin wax

Melt peanut butter and margarine in a saucepan over low heat. Stir in vanilla. Add powdered sugar and mix well. Shape mixture into balls. Melt chocolate chips and paraffin in a separate saucepan. Dip balls in chocolate and place on wax paper to set.

Yield: 9 dozen

Mildred Gray

HOLIDAY BOURBON BALLS

2	cups powdered sugar	¼	cup cocoa powder
1½	cups crushed vanilla wafers	3	tablespoons bourbon, or to taste
1½	cups crushed walnuts	3	tablespoons water
3	tablespoons light corn syrup		

Combine all ingredients and mix well. Shape mixture into bite-size balls. Let stand at least 48 hours in an airtight container.

Kathy Wiggins

CHOCOLATE LIQUEUR TRUFFLES

⅔ cup butter, softened
1 egg yolk
1¼ cups powdered sugar
1 (6-ounce) bag semi-sweet chocolate, melted and cooled, plus extra for drizzling (optional)

1 tablespoon instant coffee granules
1 tablespoon rum or liqueur
1 cup chocolate wafer crumbs

Cream butter. Beat in egg yolk, powdered sugar, melted chocolate, coffee granules and rum. Chill 3 to 4 hours. Roll by teaspoonfuls into balls. Drop balls into wafer crumbs. Drizzle with extra chocolate, if desired.

Renee Booth

GRANDMA'S CHOCOLATE CREAM DESSERT

Crust
3 cups crushed vanilla wafers
⅔ cup butter, melted

¼ cup sugar
½ teaspoon cinnamon

Filling
1 (7-ounce) milk chocolate candy bar, broken
1 (10-ounce) bag large marshmallows

1 cup milk
2 cups heavy cream
½ teaspoon vanilla

Combine all crust ingredients in a bowl and mix well. Set aside ⅓ cup of mixture for topping. Press remaining mixture into a greased 9x13-inch pan. Refrigerate until firm.

For filling, melt chocolate with marshmallows and milk in a medium saucepan over medium-low heat, stirring often. Remove from heat and cool to room temperature. While cooling, whip cream in a chilled bowl with chilled beaters. Fold whipped cream and vanilla into chocolate mixture. Pour filling over crust. Chill 3 to 4 hours. Sprinkle with reserved crumb mixture. Cut into squares and serve cold.

Lloyd Wescoat

CLASSIC KEY LIME PIE

1 (14-ounce) can sweetened
    condensed milk
6 eggs, separated
½ cup Key lime juice

Graham cracker pie crust, baked
1 tablespoon cream of tartar
1 cup sugar

Preheat oven to 350 degrees.

Whip together condensed milk and egg yolks with an electric mixer on medium-high speed for 8 minutes or until light and creamy. Add lime juice and mix on low speed for 1 second. Fold mixture a few times with a spatula to blend. Pour mixture into baked crust; set aside. Beat egg whites with cream of tartar for 5 minutes. Add sugar and beat 5 minutes longer. Spread meringue over pie. Bake 10 to 15 minutes or until meringue is brown. Cool before serving.

Serves: 6 to 8

Gary and Melissa Keyes

KEY LIME CHOCOLATE PIE

Crust
16 chocolate cookies, crushed
½   cup flaked coconut

2   tablespoons margarine

Filling and Topping
3   eggs, separated
1   (14-ounce) can sweetened
     condensed milk

2   (2-ounce) envelopes pre-melted
     unsweetened chocolate
⅓   cup Key lime juice
1   (7-ounce) jar marshmallow crème

Preheat oven to 375 degrees.

Combine all crust ingredients and press into the bottom and up the sides of a 9-inch pie pan. Bake 8 minutes. Cool. Reduce oven temperature to 350 degrees.

For filling, beat egg yolks with an electric mixer on high speed for 4 minutes or until thick and lemon colored. Add milk, chocolate and lime juice. Beat until well combined and pour into crust. With clean beaters, beat egg whites until stiff. Gradually add marshmallow crème. Beat until stiff peaks form. Spread over filling, sealing to edges of crust. Bake at 350 degrees for 12 to 15 minutes or until meringue is golden. Cool on a wire rack. Chill in refrigerator at least 2 to 3 hours.

Serves: 8

Barbara Graunke

PERFECT FLORIDA KEY LIME PIE

2	(14-ounce) cans sweetened condensed milk	2	eggs
1	cup Key lime juice	1	(9-inch) graham cracker pie crust

Preheat oven to 325 degrees.

Combine condensed milk, lime juice and eggs in a mixing bowl. Whisk until well blended and pour into pie crust. Bake 15 minutes. Chill in refrigerator at least 2 hours.

Greg Moore

 # LORELEI KEY LIME PIE

1	(14-ounce) can sweetened condensed milk	¼	cup Key lime juice Lime zest
1	(12-ounce) container frozen whipped topping, thawed	1	pie crust, baked

Combine condensed milk, whipped topping, lime juice and lime zest. Pour into baked pie crust and freeze.

Classic Cookbook Committee

BIMINI KEY LIME PIE

1	(14-ounce) can sweetened condensed milk	½	teaspoon vanilla
1	(8-ounce) package cream cheese, softened	1	(9-inch) graham cracker pie crust Whipped cream or whipped topping
½	cup Key lime juice (other limes will due, but not as tasty)		Lime slices for garnish

Combine condensed milk, cream cheese and lime juice in a blender. Blend on low speed until smooth. Stir in vanilla. Pour mixture into pie crust. Chill in refrigerator for 3 to 4 hours or until set. Top with whipped cream and garnish with lime slices.

Easy to make; my guests' favorite! No cooking; made in a blender!

Jo Durham

KEY LIME AND ORANGE PIE

1½ (14-ounce) cans sweetened
    condensed milk
7   egg yolks
½ cup Key lime juice

½ cup freshly squeezed Florida
    orange juice
1   tablespoon Key lime zest
1   tablespoon orange zest
1   graham cracker pie crust

Preheat oven to 350 degrees.

Combine all ingredients except pie crust in a bowl. Beat with an electric mixer on medium speed until thoroughly mixed and thickened. Pour mixture into pie crust. Bake 10 to 12 minutes or until filling jiggles only slightly when shaken. Cool. Cover and refrigerate 2 hours before serving. Serve topped with whipped cream.

Kirk Baker

CREAM CHEESE KEY LIME PIE

Crust
1⅓ cups graham cracker crumbs
3   tablespoons sugar

1   teaspoon cinnamon
5   tablespoons butter, melted

Filling
1   (8-ounce) package cream cheese,
    softened
3   egg yolks

1   (14-ounce) can sweetened
    condensed milk
½ cup sugar
⅔ cup Key lime juice

Preheat oven to 350 degrees.

Combine cracker crumbs, sugar and cinnamon in a bowl. Mix in melted butter. Press mixture into a pie pan. Bake 8 minutes.

Meanwhile, prepare filling. Beat cream cheese until soft. Add egg yolks. Mix in condensed milk and sugar. Stir in lime juice. Pour filling into baked crust. Bake 20 to 25 minutes longer.

Carolyn Livings

CARIBBEAN DREAM PIE

Crust

2 cups finely crushed graham crackers or ginger snaps	¼ cup finely minced pecans
½ cup shredded unsweetened coconut	6 tablespoons butter, melted

Filling

1 (14-ounce) can sweetened condensed milk	½ cup plus 1 tablespoon fresh lime juice
1 tablespoon lime zest	2 bananas, sliced
	½ ripe mango, peeled and sliced

Preheat oven to 350 degrees.

Combine all crust ingredients and mix well. Press mixture firmly into the bottom and up the sides of a 9-inch pie pan, building a smooth ½-inch ridge around the edge. Reserve some of crust mixture for topping. Bake crust 10 minutes. Cool completely.

For filling, pour condensed milk into a medium bowl. Add lime zest and juice and whisk for a few minutes until mixture thickens. Layer banana and mango slices in cooled crust. Pour milk mixture over fruit and spread evenly. Sprinkle reserved crust mixture over the top and chill.

Serves: 8

Pam Fogt

CHOCOLATE PIE DELICIOUS

3 egg whites	⅓ cup chopped pecans
Dash of salt	1 teaspoon vanilla
¾ cup sugar	1 cup heavy cream, sweetened to taste
¾ cup fine chocolate wafer crumbs	

Preheat oven to 325 degrees.

Beat egg whites with salt until soft peaks form. Add sugar and beat to stiff peaks. Fold in crumbs, pecans and vanilla. Spread mixture evenly in a greased 9-inch pie pan. Bake 35 minutes; cool thoroughly. Whip cream and spread over pie. Chill 4 to 5 hours.

Serves: 6 to 8

Jean Jacobs

TROPICAL ICE CREAM PIE

Crust

1	cup macadamia nuts	2	tablespoons sugar
1	cup sweetened shredded coconut	1	egg white
4	whole graham crackers		

Filling

1	pint mango sorbet	1	ripe mango, peeled and cut into chunks (1½ cups)
1	pint pineapple-coconut ice cream		
½	medium pineapple, peeled and cut into chunks (2½ cups)	1	ripe kiwi, peeled, halved lengthwise and thinly sliced crosswise

Preheat oven to 375 degrees.

Place nuts in a jelly roll pan. Spread coconut in a separate jelly roll pan. Bake both for 8 to 10 minutes or until toasted, stirring once; cool. In a food processor, finely crush crackers. Add toasted nuts and pulse until chopped. Add sugar and egg white and pulse until mixture is evenly moistened. Reserve ¼ cup toasted coconut. Stir remaining coconut into crumb mixture. Press mixture firmly onto the bottom and up the sides of a greased 9-inch pie pan. Bake 12 to 15 minutes; cool completely.

For filling, soften sorbet and ice cream at room temperature for 10 to 15 minutes. Pack cooled crust with layers of sorbet and ice cream using a large spoon. Freeze at least 1 hour or until ready to serve. To serve, remove from freezer and top with pineapple, mango and kiwi. Sprinkle with reserved toasted coconut.

Serves: 6 to 8

Elsie Stewart

KENTUCKY HIGH PIE

¼	cup cornstarch	1	cup chopped pecans
2	eggs	1	cup chocolate chips
1	cup sugar	1	stick butter, melted
1	teaspoon vanilla	1	(9-inch) frozen deep-dish pie crust

Preheat oven to 350 degrees.

Mix cornstarch, eggs, sugar, vanilla, pecans and chocolate chips in a bowl. Add butter and mix well. Pour mixture into pie crust. Bake 45 to 50 minutes.

Serves: 6 to 8

Melissa Neilson

PINEAPPLE FLUFF PIE

2½ tablespoons cornstarch
1½ cups pineapple juice, divided
¾ cup sugar, divided
1 cup crushed pineapple in juice, drained

¼ teaspoon orange or lemon zest
3 egg whites
1 (9-inch) pie crust, baked and cooled, or crumb crust
Whipped cream

Blend cornstarch and ½ cup pineapple juice in a bowl. In a saucepan, bring remaining 1 cup juice and ½ cup sugar to a boil. Slowly add cornstarch mixture and stir until blended. Cook until thickened. Add pineapple and zest and cook a few minutes longer. Cool completely. Beat egg whites until thick. Slowly add remaining ¼ cup sugar and beat until stiff peaks form. Gently fold whites into cooled pineapple mixture. Pour mixture into baked crust. Refrigerate until chilled. Spread whipped cream on top before serving.

Serves: 6 to 8

Jean Gallagher

FROZEN STRAWBERRY MARGARITA PIE

Crust
1¼ cups finely crushed pretzels
1 stick butter, melted

¼ cup sugar

Filling
1 (14-ounce) can sweetened condensed milk
½ cup frozen margarita mix concentrate, thawed

1 (10-ounce) package frozen strawberries, thawed
1 cup heavy cream, whipped
Lime slices for garnish

Combine all crust ingredients in a small bowl and mix well. Press mixture firmly into bottom of an ungreased springform pan. Refrigerate while preparing filling.

For filling, combine condensed milk and margarita mix in a large bowl and beat with an electric mixer until smooth. Add strawberries and beat on low speed until well blended. Fold in whipped cream. Pour filling into crust, cover and freeze 4 to 6 hours or until firm. Thaw at room temperature about 15 minutes before serving. Garnish with lime slices.

Serves: 10

Dagmar Bothwell

MACAROON PIE

3 cups chopped coconut macaroons	½ cup chopped dates
¾ cup sugar	½ cup chopped walnuts
1 teaspoon baking powder	1 cup egg whites, beaten

Preheat oven to 300 degrees.

Mix chopped macaroons, sugar, baking powder, dates and walnuts. Fold in beaten egg whites. Pour mixture into a greased and floured 8-inch pie pan. Bake 25 minutes or until top is firm to the touch. Cool. Serve with whipped cream.

Serves: 7 to 8

John Donahue
The Plaza Café, Stuart, Florida

PEANUT BUTTER ICE CREAM PIE

12 ounces crunchy peanut butter	1 quart vanilla ice cream, softened
1 (12-ounce) container frozen whipped topping, thawed, divided	2 (9-inch) chocolate crumb crusts Chocolate shavings or chocolate crumbs for garnish (optional)

Mix peanut butter and two-thirds of whipped topping. Stir mixture into softened ice cream until thoroughly mixed. Divide mixture between pie crusts. Freeze at least 4 hours. Top with remaining whipped topping. Garnish as desired and freeze until ready to serve. Thaw at room temperature 10 to 15 minutes before serving.

Amanda Tilton Martin

 MANGO PIE

3-4 mangoes, peeled	Sprinkle of nutmeg
1 pie crust, unbaked	¾ cup flour
1 Key lime or ½ Persian lime	6 tablespoons butter
1 tablespoon plus ⅓ cup sugar, divided	

Preheat oven to 400 degrees.

Slice mangoes into unbaked pie crust, using enough to fill pan. Squeeze lime juice over mangoes. Sprinkle with 1 tablespoon sugar and nutmeg. Combine remaining ⅓ cup sugar, flour and butter and mix until crumbly. Spread crumb mixture over pie. Bake 40 to 50 minutes. Delicious!

Carol Ann Snyder

PEACHES AND CREAM PIE

¾ cup all-purpose flour
1 teaspoon baking powder
½ teaspoon salt
1 (3-ounce) package vanilla
pudding mix (not instant)
3 tablespoons butter, softened
1 egg
½ cup milk

1 (20-ounce) can peaches, drained,
juice reserved
1 (8-ounce) package cream cheese,
softened
½ cup plus 1 tablespoon sugar,
divided
½ teaspoon cinnamon

Preheat oven to 350 degrees.

Combine flour, baking powder, salt, pudding mix, butter, egg and milk in a large bowl. Pour mixture into a greased pie pan. Arrange peaches over batter in pan. Mix cream cheese, ½ cup sugar and 3 tablespoons reserved peach juice. Spoon mixture into the middle of pie, leaving a 1-inch border around the sides. Combine remaining 1 tablespoon sugar and cinnamon and sprinkle over the top. Bake 30 to 35 minutes or until golden brown.

Joanna Florio Huffman

 LEMONADE PIE

1 (¼-ounce) envelope unflavored
gelatin
½ cup cold water
⅛ teaspoon salt
4 eggs, separated

1 (6-ounce) can frozen lemonade
concentrate, thawed
½ cup sugar
½ cup heavy cream, whipped
1 pie crust, baked

Sprinkle gelatin over cold water in the top of a double boiler. Add salt and egg yolks and mix well. Place over boiling water and cook, stirring constantly, for 3 minutes or until mixture thickens slightly and gelatin dissolves. Remove from water and add lemonade. Chill, stirring occasionally, until mixture mounds slightly when dropped from a spoon. Beat egg whites until stiff, but not dry. Gradually add sugar, beating well after each addition. Fold gelatin mixture into egg whites. Fold in whipped cream. Pour mixture into baked pie crust and chill.

Alice Hoke

CHESS PIE

An old Southern recipe — like pecan pie without the pecans.

1½ cups sugar	1 teaspoon vanilla
4 eggs	1 teaspoon lemon extract
1 stick butter, melted	1 tablespoon vinegar
5 teaspoons cornmeal	1 pie crust, unbaked
5 teaspoons milk	

Preheat oven to 350 degrees.

Beat sugar and eggs. Add butter, cornmeal, milk, vanilla, lemon extract and vinegar. Pour mixture into unbaked pie crust. Bake 45 minutes.

Melissa Keyes

 ## A STUART PIONEER'S PUMPKIN PIE

1 cup sugar	1½ cups canned pumpkin
1 teaspoon cinnamon	2 eggs, beaten
1 teaspoon ground ginger	1½ cups milk, heated without boiling
½ teaspoon salt	1 pie crust, unbaked

Preheat oven to 400 degrees.

Combine sugar, cinnamon, ginger and salt in a bowl. Add pumpkin and mix thoroughly. Add beaten eggs. Blend in heated milk. Pour mixture into unbaked pie crust. Bake 15 minutes. Reduce heat to 375 degrees and bake 30 minutes longer or until done.

Mrs. Harry Dyer
Mother of Virginia Dyer Brock

We need quiet, wild places to cut ourselves down to size. They have the therapy that restores a proper sense of values: that all men and all creatures are common passengers on a wondrous space ship, living in that strange river of light always flowing from the sun. We need to lift our eyes to the mystery of a starry sky at night and to wonder.

~ Ernest Lyons

Pet
Pages

HOMEMADE DOG FOOD

3 pounds ground beef, pork, chicken or turkey
3 tablespoons garlic powder (not garlic salt)
1 (28-ounce) can crushed tomatoes

1 (28-ounce) can diced tomatoes
2 (15-ounce) cans beans, any type
2 (15-ounce) cans carrots
2 (15-ounce) cans peas

Cook meat until brown. Add all remaining ingredients and mix well. Cool before serving. Divide mixture into containers; freeze half of the containers, refrigerate other half.

You should consult your vet before switching to a homemade diet for your pets.

Bread crumbs and rice can also be used. About every other batch, I cook up a package of chicken livers along with the beef and add them to the mixture. Dogs love it.

Meko

LIVER COOKIES

1½ pounds chicken livers
1 teaspoon garlic powder (not garlic salt)

2 eggs
3 cups white flour

Preheat oven to 350 degrees.

Mix livers, garlic powder and eggs in a food processor or blender until smooth. Pour mixture into a bowl and stir in flour, a little at a time, until batter is thick but still pourable. Spread batter in a greased baking dish. Bake 30 to 45 minutes or until done. (Dogs love these soft or dry so the cooking time will vary depending on how your dog likes the treats.) Cut into squares. Refrigerate or freeze; can be served frozen.

Whatney

DOGGIE COOKIES

¾ cup wheat germ
¾ cup powdered milk

1 egg
1 cup puréed chicken livers

Preheat oven to 350 degrees.

Combine all ingredients and mix well. Drop by spoonfuls onto a baking sheet; the cookies should be about the size of a quarter. Bake 20 minutes. Refrigerate.

Charlie

WHEAT AND TOMATO DOG BISCUITS

8	chicken bouillon cubes	1½	cups whole wheat flour
¼	cup hot water	2	cups wheat germ
1	envelope dry yeast	1	teaspoon sugar
2	cups all-purpose flour	1½	cups tomato juice

Preheat oven to 300 degrees.

Dissolve bouillon cubes in hot water. Stir in yeast and allow to stand 5 minutes. Stir in both flours, wheat germ, sugar and tomato juice and blend well. Divide dough in 2 parts. Roll dough on a lightly floured surface to ¼-inch thick. Cut into shapes with a cookie cutter or the top of a glass, or cut into squares. Place on a greased baking sheet. Bake 1 hour. Allow to cool before storing in an airtight container.

Hoku

CHEESY PET BISCUITS

1	cup boiling water	2	teaspoons garlic powder (not garlic salt)
1	cup rolled oats		
5	tablespoons margarine	1	egg, beaten
1	cup shredded Cheddar cheese	1	tablespoon sugar
¾	cup cornmeal	2	teaspoons chicken or beef bouillon granules
½	cup milk		
		2½-3	cups white or wheat flour

Preheat oven to 325 degrees.

Stir together boiling water, oats and margarine. Allow to stand 10 minutes. Stir in cheese, cornmeal, milk, garlic powder, egg, sugar and bouillon. Stir in flour, ½ cup at a time, mixing well after each addition until dough is stiff. Turn dough onto a floured surface and knead in remaining flour and continue to knead for 4 minutes total or until dough is no longer sticky. Roll dough out to ½-inch thick. Cut dough into shapes or squares. Place on a greased baking sheet. Bake 35 to 45 minutes or until golden brown.

Hoku

FANCY DOG BISCUITS

12-16	ounces raw liver	3	chicken or beef bouillon cubes
1½	pounds white flour	2	eggs, beaten
8	ounces oats	1	cup water

Preheat oven to 350 degrees.

Chop liver in a food processor or finely chop by hand. In a large bowl, combine flour and oats. Crumble in bouillon cubes. Add eggs and liver. Stir in enough water to make a firm, but sticky dough. Spread evenly on a work surface to about ½-inch thickness. Cut with a floured cookie cutter or top of a glass, or cut into squares. Place on a greased baking sheet. Bake 1 hour. Store in refrigerator.

Meko

BABY FOOD DOG BISCUITS

3	jars baby food, beef and carrots or chicken	¼	cup cream of wheat
		¼	cup dry milk powder

Preheat oven to 350 degrees.

Combine all ingredients in a bowl and mix well. Roll into small balls and place on a well greased baking sheet. Flatten balls slightly with a fork. Bake 15 minutes. Cool and store in refrigerator.

Whatney

PEANUT TREATS

2¼	cups whole wheat flour	1¼	cups peanut butter
¾	cup all-purpose flour	1	cup milk
1¼	teaspoons baking powder		

Preheat oven to 400 degrees.

Combine both flours and baking powder in a large bowl. In a separate bowl, combine peanut butter and milk until well blended. Gradually stir peanut butter mixture into dry ingredients. Knead dough for a couple minutes. Roll dough out on a floured surface to desired thickness. Cut out treats and place on a foil-lined baking sheet. Bake 15 to 20 minutes; cooking time will vary depending on thickness. Cool before storing.

Charlie

CHEESE DOG BONE BISCUITS

2 cups flour	½ cup vegetable oil
1¼ cups shredded Cheddar cheese	4½ tablespoons water
2 cloves garlic, finely chopped	

Preheat oven to 400 degrees.

Combine flour, cheese, garlic and oil in a food processor and blend to a coarse meal consistency. Slowly add water for form a ball. Divide dough into 12 parts. Form each part into any shape about ½-inch thick. Transfer to an ungreased baking sheet. Bake 10 to 15 minutes or until bottom is brown. Refrigerate in an airtight container when cool.

Hoku

KITTY HASH

1 cup water	⅔ cup ground turkey or flounder
⅓ cup dry brown rice	2 tablespoons chopped liver
2 teaspoons corn oil	1 tablespoon bone meal
Pinch of salt	

Bring water to a boil in a medium saucepan. Stir in rice, corn oil and salt. Reduce heat to low. Cover and simmer 20 minutes. Add turkey, liver and bone meal. Simmer 20 minutes longer, stirring frequently. Cool before serving. Store in refrigerator.

Maggie

TUNA PATTIES FOR CATS

2 eggs	1 teaspoon brewer's yeast
1 (6-ounce) can water-packed tuna, drained and flaked	1 teaspoon bone meal
	Pinch of salt
1 cup bread crumbs	2 tablespoons margarine

Whip eggs in a medium bowl. Add tuna, bread crumbs, yeast, bone meal and salt and mix thoroughly with a spoon until all is moistened. Form mixture into 5 patties. In a skillet, melt margarine over medium heat. Add patties to skillet and cook 3 to 5 minutes per side or until golden brown. Cool patties and crumble to serve. Store remaining patties in refrigerator.

Maggie

CAT COOKIES

1	cup whole wheat flour	1	egg
¼	cup soy flour	⅓	cup milk
1	teaspoon catnip	1	tablespoon unsulferated molasses
2	tablespoons wheat germ	2	tablespoons vegetable oil
⅓	cup powdered milk		

Preheat oven to 350 degrees.

Combine both flours, catnip, wheat germ and powdered milk. Add egg, milk, molasses and vegetable oil. Roll out dough onto a greased baking sheet and cut into small, cat bite-size pieces. Bake 20 minutes. Cool and store in an airtight container.

Maggie

INDEX

INDEX

INDEX

INDEX

INDEX

335

INDEX

INDEX

Mail to:

The Environmental Studies Council, Inc.
2900 N.E. Indian River Drive
Jensen Beach, FL 34957

Please send _____ copies of *Florida Flavors II*   @ $22.95 each _____
                            Postage and handling   @ $ 3.50 each _____
                            Florida residents please add sales tax   @ $ 1.38 each _____
                            Total _____

Make checks or money orders payable to ESC, Inc.

Name _____

Address _____

City _____ State _____ Zip _____

Mail to:

The Environmental Studies Council, Inc.
2900 N.E. Indian River Drive
Jensen Beach, FL 34957

Please send _____ copies of *Florida Flavors II*   @ $22.95 each _____
                            Postage and handling   @ $ 3.50 each _____
                            Florida residents please add sales tax   @ $ 1.38 each _____
                            Total _____

Make checks or money orders payable to ESC, Inc.

Name _____

Address _____

City _____ State _____ Zip _____

Mail to:

The Environmental Studies Council, Inc.
2900 N.E. Indian River Drive
Jensen Beach, FL 34957

Please send _____ copies of *Florida Flavors II*   @ $22.95 each _____
                            Postage and handling   @ $ 3.50 each _____
                            Florida residents please add sales tax   @ $ 1.38 each _____
                            Total _____

Make checks or money orders payable to ESC, Inc.

Name _____

Address _____

City _____ State _____ Zip _____